Unity in Diversity

A third of all children in our schools are from racially minoritised backgrounds. Yet the data on attainment, exclusion, progression and representation indicates that our education system is structurally racist. *Unity in Diversity* explores the unconscious biases at play in our schools and demonstrates how educators can address this by improving representation in the curriculum, staffroom and on the governing/trust board. Drawing on case studies from leaders, this book demonstrates what schools are already doing to create an impactful anti-racist ethos and how these strategies may be applied in practice.

Written by an experienced headteacher who has supported a diverse range of schools in improving their race equity, each chapter addresses a different aspect of race inequality and provides practical strategies for overcoming it. This book empowers readers:

- To acknowledge that systemic race inequality exists in schools and that this necessitates an anti-racist approach

- To become comfortable talking about race and to create safe spaces for staff and students to engage in discussions about race

- To address unconscious biases and white fragility and to examine the inequality and underrepresentation of ethnic groups

- To audit all aspects of educational provision to determine what needs to change and to action and implement this change with lasting impact.

Schools and teachers can play a major role in eliminating systemic racism in society. This book is an essential read for any teacher, leader, governor or trustee who is restless to address race inequity in our education system, creating a more equal and represented school community.

Rachel Macfarlane, previously a teacher with over 30 years of experience, is currently a trainer, author and Director of Education Services at HFL Education. She was a headteacher of three contrasting schools over a 16-year period. She is committed to social mobility and equity for all in education.

'The fight against racial inequity and institutional racism starts in our schools. *Unity in Diversity* is an essential tool for all of those who want to join in that fight.'

David Lammy, MP for Tottenham and Shadow Secretary of State for Foreign, Commonwealth and Development Affairs

'Macfarlane challenges us to understand that racism is affecting staff and students in our institutions, whilst also inviting us to challenge and change systems, processes and peoples involved in fomenting racism. This book is thoughtfully written, combining theory with case studies of practice and is a must read, especially for those working in schools, who have an interest in and passion for anti-racism.'

Professor Paul Miller, Institute for Educational & Social Equity

'Addressing racial inequity in schools is urgent and necessary. Informative, engaging, practical and clearly written, this compelling book is a valuable resource for all head teachers and senior leaders.'

Professor Louise Archer, University College London

'Addressing race inequity in schools is a difficult thing to do with authenticity: unpacking the real issues which plague us as a society, whilst also presenting pragmatic solutions to help address these problems. I am often asked by MAT and education leaders what book I would recommend to help them on their journey. My answer will now be *Unity In Diversity*; it's engaging for the activist and a great choice for the novice looking to learn and make a difference.'

Sufian Sadiq, Director of Teaching School at Chiltern Learning Trust

'This book is a must read for educationalists promoting race equity in Britain. It covers factual data, lived experiences and practical strategies for a much-needed way forward.'

Bushra Nasir, CBE DL and CEO Drapers' MAT

'This will be a useful guide for teachers and educators seeking to deepen their anti-racism journey. Used properly, it will provide real support for anyone needing guidance in this area – a solid starting point for deeper engagement.'

Jeffrey Boakye, Author, Broadcaster and Educator

Unity in Diversity

Achieving Structural Race Equity in Schools

Rachel Macfarlane

Routledge
Taylor & Francis Group

LONDON AND NEW YORK

Designed cover image: © Getty Images

First published 2023
by Routledge
4 Park Square, Milton Park, Abingdon, Oxon OX14 4RN

and by Routledge
605 Third Avenue, New York, NY 10158

Routledge is an imprint of the Taylor & Francis Group, an informa business

© 2023 Rachel Macfarlane

British Library Cataloguing-in-Publication Data
A catalogue record for this book is available from the British Library

ISBN: 978-1-032-23015-3 (hbk)
ISBN: 978-1-032-23016-0 (pbk)
ISBN: 978-1-003-27522-0 (ebk)

DOI: 10.4324/9781003275220

Typeset in Melior
by Newgen Publishing UK

Contents

Part Four: Recruiting, retaining and developing a diverse body of staff, governors and trustees

Foreword by
Evelyn Forde MBE

I first met Rachel in the spring of 2022 when I was invited to deliver a keynote speech as part of HFL's annual leadership programme, Great Representation, designed to address race equity in schools. At the time, I was struck by the number of delegates who had signed up for the programme and then by the range of keynote speakers who had all agreed to contribute. After my keynote, I was contacted by a delegate who told me how much the conference meant to her and how she had been inspired to apply for a more senior position in her school. She had decided to rethink the narrative she tells herself. So, when Rachel asked me to write the foreword to this book, I knew the impact she had already made with the delegates that were part of Great Representation and therefore how wide her impact and influence could be when people read this book.

It is an honour and privilege to write this foreword.

Where this book stands out from others is in the humility and candour which Rachel portrays right from the start. She owns the narrative as to how a white woman is able to write a book like this, albeit with over 30 years in the sector, when not enough writers from an ethnic diversity background are able to secure publishing deals. Simply put, Rachel says 'it is important that I use this privilege as a force for good.' This book *is* a force for good, as it outlines the uncomfortable truth that we have a problem with structural racism and race inequality in the UK which is as evident in the education system as it is in many other institutions. But this book moves beyond stating the obvious: it gives a voice to racially minoritised educators, which is sometimes painful but necessary to read. The reader will have an opportunity to read this book, which is divided into four parts, all in one go or to dip into the different sections as and when. What is also great about this book is that it gives the reader time to reflect on their own practice and that of their school(s). Perhaps most importantly, it gives one the chance to consider what small changes might be taken to address the big issues that *Unity in Diversity* wrestles with.

The book is underpinned by hard data and facts, quotes from esteemed educators and writers; you will be hard pressed not to want to re-read many of the case studies this book provides. I was particularly struck by the case study on school uniform which reminds us of how sometimes we as the adults over-complicate things when our young people really want to keep things simple. Speaking truth to power, the students in this case study wanted to feel included and to ensure that their rights were protected. We can learn a lot from this case study alone.

The role that school leaders and governors play is also laid bare as we are challenged to review our curriculum, to consider our policies and to reflect on the books and resources we use in our schools. These sections give clear examples of how to make those changes and signpost the reader to do more reading to further understand the issues.

My view is that *Unity in Diversity* should become 'your go to/bedside reading' because, regardless of where you are on your journey from understanding to addressing the structural racism and race inequality the education system, as Rachel says 'The key thing is to dip your toe into the water, or even dive straight in. Little by little, your understanding will grow.'

Acknowledgements

This book is dedicated to everyone who is striving to bring about race equity in education and in society.

I owe thanks to so many people.

Some of those whose mark is on this book wish to remain anonymous. For that reason, I shall not mention names, but you know who you are.

Firstly, thanks to all those people who shared their lived experience with me and trusted me to include their stories in the book. Your voices are so powerful.

Secondly, thanks to everyone who read the manuscript and gave feedback to me. Your encouragement, candour and advice were invaluable.

Next, thanks to those Hertfordshire leaders on the two Great Representation cohorts, with and from whom I have learnt such a lot. The work you are doing in your schools is uplifting and vital.

Also, thanks to my HFL Education colleagues. Your work on race equity is inspirational.

Lastly, thanks to my husband and my parents, for their immeasurable support.

Introduction

Our ability to reach unity in diversity will be the beauty and the test of our civilization.

Mahatma Gandhi

It is not those differences between us that are separating us. It is rather our refusal to recognise those differences and to examine the distortions which result from us misnaming them.

Audre Lorde (2017:95)

What is this book about and who is it for?

This book is for leaders and teachers in all types of schools and settings who are restless to address race inequity in our education system and in their own institutions. It explores the unconscious biases, uncertainties and fragilities at play in conference rooms, staffrooms and classrooms up and down the country. It considers the myriad manifestations of race inequity through the examination of data and the testimony of some of the Black, Asian and minority ethnic educationalists I have worked with over a 35-year career in education. Through reference to research and writing on the subject, as well as the use of case studies from a range of schools already well on the way to confronting and tackling racial inequity, it offers suggestions as to what can be done to achieve greater representation in the curriculum, in the staffroom and on governing bodies and trust boards and to create an impactful anti-racist ethos and culture in the whole school community.

The book aims to empower teachers, leaders, governors and trustees in schools

- to acknowledge the existence of systemic race inequality in schools and understand the need for an anti-racist approach

- to become comfortable talking about race and create safe and brave spaces for staff and pupils to do likewise

- to address unconscious bias and white fragility and examine inequities between and under-representation of racial groups

- to audit all aspects of their provision to determine what needs to change

- to be equipped with ideas, strategies and approaches to address any aspect of inequity that is relevant to their school/setting

- to action plan and implement change effectively and with lasting impact.

It can be read a section or a chapter at a time. It is designed to generate reflection and thought, with questions posed to the reader at regular intervals. It is intended to stimulate discussion and debate within senior teams, amongst leaders in a school, between staff and governors/trustees. It contains suggestions for training activities as well as audit and evaluation exercises. It aims to inspire and to provide practical assistance by presenting case studies and examples of ways in which schools have tackled elements of anti-racism work, showing their learning along the way.

How is the book structured?

The book is divided into four sections.

Part One lays the foundations, examining the evidence of race inequity in our education system and making the case for leaders to take action to effect change. Chapter 1 presents the hard data: facts and figures that illustrate the under-representation of people of colour in staffrooms, on our governing and trust boards and in our curriculum; evidence of over-representation of children of colour in suspension and exclusion records; data on the prevalence of incidents of racism in schools; evidence of the under-performance of certain ethnic groups in tests and exams. In Chapter 2 we hear the testimony of interviewees, people of colour who share their lived experience and memories of their school days.

Parts Two, Three and Four each address a different aspect of race inequity in more detail and give practical strategies and advice for overcoming it.

Part Two is focused on developing racial literacy through staff training and by creating safe spaces for adults and pupils to talk about race. Chapter 3 explores the vital role of the head, CEO and senior staff in leading anti-racism action in school. Chapter 4 addresses the issue of language. Chapter 5 considers ways to address assumptions, biases and privileges. Chapter 6 looks at the impact and effects of both positive and negative racial stereotypes.

Part Three is all about the curriculum. In Chapter 7 I explore the groundwork required to be ready to diversify and decolonise the curriculum. Chapter 8 considers various approaches to designing and implementing an anti-racist curriculum and Chapter 9 focuses on resourcing an anti-racist curriculum.

Part Four addresses the issue of the national under-representation of people of colour on staff and governing bodies and on trust boards. Chapter 10 looks at strategies for attracting racially minoritised staff to apply for posts. Chapter 11 considers the conditions needed to retain staff and governors/trustees of colour. Chapter 12 explores effective ways of supporting and developing racially minoritised staff to be promoted and to progress to senior positions in schools and trusts.

Why this book, now?

I have worked in seven contrasting schools. Most had very ethnically diverse student cohorts; one was 97% Bengali. In two I was the teacher with responsibility for Equal Opportunities (as EDI Leads were called in those days). In three I was headteacher and one (a 4–18 all-through school in East London) I built from scratch, striving to establish an anti-racist ethos. In my current role, as a Director of Education Services in Hertfordshire, I work with heads from a wide range of schools, from mono-ethnic to multi-ethnic.

At no point in my career have I been more aware of school leaders seeking direction and guidance as to how to address and educate about racism and how to be effective anti-racist allies.

Why is this?

Many of the leaders I talk to point to May 2020 as a catalyst, although often their journey towards making their schools anti-racist institutions began well before then. It would be fair to say that the murder of George Floyd on 25 May 2020 and the subsequent Black Lives Matter protests fired my resolve to write on the matter of the leadership of anti-racism in schools.

Although George Floyd was, sadly, just one individual in a long list of people of colour to die in recent years at the hands of the police (on both sides of the Atlantic), his death was particularly significant, being captured on camera and witnessed by the world, from their lockdown homes. It showed in stark technicolour the price of racial inequality. June Sarpong, in *The Power of Privilege*, makes the important point that 'Generally, white people in majority-white countries will have had limited exposure to racism' but that 'witnessing the same incident through the same mobile-phone lens meant that the racism experienced by black Americans suddenly became a visual reality for white people. There was no escaping it, no justification or narrative to present the killing as accidental or in some way caused by the action of the victim' (2020:11–12).

Paul Miller, in an article entitled *System Conditions, System Failure, Structural Racism and Anti-Racism in the United Kingdom: Evidence from Education and Beyond*, reflected that George Floyd's death has 'fuelled countless debates about racism and anti-racism in every facet of global society, leading to two important interrelated outcomes.' The first is that 'these debates have led many organisations … to consider and examine their complicity in racism, the degree to which their engagement in anti-racism work is deep or shallow and/or the absence of their engagement in anti-racism work.' Secondly, 'these debates have also led many individuals and organisations to commit to active anti-racism work.' He concludes that 'The attendant enthusiasm, whether construed as a "push" or a "pull" cannot be denied, and it is clear that the "conscience" of society and organisations has been stirred' (2021:1).

Thousands of school leaders and teachers were directly inspired by the Black Lives Matter Movement to give serious thought as to how they could effect change and stand up to racism. At my organisation, HFL Education, a brave leader, Andrew Brown, urged the Executive to take action. Through a collaborative process, a statement of intent was written in the days following the murder and publicised on HfL's website, an extract from which is given below. Similar action was being taken in schools across the land.

HfL's purpose is founded on our belief that every young person, through access to a great education, should be able to realise their potential, regardless of where they live or their circumstances. We deplore the murder of George Floyd, Ahmaud Arbery, Breonna Taylor, Manuel Ellis and countless others who have lost their lives due to unrelenting racial injustices and we recognise the uncomfortable truths that we all must face.

HfL acknowledges that systemic racism is a problem that must be addressed everywhere. We have a duty to face up to the difficult conversations that ultimately result in the lifting of Black, Asian and minority ethnic (BAME) voices. We know that in Britain, Black children are more likely to experience poverty, have poorer educational outcomes, be excluded from school, be unemployed, and come into contact with the criminal justice system. They are less likely to access the care they need if they are struggling with mental health problems, and Black children are more likely to act as carers for ill and disabled family members and to miss out on support. We know that the Black community is under-represented in teaching staff, even more so at a leadership level and we acknowledge that that impacts upon Black children's experience of education. We acknowledge the position we are in today and we refuse to fail to learn.

It is crucial that we take action beyond statements. We welcome challenge on our practices and will not be afraid of robust questioning. Furthermore, HfL pledges that, with immediate effect, we will:

- *Promote the comprehensive review of the curriculum coverage of Black history in Hertfordshire schools, to ensure that, at every key stage, Black voices are heard, Black stories are told and Black achievements and contributions to society are celebrated.*

- *Support school leaders, through our school improvement work, to review the entire curriculum experience to ensure that there is good representation of Black voices and experiences: in and outside the formal taught curriculum, in each subject area, through trips and visits coverage and the profile of speakers.*

- *For all internal recruitment and recruitment that we support schools with…we commit to doing all that is possible to ensure that ethnicity is unknown throughout all hiring processes.*

> ● *Monitor, report and take action upon any differences in successful hires, performance results, promotions and pay between our Black and non-Black colleagues.*
>
> ● *Invite all colleagues that identify as BAME to form a BAME forum. This forum will be given an Executive level platform to make robust recommendations that seek to further the cause of ending systemic racism both internally and with the work that we do.*

(NB: The term 'Black' here is used to represent all racially minoritised groups. In Chapter 4, I examine terminology in much more detail.)

And so began a concerted effort on the part of all at HFL Education to progress an anti-racism agenda. All staff now set themselves a race equity performance objective as part of the annual appraisal cycle and all colleagues receive regular training on unconscious bias, discrimination and equality issues.

In spring 2021, I secured funding to run an annual leadership programme which I called Great Representation. The key aims of the programme were to bring together leaders of Hertfordshire primary and secondary schools (mainstream and special):

● to encapsulate the key features, structures and practices of schools (from nursery to secondary) which have a strong ethos of anti-racism, to better understand how schools become great at inclusion, diversity and equity

● to explore strategies, review literature and hear from expert speakers on how to achieve great representation of people of colour in the curriculum and the school community and

● to share great practice and ensure that schools engaged in exciting race equity practice are contributing to system leadership in Hertfordshire.

The format of the programme, launched in September 2021, comprised a series of seminars over the course of the academic year, attended by the headteacher/principal and another member of the senior leadership team (SLT) of each school on the programme. At each seminar, a keynote speaker (or two) gave a presentation or ran a workshop on an aspect of race equity in education, as inspiration, stimulation and provocation for the leaders attending. The delegates then shared and discussed the keynote talks and other reading and research about impactful anti-racism action in schools. They also conducted activities to scrutinise in detail and reflect on their specific context, practices and challenges. Between seminars, delegates conducted visits with their peers to three other schools on the programme, to learn from their best practice and to form links for ongoing school improvement collaboration. Each school on the programme also wrote a case study over the course of the year, on an initiative that they had successfully introduced and evaluated at their school to increase race equity.

In reading as preparation for the Great Representation programme, I became aware that plenty has been written in recent years about race inequality in our society, and about the importance of Equality, Diversity and Inclusion (EDI) in education. But there are surprisingly few books offering practical advice to school leaders determined to run anti-racist schools.

What gives *me* the right to write on this subject?

I have wrestled long and hard with this question. There will be some who, understandably, will question my credentials to author a book on race equity. I am a White, middle class, straight ex-headteacher with all the advantages and privileges that come with my race, class, status and sexuality. I have not experienced racism and cannot claim to understand how that feels.

But I do have 16 years of experience of leading schools and some understanding of how White school leaders (and 93% of them are White) can feel: fragile and uncertain about how to approach discussions around race, anxious about causing offence, unskilled as to how to start to tackle systemic racism, unsure about what to prioritise and how to action plan.

Not enough minority ethnic writers get book contracts. It is an uncomfortable truth that my race may well have advantaged me when seeking a publisher. This is obviously wrong, as is the fact that my whiteness affords me influence. Whilst acknowledging this fact, it is important that I use this privilege as a force for good.

Recognising my inability to write from personal experience of racial prejudice or discrimination as a pupil or member of staff, this book cites the words and thoughts of many people of colour, which hopefully gives my writing legitimacy. In particular, the reader will find projected the voices of 10 former and current colleagues who kindly agreed to be interviewed by me as part of my research. Their stories are woven throughout the book; their testimony is harrowing but their voices powerful.

In conversation with Professor Paul Miller in the summer of 2021, I was introduced to his concept of White Sanction. His argument is that white power should be used by people like me to promote anti-racism. He elaborated on this concept when he came to address the Great Representation programme in September 2021, saying 'You can't feel guilty for having a privilege you didn't ask for. White people have to use their privilege. White sanction confers legitimacy. In an equitable system we wouldn't need white sanction but we don't all have the same level of power. Any White person who engages in white sanction is standing aside Black people. They won't gain anything from it or lose anything by not doing it.'

Racism is a white problem. It was created by White people and the ultimate responsibility for it lies with White people. So perhaps it is appropriate that a White education leader should author this book. Reni Eddo-Lodge makes a similar point when she argues that the load should not fall on people of colour to effect change: 'The onus is not on *me* to change. Instead, it's the world around me' (2017:184).

I was also spurred on by a British Pakistani friend who wrote to me: 'White people in charge of change listen to other White people. So, I would definitely say please do write the book!'

This book is a response to a belief that there is an urgent need for us to address race equity in schools and to ensure that those in education today affect systemic change for the future. The key to eliminating systemic racism in society surely lies with our educators. I hope that this book will, in some small way, empower school leaders to create an anti-racist legacy.

References

Eddo-Lodge, R. (2017). *Why I'm No Longer Talking To White People About Race.* (London: Bloomsbury).

Lorde, A. (2017). *Your Silence Will Not Protect You.* (UK: Silver Press).

Miller, P. (2021). *'System Conditions,' System Failure, Structural Racism and Anti-Racism in the United Kingdom: Evidence from Education and Beyond.* MDPI Available at: www.mdpi.com/2075-4698/11/2/42

Sarpong, J. (2020). *The Power Of Privilege: How White People Can Challenge Racism.* (London: HQ).

PART ONE
Race inequity in education

The problem laid bare

My son was murdered because of racism and you cannot forget that. Once you start covering it up, it is giving the green light to racists.

Doreen Lawrence
(in response to the Sewell Report 2021)

The master's tools will never dismantle the master's house.

Audre Lorde (2017:89)

The uncomfortable truth

Let's start with an uncomfortable truth: we have a problem with structural racism and race inequality in the UK and it is as evident in the education system as it is in many other institutions. We won't get anywhere if we skirt around the issue or allow ourselves to feel bruised or under attack on hearing this.

Whilst all schools are committed to equality of opportunity and very few have systems or procedures that are overtly or intentional racist, racial inequality is illustrated by a multitude of indicators:

- The low attainment levels from Early Years to A level of many ethnic minority groups

- Evidence of unconscious teacher race bias in assessment grading and pupil grouping decisions

- The number of race incidents reported in schools annually

- Over-representation of certain racially minoritised groups in suspensions and permanent exclusions and those who become NEETs (not in education, employment or training)

- Lack of protagonists of colour in children's literature, picture books and fiction textbooks

DOI: 10.4324/9781003275220-2

- Under-representation of people of colour in the curriculum

- Under-representation of students from minority ethnic backgrounds in admission rates to university and over-representation in drop-out rates from university

- The low percentage of adults from minority ethnic backgrounds working in schools, especially as teachers and even more so as leaders and governors/ trustees

- Racism being a key factor leading to teachers of colour leaving the profession.

We will look into each of these in more detail shortly.

Facts and figures

As educators, we are painfully aware of the race inequalities in wider society, as illustrated in the following statistics:

- 41% of Pakistanis, 35% of Bangladeshis and 27% of Black people in the UK live in low-income households, compared to 16% of White British people and 17% of all people in the UK (Gov.uk 2022)

- In 2020, death rates in people known to have Covid-19, after taking into account age, sex, deprivation and region, were twice as high among those of a Bangladeshi background and 10–50% higher among other ethnic groups compared with white British people (BMJ 2020)

- Black women are five times more likely to die in childbirth in the UK than White women (Knight et al. 2019)

- People of colour were disproportionally affected by redundancies through Covid. The unemployment rate for Black young people reached 40% in April 2021, compared to 12% for White young people (Thomas 2021)

- In 2016, the pay gap between White and Black people with education up to GCSE level was 11%, the pay gap between White and Black people with education up to A level was 14% and the pay gap between White and Black people with education up to degree level was 23% (TUC 2016)

- Black women in the UK are three to six times more likely to be submitted to mental health units (Linton 2017)

- In 2017 12% of the prison population was Black, despite making up only 3% of the population (Kentish 2017).

And the data around education and race shows that we have not yet been able to compensate adequately for, or affect an overturning of, the inequities experienced outside of the school gates: we are not ensuring a consistently equitable provision for our children of colour in schools.

An institutionally racist society?

The Commission on Race and Ethnic Disparities, chaired by Tony Sewell, which reported in March 2021, accepted that racism in the UK is a 'real force' (2021:8), but challenged the concept of the UK as an institutionally racist society, stating that 'The country has come a long way in 50 years and the success of much of the ethnic minority population ... should be regarded as a model for other White-majority countries' (2021:9). Yet when we consider the definition of institutional racism as defined in the Stephen Lawrence Inquiry Macpherson Report (1999) – especially those words highlighted in italics below – against the data shown above, it is hard not to accept that institutional racism, albeit predominantly unintentional, is still very much in evidence in our systems and structures:

> The collective failure to provide an appropriate and professional service to people because of their colour, culture or ethnic origin. *It can be seen or detected in processes, attitudes and behaviour which amount to discrimination through unwitting prejudice, ignorance, thoughtlessness and racist stereotyping which disadvantage minority ethnic people.*
>
> *para 6.34*

Claire Stewart-Hall, in her essay in *Diverse Educators: A Manifesto* (2022: 282) argues that the Sewell report redirected 'attention away from structures towards individuals' perceived failures. Black and Brown people become positioned as self-limiting and self-defining, responsible for determining their futures as if racism had not existed.' She suggests that the report 'enables a distancing of any structural cause, strategically avoiding discussion of Whiteness and its ability to manifest, uphold and underpin racism within institutions.'

The Sewell report was widely condemned by academics, MPs, experts, NHS providers and even some of those cited and quoted within it. The Joint Teaching Unions called it an 'insult to all those in Britain who experience racism every day of their lives.' Jeffrey Boakye tweeted: 'The racism within this country's institutions is so structural that even acknowledging it brings out the government's fear of being dismantled.' Rehana Azam from the GMB stated: 'Institutional racism exists – it's the lived experience of millions of Black and Ethnic Minority workers.'

In February 2021, a month before the Sewell report was published, a poll conducted by the Henry Jackson Society found that 29% of the public consider Britain to be a fundamentally racist society, with 58% of Black Britons polled saying so. Factors likely to have influenced these figures include the xenophobia manifested at the time of and following the Brexit vote (with a 41% increase in racially and religiously aggravated crime in the month following the vote (2018:274)), the murder of Jo Cox by a far right extremist in June 2016, the

Windrush Scandal, George Floyd's murder and the Black Lives Matter movement, the disparities between the impact of Covid-19 on White people and those from Black, Asian and ethnic minority groups, the institutional racism uncovered at the Yorkshire Cricket Club, a number of high profile incidents of racism in the Metropolitan police and the racism shown towards Rashford, Saka and Sancho after the Euro 2020 Cup Final in July 2021. Rashford alone received 23,000 racially abusive tweets.

Yet it was reported by Simon Murphy and Amy Walker in September 2020 that *The Times* had picked up that 40 Conservative MPs were set to refuse to undertake unconscious bias training, accusing parliamentary authorities of 'pandering to the woke agenda.' How could the views of key political leaders and their commissioners be so at odds with their critics? Richard Beard, author of *Sad Little Men*, argues that there is a fundamental problem with the ruling elite, many educated at top private schools and enjoying a highly privileged lifestyle, pronouncing on the state of the nation. Himself a product of the public school system, Beard comments 'How could we know anything of the Great Britain outside these walls, without making an immense effort from the day we left on nothing else but that?' (2021: 54) 'What did we know ... of the world as it really was? By the end of our school days, it had been a while since we confronted the realities of social inequality (2021: 190). The lived experience of the majority of politicians does not lead them to sense that society is structurally inequitable and there is little incentive, as suggested by the Audre Lorde quote at the opening of the chapter, to suggest otherwise.

The stance taken by certain government ministers to the taking of the knee by the England team in the run up to and during the Euros was notable: George Eustace and Prime Minister Boris Johnson, like Donald Trump in the US, refused to condemn those who booed this moral stance. Jon Stone, in *The Independent*, reported that Priti Patel said fans had a right to call such action 'gesture politics.' David Olusoga, in *The Guardian* on 13 July 2021, wrote about the stubborn minority of our population with racist views: 'During the tournament the think tank British Future released the results of a survey that showed that one in 10 people regard Englishness as a racial identity. In their minds, black people can never truly be English...Although outnumbered, that 10% are never silent.' He went on to say that 'While England were winning, their hate was largely exiled to the toxic margins of social media. But literally within minutes of the team's first and only defeat...those who believe blackness and Englishness are mutually exclusive unleashed their fury against the black players who missed penalties.'

Gary Younge, writing in *The Guardian* in 2018, had said much the same thing about the World Cup: 'When diversity is related to something successful then it is a sign of the nation's genius in allowing, nurturing and managing it; when it is attached to a national calamity, diversity is the reason for the failure.'

Olusoga reflected that, in 2021, racists had been 'given a free pass by the government to target their national team.' He argued that 'The rot has grown deeper in recent months, in part because our political leaders have allowed that poison to fester and – when they calculated that it was in their electoral interests – cynically refused to condemn it.'

The post-Euros outpouring of racist hatred on social media was particularly stark proof that overt expression of racism is, sadly, not consigned to history in our country. David Baddiel reminds us, in *Jews Don't Count*, that racist abuse against Jews is heard every week at football matches, and often goes unchallenged. He does not deny the significant efforts to kick racism out of football – 'In the 1970s, football fandom was unbelievably racist, and immense strides were made to eradicate it over the next decades' (2021:13–14) – but he makes an important point about the way still to go.

The evolution of racism

What we, as educators as well as members of UK society, are dealing with is the changing nature and manifestation of racism. Afua Hirsch, in *Brit(ish)*, quotes Benjamin Zephaniah: 'Time has moved on. And racism has evolved. We don't really see gangs of racist thugs roaming the streets like they did back in the day. They now wear suits and ties. Some form political parties. Some build websites' (2018: 119). Omar Khan and Faiza Shaheen point out that 'It's not the white working class that make people with African and Asian-sounding surnames send in twice as many CVs; it's not the white working class who award white British graduates nearly three times as many firsts as Black British graduates' (2017: 6). In *Sway*, Pragya Agarwal picks up on this idea: 'The 'post-racial' world-view is that racism has no value or place in today's world, with its liberal democracies, and decline in explicit racial prejudices and expression.' She continues, 'Thus, a post-racial illusion of the world is created where there is no structural racism or bigotry, and therefore any acts of racism are more aversive, less explicit, and seemingly "non-racial".' Agarwal concludes that 'Racism has not disappeared, but the nature of racism has changed – "racism without racists" – and its expression and articulation is different' (2020:292–3). Hirsch suggests that there is something unique about Britain in terms of 'the convoluted lengths we are willing to go to, to avoid confronting the problem. We will not name it, we avoid discussing it and, increasingly, we say we can't see it. We want to be post-racial, without ever having admitted how racial a society we have been' (2018:125). She talks of the challenge of, and pressure caused by 'experiencing race, while being encouraged to ignore race' and reminds us that 'racial prejudice is alive and well' (2018: 124).

We need to confront the fact that racism exists, for the good of all our pupils. The demography of the UK is changing rapidly. A third of all school children are from ethnic minority groups; indeed the 2011 census revealed that people identifying as 'white British' are now a minority in London. The same census shows that the fastest growing ethnic group is people who are mixed race. Children of colour need to feel represented in the curriculum they study, and their white peers need to hear, understand and be enriched by the stories, cultures, achievements, struggles and contributions of people of colour. Racially minoritised students need to see educators around them to whom they can relate and who understand their lived experience and heritage. They need to feel respected and protected from all forms of racism as they grow up and pass through our schools. Yet the 2020 report *Making Progress? Employment and Retention of BAME Teachers in England* found that almost half of English schools have no teachers from Black, Asian or ethnic minority backgrounds at all (2020:8). In 2021 The Runnymede Trust reported that 'just 14.3 per cent of teachers are from a BME group and over 96 per cent of male and female headteachers are white' (2021:35). And the majority of staff in schools feel unprepared and ill-equipped with the skills to address racism sensitively and effectively. Most have not been trained in how to design and deliver a diverse and decolonised curriculum (or even the knowledge as to what that means!).

June Sarpong quotes a letter written to the British government by Sandra Kerr, CEO of Race for Opportunity: 'By 2051, one in five people in the UK will be from an ethnic minority background... The (attainment) gap must not be allowed to widen further, but without action little will change' (2020:53).

Race inequity in education

Let's examine the gaps and inequalities referenced at the start of this chapter in more detail.

The low attainment of many racially minoritised groups

It is important to stress that analysis of attainment data by ethnicity is problematic and it reveals significant complexities. Professor Louise Archer of UCL reminds us that 'Whilst, undoubtedly, there are identifiable, racialised patterns of attainment among different "ethnic groups", the picture is highly complex and nuanced.' She says that

> the notion of 'an ethnic group' is, in itself, a complex and contested one, since the boundaries of ethnic collectivities are porous, shifting and contestable. Racialised patterns of achievement are cross-cut by gender and social class and are shaped by histories of migration, arrival, settlement and schooling – and must, therefore, be treated with care.
>
> *2008:90*

In 2019, the last year of public exams prior to Covid disruption, some racially minoritised groups performed better than the national average at Early Years Foundation Stage, in Key Stage 2 SATs and at GCSE. These were: Indian, Chinese, Mixed White/Asian and White Irish. The ethnic groups that performed less well than the national average and less well than White British pupils at all key stages were: Gypsy Roma, Irish Traveller, Pakistani, Black Other, Black Caribbean and

Mixed White/Black Caribbean. The attainment of Gypsy Roma children was, and habitually is, the lowest of all ethnic groups.

An examination of GCSE performance by ethnicity shows that some ethnic groups perform less well than others, year after year. The 2020 EPI report into Education in England stated that 'Since 2011, the gap between pupils from Black and White British backgrounds has increased in the order of 60–70 per cent' (Hutchinson et al. (2020:32)), with a 'widening of the gap by three months (77 per cent) for pupils from Any Other Black Background and by 4.4 months (68 per cent) for Black Caribbean pupils' (2020:20). Only Black African students (of all Black groups) achieved in line with their White counterparts at GCSE in 2019. Irena Barker, writing in TES on 6 August 2021, pointed out that 'only 29.2 per cent of boys from black Caribbean backgrounds gain a grade 5 or higher in both English and maths at GCSE, and the figures for some other black and mixed ethnicity categories are not much higher.'

In 2022, White British students gained an average grade of 4.76 score in their best eight GCSEs. Students from a number of ethnic groups (including Indian, Bangladeshi, Pakistani and Chinese) gained a higher average grade. However, the average grade for children from Mixed White and Black Caribbean heritage was 4.2, for Caribbean students was 4.16 and for pupils in the Black Other category was 46.8. Most shockingly the average grade for the best eight GCSEs for Gypsy Roma learners was 20.9 (way below a standard pass) and for Traveller children was 2.9 (DfE 2022).

The 2021 *Runnymede Trust Civil Society report to the UN: Race and Racism in England*, stated that 'The continuing disparities in educational attainment between some BME groups, particularly Gypsy, Roma and Traveller and Black Caribbean pupils, and their white counterparts, are deeply concerning' (2021:37). The report cited the fact that 'By the end of secondary school, Gypsy, Roma and Traveller pupils are almost three years behind their white counterparts, and Black Caribbean students are 11 months behind their white British counterparts' (2021:37).

In Chapter 6 we will return to the implications of the attainment gap between the performance of students of certain ethnic groups – on student self-perception and behaviour and on teacher assumptions and biases. We will, throughout the book, be considering strategies to eliminate variation between the performance of students of different ethnicities.

Unconscious teacher race bias

David Gillborn, emeritus professor of critical race studies at the University of Birmingham, quoted by Irena Barker in the TES, talks of teachers' lower expectations of Black children. He argues that, 'as children move through the system, ... black pupils (are) more likely to be channelled into lower-ability groups and entered for the foundation tier at GCSE, making it more difficult for them to succeed' (2021). In her book *Equitable Education*, Sameena Choudry quotes research conducted by Gillborn and Youdell (2020) which found that 'white students were significantly more likely to be entered for the top tiers compared to their black Caribbean, Pakistani, black African and Bangladeshi classmates' (2021:206), despite some of these ethnic groups achieving more highly than White pupils overall.

The Runnymede Trust report of 2021 echoed these concerns regarding teacher bias in relation to the system of teacher assessed grades adopted by the government as a result of the cancellation of GCSE and A level examinations: 'There is significant evidence that students with lower socio-economic status are at a particular disadvantage because their grades are more likely to be under-predicted. Research by Ofqual, England's exam regulator, found that the replacement of exams with teacher assessments is biased against disadvantaged students' (2021: 38).

The phenomenon of unconscious teacher bias in decisions around pupil groupings, tiers of entry in exams and marks allocated in teacher assessments has been explored in a number of research studies. A study by Simon Burgess and Ellen Greaves in 2009 found evidence that some ethnic groups are systematically 'under-assessed' relative to their White peers (Black Africans and Black Caribbeans), while others are 'over-assessed' (Indians and Chinese) in Key Stage 2 SATs tests. Once the ethnicity of the students was anonymised, the grades awarded were much more reflective of their performance. In *Black, Listed*, Jeffrey Boakye talks of 'the black boy assessment trap, whereby black boys are consistently undermarked in their formal assessments due to unspoken biases and assumptions of intellectual inferiority.' He argues that these biases 'run deep in the DNA of (the) education system' (2019:92). In 2008, a research study conducted by The University of Warwick, involving 15,000 pupils, examined the profile of pupils entered for the higher and foundation tiers of the Key Stage 3 maths and science tests. It found that Black Caribbean, Pakistani, Black African and Bangladeshi pupils were significantly less likely to be entered for the top tiers than their White classmates. Although for many the choice of tier could be explained by the pupils' prior academic performance, for a significant proportion of Black Caribbean pupils, there was no academic justification for the teacher's decision. In an audio interview with Jon Dennis for *The Guardian*, Dr Steve Strand, the author of the study, explained that, once all measured factors had been accounted for, the most likely reason was low teacher expectations. He described what was found as institutional racism in that organisational policies or actions were having an unintentional negative impact on some ethnic groups (2008). Twelve years later, Gillborn and Youdell found the same pattern with tiers of entry for GCSEs: Black Caribbean, Black African (and Bangladeshi and Pakistani) pupils were far less likely to be entered for higher papers (2000).

As part of a 2019 Best Practice in Grouping Students project, Becky Taylor found that Black pupils were more than 2.5 times more likely than White pupils to be allocated to a lower maths group in Year 7 than predicted by their attainment in Year 6. Asian pupils were 1.8 times more likely to be allocated to a lower set than their prior attainment would have indicated. Her conclusion was that stereotypes were at play in the allocation of pupils to sets. This study found that there was an added disadvantage for pupils wrongly placed in lower sets in that these groups were disproportionately likely to be allocated weaker or less highly qualified teachers. Furthermore, Taylor found that students perceived the teachers of higher attaining sets to have more rigorous expectations, to 'push' learners more and to show more respect for their pupils. In contrast, the pedagogy in the lower sets was seen as more tolerant and relaxed and the pace of teaching slower and less demanding (2019).

Chapter 6 will explore further the implications of unconscious teacher bias and what school leaders can do to create a culture where it is acknowledged, explored and addressed.

University admission and drop-out rates

In the Runnymede Trust report of 2021, it was noted that

> At current levels, British-born BME people aged 18 to 30 have better qualifications at university level than their white counterparts. Despite this, BME graduates, particularly Black, Pakistani and Bangladeshi students, are less likely to attend higher-status, more selective Russell Group universities or to be awarded higher degree classifications (first or 2:1).

The report stated that 'Black students are also the least likely to continue into a second year of study in higher education in both STEM and non-STEM subjects. An EHRC inquiry found that one in four students have experienced racial harassment at university. Without effective redress mechanisms, the EHRC found that 1 in 20 students and 3 in 20 staff members left universities because of racial harassment' (2021:39).

Volume of race incidents

It is hard to assess the prevalence of racist incidents in schools. Many will go unreported: this is one of the messages that you will receive loud and clear in the next chapter when we hear the school day recollections from a number of educators of colour. In *Living While Black*, Guilaine Kinouani talks of a rule, silently enforced, which states 'that we must remain silent when subjected to racism, that we must adapt, that we must over-look microaggressions and generally that we must keep white people comfortable' (2021:120). Furthermore, of those incidents of racism that occur in school and are reported, only a proportion will be recorded. In 2012 the government advised schools that they were no longer required by law to report racist incidents to the local authority, with the effect of raising questions as to the validity of any published data. Even so, David Batty and Nazia Parveen reported in *The Guardian* on 28 March 2021 that UK schools have recorded over 60,000 racist incidents in the past five years, with the 'true scale thought to be far higher.'

In Chapter 5 we will examine the issues around effecting a culture in which all members of the school community understand the importance of and feel safe reporting incidents of racism, as well as what constitutes best practice in terms of recording, tracking, responding to and resolving racist incidents.

Suspensions and permanent exclusion rates

The most recent data from the Department of Education (2021) showed that White Gypsy and Roma pupils had the highest school permanent exclusion rates in the 2018 to 2019 school year at 0.39%, or 39 per 10,000 pupils. This compares with 0.10% of White and White British pupils. The ethnic group with the second highest exclusion rate was Irish Traveller (0.27%), then Black Caribbean (0.25%), Mixed White and Black Caribbean (0.24%), Black Other (0.13%), Mixed White and Black African (0.12%) and Black (0.11%).

Naimh McIntyre, Nazia Parveen and Tobi Thomas, writing in *The Guardian* in March 2021, reported that 'Exclusion rates for black Caribbean students in English schools are up to six times higher than those of their white peers in some local authorities... Gypsy, Roma and Traveller children were also excluded at much higher rates, with Roma children nine times more likely to be suspended in some areas.' They found that 'exclusion rates for mixed-race white and black Caribbean students were more than four times higher than their white peers in several local authorities...In Gloucestershire, 12.4% of all black Caribbean students were given an exclusion in the 2018–19 school year, compared with just 2.4% of white British students.'

Whilst more boys than girls are permanently excluded from school, Aamna Mohdin, in a *Guardian* article of 23 September 2021, cited data which shows that 'black Caribbean girls were permanently excluded from school at a rate double that of white British girls during the academic year 2019–20, with this tripling for mixed white and Caribbean girls.' Furthermore 'girls from Gypsy, Roma and Traveller communities faced rates of permanent exclusion that were four times higher than those of white British girls.' She stated that 'the number of girls excluded is increasing, with permanent exclusions of girls rising by 66% over the last five years, compared with a 32% increase among boys.'

All educators know of the correlation between exclusion from school, poor academic qualifications, likelihood of becoming a NEET, vulnerability to exploitation, crime and poverty. In effect, exclusion directly impacts a student's life chances; if exclusions are meted out to students of colour without impartiality or sufficient attempt to seek alternative interventions or sanctions, the education system is fuelling the perpetuation of the societal racial inequalities considered earlier in the chapter.

In Irena Barker's *TES* article, David Gillborn talks of White teachers' hypervigilance over Black students, leading to them facing harsher discipline: '"black students, especially boys, are subjected to more surveillance. They're watched more closely."' Gillborn asserted that White staff "tend to come down on them more harshly and they tend to underestimate what they're capable of academically"' (2021).

We will explore the dangers of unconscious staff stereotyping and racial bias – in favour of some racially minoritised groups and against others – in Chapter 6, as well as considering ways of implementing effective staff unconscious bias training and examining what anti-racist behaviour policies and procedures might look like.

Under-representation in books and in the curriculum

At the end of 2020, the National Literacy Trust published a report into children's reading habits. Based on a survey of 58,000 young people, it concluded that 'almost a third of children and young people between 9 and 18 don't see themselves in what they read – and two fifths would like to read more books with characters similar to them' (2020). The Centre for Literacy in Primary Education (CLPE) undertakes an annual survey of ethnic representation in children's books. In 2020 they found only 15% of children's books published that year featured any minority characters, with just 5% having a protagonist from an ethnic minority background. The 2020 report argues that 'It is crucial that all readers are able to encounter characters of colour as a meaningful part of the mainstream.' It explains that this 'serves as affirmation in one instance and broadens world outlook in another.' It concludes that 'A representative and inclusive shelf therefore benefits all readers and should be an entitlement for all of our pupils' (2020:7–8).

Chapters 7 and 8 focus on arguments for and suggested methods of effectively diversifying and decolonising the curriculum, referencing a number of school case studies. Chapter 9 examines ways to ensure broad representation of people of colour in school resources and materials, including picture, fiction and non-fiction books.

The low percentage of racially minoritised teachers, leaders and governors/trustees

In NFER research into racial diversity in the teaching profession, Jack Worth, Dawson McLean and Caroline Sharp reported that six in 10 English state secondary schools have an all-white teaching staff, while nearly seven in 10 primary schools have only white teachers. The report found that Black, Asian and minority ethnic applicants are over-represented in applications for first teaching posts, yet teachers of colour are under-represented right from Early Career Teachers (ECTs) right through to senior leaders. Ninety-six per cent of heads are from white backgrounds, compared to 83% of the wider population. Eighty-six per cent of state schools have an all-white senior leadership team and 60% have an all-white teaching staff (2022).

This led the authors to conclude that there was a high probability that children starting school today would rarely or never be taught by a racially minoritised teacher (2022).

Interviewed by Habiba Katsha of the Huffington Post on 18 May 2022, Michaela Lawson, the founder of Prosperity Project,

> said that if children of colour don't see themselves represented in schools they won't feel that it's a profession they can enter. 'Children can only be what they see...People of colour in schools tend to only be in the lowest paid positions, so teaching assistants, site staff and admin staff.'
>
> *2022*

The NFER report also identified under-representation of volunteer governors from minority ethnic backgrounds.

Tom Belger, in *Schools Week* on 28 April 2022, referring to DfE research entitled *School Leadership in England 2010 to 2020: Characteristics and Trends* reported that 'after controlling for other factors, non-white teachers were 18 per cent less likely to be promoted to middle leadership than white British ones, and 21 per cent less likely to be promoted to headship.' He noted that the research found that 'Ethnic minority staff overall were also disproportionately represented in London, even when factoring in its more diverse population. But, interestingly, diversity among inner London secondary heads has actually fallen, from 34 per cent in 2010 to 25 per cent a decade on.'

Over half of respondents participating in research for a NASUWT report of 2011 said they had experienced discrimination during their career (44% experiencing ethnic discrimination) and in *Making Progress?*, Tereshchenko, Mills and Bradbury found that 'racism and associated inequalities are at the forefront of BAME teachers' minds in conversations about retention, not workload' (2020:4).

Chapters 10, 11 and 12 respectively address the key issues of recruitment, retention and development/progression of staff and governors/trustees of colour and consider effective practice through examining a number of case studies and personal testimony.

If you have read this far, I am confident that you will be in agreement that, however well-intentioned our staff may be and however much our school and trust leaders may feel that they are driven by a commitment to equality, diversity and inclusion, we have a problem with race inequity in our educational system and institutions. However, to reinforce the point, in Chapter 2 we will hear the testimony of a number of school teachers and leaders of colour, reflecting on their experiences of their own education.

Before we move on, however, you might like to reflect on the following questions:

How do you feel when confronted with the hypothesis that the UK's education system is institutionally racist? Do you agree?

How aware were you of the various manifestations of race inequity that we have considered in this chapter?

How aware would your a. senior leaders and b. governors/trustees be of this data? How might you look to share and discuss this data with them?

What further reading might you seek to do as a result of reading this chapter?

What questions is it raising for you as a leader?

References

Agarwal. P. (2020). *Sway: Unravelling Unconscious Bias.* (London: Bloomsbury).

Archer. L. (2008). *The Impossibility of Minority Ethnic Educational 'Success'? An Examination of the Discourses of Teachers and Pupils in British Secondary Schools.* (EERJ Vol 7 No 1). Available at: https://journals.sagepub.com/doi/10.2304/eerj.2008.7.1.89

Baddiel. D. (2021). *Jews Don't Count.* (London: TLS Books).

Barker. I. (2021). *Racial Bias and Attainment.* (TES). Available at: www.theguardian.com/education/2021/sep/23/black-girls-in-england-twice-as-likely-to-be-excluded-from-schools-as-white-girls

Batty. D. and Parveen. N. (2021). *UK schools record more than 60,000 racist incidents in five years.* (The Guardian). Available at: www.theguardian.com/education/2021/mar/28/uk-schools-record-more-than-60000-racist-incidents-five-years

Beard. R. (2021) *Sad Little Men* (London: Harvill Secker).

Belger. T. (2022). *Women and non-white staff far less likely to be promoted, DfE leaders study shows.* (Schools Week). Available at: https://schoolsweek.co.uk/women-and-non-white-staff-far-less-likely-to-promoted-dfe-leaders-study-shows/?mc_cid=3b420f392c&mc_eid=24623934f7

Boakye. J. (2019). *Black, Listed.* (Great Britain: Dialogue Books).

British Medical Journal (2020). *Ethnicity And Covid 19* (BMJ 2020;369) Available at: www. bmj.com/content/369/bmj.m2282

Burgess. S. and Greaves. E. (2009) *Test Scores, Subjective Assessment and Stereotyping of Ethnic Minorities* (IFS) Available at: https://ifs.org.uk/publications/7932

Choudry. S. (2021). *Equitable Education*. (St Albans: Critical Publishing).

CLPE Annual *Reflecting Realities* Report 2020 https://clpe.org.uk/research/clpe-reflecting-realities-survey-ethnic-representation-within-uk-childrens-literature-0

Dennis. J. (2008). Audio Interview with Dr. Steve Strand for The Guardian. Available at: www.theguardian.com/global/audio/2008/sep/05/raceineducation

Department For Education (2021). *Permanent Exclusions* (for 2018–19 school year) Available at: www.ethnicity-facts-figures.service.gov.uk/education-skills-and-training/absence-and-exclusions/permanent-exclusions/latest

Department For Education (2022) *Key Stage 4 Performance 2022*. Available at: https://expl ore-education-statistics.service.gov.uk/find-statistics/key-stage-4-performance-revised/ 2021-22

Gillborn. D. and Youdell. D. (2020). *Rationing Education: Policy, Practice, Reform and Equity*. (Buckingham: Open University Press).

Gov.UK (2021) *The report of the Commission on Race and Ethnic Disparities.* Available at: www.gov.uk/government/publications/the-report-of-the-commission-on-race-and-eth nic-disparities

Gov.UK (2022). *Ethnicity Facts And Figures: People Living in Low Income Households.* Available at: www.ethnicity-facts-figures.service.gov.uk/work-pay-and-benefits/pay-and-income/people-in-low-income-households/latest#by-ethnicity

Hirsch. A. (2018). *Brit(ish): On Race, Identity and Belonging.* (London: Vintage).

Hutchinson, J., Reader, M. and Akhal. A (2020). *Education In England Annual Report 2020.* (London: Education Policy Institute). Available at: https://dera.ioe.ac.uk/36268/

Katsha. H. (2022) *Most English School Kids Will Only Ever Be Taught By White Teachers There aren't enough teachers of colour in the UK (and it's not for want of applications).* *Huffington Post.* Available at: www.huffingtonpost.co.uk/entry/state-school-all-white-teachers_uk_62835f73e4b050d951964f42

Kentish. B. (2017) *Revealed: How 'racial bias' at the heart of criminal justice system means black people in UK more likely to be in prison than those in US* (The Guardian). Available at: www.independent.co.uk/news/uk/home-news/black-people-prison-uk-more-likely-us-lammy-review-a7935061.html

Khan. O. and Shaheen. F. (2017) *Minority Report: Race and Class in post-Brexit Britain* (The Runnymede Trust).

Kinouani, G. (2021) *Living While Black.* (London: Ebury Press).

Knight. M., Bunch. K., Tuffnell. D., Shakespeare. J., Kotnis. R., Kenyon. S. and Kurinczuk. J. (Eds.) (2019). *Saving Lives, Improving Mothers' Care.* (MBRRACE-UK) Available at: www. npeu.ox.ac.uk/mbrrace-uk/news/1834-npeu-news-black-women-are-five-times-more-lik ely-to-die-in-childbirth-than-white-women-why

Linton. S. (2017) *#16daysofactivism: beyond 'resilience' – black women and mental health.* Fawcett Society). Available at: www.fawcettsociety.org.uk/blog/16daysofactivism-bey ond-resilience-black-women-mental-health

Lorde, A. (2017). *Your Silence Will Not Protect You.* (UK: Silver Press).

McIntyre. N., Parveen. N. and Thomas. T. (2021). *Exclusion rates five times higher for black Caribbean pupils in parts of England.* (The Guardian). Available at: www.theguardian.com/education/2021/mar/24/exclusion-rates-black-caribbean-pupils-england

McPherson. W. (1999) *The Stephen Lawrence Inquiry Report* Gov.uk. Available at: www.gov.uk/government/publications/the-stephen-lawrence-inquiry

Mohdin. A. (2021). *Black Caribbean girls in England 'twice as likely to be excluded from schools as white girls.'* (The Guardian). Available at: www.theguardian.com/education/2021/sep/23/black-girls-in-england-twice-as-likely-to-be-excluded-from-schools-as-white-girls

Murphy. S. and Walker. A. (2020) *MPs urged to do unconscious bias training as dozens of Tories set to reject it.* (The Guardian). Available at: www.theguardian.com/world/2020/sep/21/mps-urged-to-do-unconscious-bias-training-as-dozens-of-tories-set-to-reject-it

National Literacy Trust (2020). *Children' and Young People's Reading in 2020 before and during the COVID-19 lockdown.* Available at: https://literacytrust.org.uk/research-services/research-reports/children-and-young-peoples-reading-in-2020-before-and-during-the-covid-19-lockdown/

Olusoga. D. (2021) *Southgate showed us a new England. But the old one hasn't gone away* (The Guardian). Available at: www.theguardian.com/commentisfree/2021/jul/13/southgate-showed-us-a-new-england-but-the-old-one-hasnt-gone-away

Sarpong, J. (2020). *The Power Of Privilege: How White People Can Challenge Racism.* (London: HQ).

Stewart-Hall. C. *Institutional Racism and Whiteness in Schools* in Wilson. H. and Kara. B. ed. (2022) *Diverse Educators: A Manifesto* (London: University of Buckingham Press).

Stone. J. (2021) *Priti Patel says fans have right to boo England team for 'gesture politics' of taking the knee.* (The Independent). Available at: www.independent.co.uk/news/uk/politics/priti-patel-taking-knee-boo-england-b1865409.html

Taylor. B. *The Best Practice in Grouping Students Study* in Francis. B, Taylor. B and Tereshchenko. A. (2019) *Reassessing Ability Grouping* (Abingdon: Routledge).

Tereshchenko. A., Mills. M., Bradbury. A. (2020) *Making Progress? Employment and retention of BAME teachers in England.* (UCL Institute of Education: London, UK). Available at: https://discovery.ucl.ac.uk/id/eprint/10117331/

Thomas. T. (2021) *Black youth unemployment rate of 40% similar to time of Brixton riots, data shows* (The Guardian). Available at: www.theguardian.com/society/2021/apr/11/black-youth-unemployment-rate-brixton-riots-covid

The Runnymede Trust (2021). *Civil Society Report To The United Nations CERD.* Available at: www.runnymedetrust.org/publications/civil-society-report-to-united-nations-cerd

TUC Report (2016). *Black workers with degrees earn a quarter less than white counterparts, finds TUC.* Available at: www.tuc.org.uk/news/black-workers-degrees-earn-quarter-less-white-counterparts-finds-tuc

Younge. G. (2018). *Welcome to the World Cup, where national failure unleashes dark forces* (The Guardian). Available at: www.theguardian.com/commentisfree/2018/jun/15/world-cup-national-failure-dark-forces-race-scapegoats

Worth. J., McLean. D. and Sharp. C. (2022) *Racial Equality In The Teacher Workforce* (NFER, Ambition Institute and Teach First). Available at: www.nfer.ac.uk/racial-equality-in-the-teacher-workforce/

2 Experiences of being a child of colour in an English school

Every person needs a place that is furnished with hope.

Maya Angelou

While race is a figment of our imagination, racism is not.

Guilaine Kinouani (2021:7)

At this point, let me introduce you to Yasmin, Cynthia, Bonolo, Nigel, Ayeesha, Rubia, Tom, Nabeela, Adarsh and Lucky – ten colleagues, ex-colleagues and friends who agreed to be interviewed as part of my research and whose voices appear at regular intervals in this book. At times their stories are directly attributed to them by name; at other points their identity is anonymised. They span a wide age range, from late sixties to early twenties. They hold a variety of positions from classroom teacher to middle leader, to adviser, to governor, to senior leader. Some work in the primary phase (one in Early Years) and others in secondary schools. Some are Black, some are Asian and some are of mixed heritage. Three are ex-pupils of mine (of whom one has become a school governor, one a head of faculty and one a headteacher).

Most of the questions I asked of my interviewees were about their experiences as adults and educators. However, the early questions invited them to share their memories of their schooldays. Some of these reflections are recounted later in the book, but a number are captured here. Everyone's school experiences are, of course, different. And the events that stick as memories and shape us as people are just a microcosm of what took place. My interviewees grew up and were educated in different parts of the country, in different types of schools and at different times in the past 60 years.

The context inevitably shapes the experience. But so does serendipity. Some children of colour are lucky to encounter teachers who are committed to championing their rights and are true anti-racist allies. Others are less fortunate. In his book *Natives*, Akala shares heart-breaking memories of his education in Camden in the 1980s: 'Some of my white middle class teachers made my school life extremely difficult and penalised me for the very thing they were supposed to

DOI: 10.4324/9781003275220-3

be nurturing: my intelligence' (2019:19). Sadly, few of the people of colour with whom I have discussed memories of their school days in the UK passed through the education system unaffected by racism. I am therefore completely respectful of those who decided not to share testimony, but supremely grateful to those who did.

Some school experiences of my interviewees

Nigel

Nigel's parents came to England from Barbados in the 1950s. After he and his brothers were born, the family moved to Letchworth. Nigel and one of his brothers attended an infants' school where they were the very first Black children in the area and the school. The headteacher got them up on stage to join him for the assembly on their first day. As all the children processed in to sit on the floor they 'oohed' and 'aahed' and pointed at the brothers with a mixture of excitement and amazement. The headteacher explained who Nigel and his brother were, saying that they were special children and that everyone in the school community had a responsibility to look after them and care for them. Nigel reflected, 'This was such a change from the colour-blind attitude of the 70s and 80s!' Nigel never felt that expectations were different for him at school. Race was not a big issue to him at this time.

At secondary school, race became more significant, and at university Nigel faced direct racial discrimination from one of his tutors who made sinister references to eugenics and natural selection in his lectures. This tutor marked Nigel down during his PGCE, giving his final assessment 40%. Nigel took his name off the essay and asked a more senior tutor to read and assess it. The essay was awarded 75% plus.

Yasmin

In contrast to Nigel, Yasmin grew up in a part of London where the majority ethnic group was Asian Indian – her ethnicity. She reflects, 'I thought I was normal. There were about three white families on the road – proper English people.' Like Nigel, she can remember in the late 1970s, the National Front riots and Blair Peach. 'My part of London was attacked. When I was eight, my family had to leave home one weekend and go to stay with an uncle. The National Front smashed shop windows. It felt a bit like a movie. I wondered, "Why do these people hate us?"'

'I attended a three to four-form entry primary school with predominantly Punjabi Indians, yet the curriculum was very Anglicised. There was an occasional Diwali assembly but it was very tokenistic. There were only two Asian staff members. I became aware that I was not "proper English". In secondary school, too, the curriculum was not culturally diverse or reflective of my heritage, despite most of the pupils again being Asian Indian. All of the food was traditional British food, but I liked that! When I went to university, I had never seen so many white people!'

Ayeesha

Ayeesha writes: 'I attended primary school in Blackburn in 1979 and society at the time was rife with racism. Even at that age, I was aware of language which was racist that would be spoken by people we would pass on the street, in the shops and on the TV. I remember young people (possibly teenagers) setting their dogs on us. At school there was an optional uniform; most of the white children wore a uniform and most of the Asian Muslim children didn't, including myself. The Asian Hindu children did wear the uniform. I don't recall any Sikh children. This was a Christian primary school, and I knew I was not the same as everybody in my school; some children in my class were white and some were brown. We couldn't afford uniform so I would wear many of my older sister's hand-me-downs and most of these were Asian dresses. The headteacher told me off in front of the whole school and told me never to wear one particular dress again. I think the headteacher was telling me off for wearing a flary dress with flary sleeves which was going into my soup, so she may not have meant to sound racist – but this was what I thought at the time.

I was invited to a white girl's house one Saturday. I went in my best pink dress because that's what I thought you did. We played on roller skates – which was my very first time – and I was given food with ham/bacon. I don't remember what my reaction was – whether I did or didn't eat it. I didn't receive an invite again but I was very close to a Hindu girl who lived a few streets away. I did go to her house but I don't think my parents were too keen because she was a Hindu and my parents were very strict Muslims. The Muslim Asian children also attended mosque from 5pm to 7.15 pm every day, including me.

The teachers were all white. I remember reading to my Year 1 teacher at the front of the class and I didn't know what the countryside was so she organised a trip to the local farm. On the day we were leaving, the teacher reminded everyone why we were going because "she" (pointing at me) "doesn't know what the countryside is". I remember my Year 6 teacher pointing at all the white children in the class and saying, about me "If her sister can do that, then so can all of you". For dinner, white children would line up separately to Muslim Asian children, due to Muslims eating vegetarian food (because the school did not provide halal food, we were given the vegetarian option.)

In secondary school, I took part in Duke of Edinburgh. I was the leader of my group and everyone in my group was Asian. The remaining groups were mainly white. I mentioned something about this and it got back to the teacher who was organising the expedition. She told me off for accusing her of being racist. When we went on the actual expedition, we were placed in mixed groups.'

Rubia

Rubia recalls having a very early awareness of race: 'My parents made me aware of who I was as soon as I was able to comprehend this – I was fully aware of being Muslim which immediately set me apart from my non-Muslim peers. There were often comments such as "We are different, we have different values. Pakistani people have a different way of life, Muslims don't do that". We visited Pakistan for the first time when I was three and my parents' circle of friends were mostly Asian so I had a sense of race/ethnicity/faith from a very early age. Also, my parents bought me the "black Pippa doll" and we brought back dolls dressed in Asian outfits from Pakistan. I had a sense from around age four of being treated differently by white neighbours when playing with their children. I would say I became fully aware as a young adult when I went to a party and stopped dead because I was the only non-white person there.

At school I was shouted at for having hennaed hands, accused of graffitiing my hands and sent to the bathroom to scrub it off (which was an impossible task!). I wasn't given the opportunity to explain fully what mendhi is and was not believed even when I tried. In a couple of incidents between myself and white students the white students were believed/sided with over me (white girl tears). I was once called a "Paki" at primary school by another Asian student which amused and bewildered me; I shouted back "But you're one too!"

I do not believe that teachers at school had the same expectations of me as other students. I had no feeling/experience that they had any knowledge or understanding of my heritage. I was, to all intents and purposes, a "brown" white student. When moving from a grammar school in the Midlands to a grammar school in Kent (which was 99% white) I was immediately placed in the bottom set for English and maths without any assessment. The history curriculum was completely Eurocentric. There was never any conversation or learning around world history or events. I suppose I felt numb. I asked to participate in the Duke of Edinburgh scheme and was overlooked without any explanation. Generally, there was a lack of encouragement to participate in curriculum enrichment activities.

There were some cultural barriers to residential trips but I did go on a weekend French exchange twice – perhaps if the school had liaised more with my family, further opportunities could have been availed. Visits to souvenir shops on school trips were frustrating as I never had anything with my name printed on it, that "Bella" or "Francesca" were able to purchase. At university, when I had to repeat my first year, my lecturer informed me that there was not much point in retaking the year as most people failed on the retake.

There were no teachers of colour at my schools or at university. At the time, when you are living through it and lack life experience, you don't always understand or appreciate the significance; now, in hindsight, I can see it probably stifled my ability to express concerns – such as conversations around dietary, dress or prayer requirements.'

Bonolo

In contrast to Rubia, Bonolo first became aware of the concept of race when he was about 11 years old, 'which seems a little old compared to other black people. Living in a household with a black mother, a white step-father and mixed siblings meant that conversations around race rarely happened. My parents focused on character and content building rather than skin colour. I think this was a conscious effort not to highlight differences in the family unit. A fellow pupil highlighted the differences in race within my family by asking me why I had a "white dad" when I was clearly black. I knew that my step-dad was not my biological dad but did not understand why his colour was relevant and why a student in my school was clearly concerned with the colour of his skin compared to mine. I went home and my mum explained the concept of race to me.

When I first joined secondary school I faced a challenging time during P.E. lessons. I was overweight. The teachers expected me to be good at P.E., even though I found it physically challenging. I was often mocked and teachers looked disappointed. My P.E. teacher would call me "coloured" and I knew that this was not right but kept quiet. When I lost weight a few years later, I began to do a little better in sport. I began to get frequent praise that was not equal to my performance. Teachers would then use plenty of praise and compare me to sportsmen, but they didn't do this for other students. The teachers in P.E. had totally unrealistic expectations of me based on what they saw Black sports people doing in wider society. This actually made me feel weak or inadequate when I did not fit the stereotype. I look back on it and realise that this was one of the few subjects in school where I was given high aspirations to work towards.

Throughout school I faced unwarranted personal questions, jokes and comments from other students about my race and background. When students called me names, nine times out of ten I did not report it. This was because the majority of teachers were white and I thought that no action would be taken. When I did report it, teachers often would try to justify it. I remember when a student said that my skin was "dirty", I reported this. The teacher told me that it was probably said because I was playing outside and maybe the boy was being inquisitive. I knew that the teacher understood and clearly did not want to see my point of view. This made me feel unheard and unseen, but I quickly got used to it and learned to deal with instances like this on my own.'

Lucky

Like Bonolo, Lucky (who is British Indian Sikh) didn't report incidents of racism towards her to her parents or teachers: 'I didn't tell my family when I was the target of racist slurs. It hurt but I didn't know how to share. I was not sure what the response would be. I didn't want my parents to be hurt. I didn't know if my teachers would dismiss what I said or whether there would be repercussions. I remember being emotionally affected. I took a certain route home from school. One day a group of children intercepted me. They called me a "Paki" and slashed at my legs. There were three girls and one on the wall, not involved. On another occasion, I was mistaken for another girl when I went to some local shops. A group of children insisted I was the girl they were looking for because of my skin colour, repeatedly chanting "Paki". I didn't share this with anyone as I didn't know how to or how my teachers would respond.

My name in full is Lakhbir. I remember occasions where my name was mocked, with comments like "Do you want a beer?" or "Blackbeard". At school, I was referred to as "Laky" until a teacher commented, "Are you a slave?" My family have always called me Lucky and it seemed to "fit" better than Lakhbir or Laky. Also, Lucky as a name appeared to be more acceptable and to "conform", without the fear of my name being mispronounced or mocked.'

Tom

Tom also experienced issues with his name as a teenager: 'I had felt very conscious of my foreign surname (Hassan) for a while. Most of my friendship group were white British and I didn't want to feel different to them. I began to see this as an opportunity to change my name and take my mum's maiden name (Coleman – how very English!). I didn't want to have to be hyper-vigilant for people using terms like "Paki", and naively thought this was the answer. Deep down, I knew it was because I wanted to be like everyone else, not having to explain my heritage each time I met someone. I spoke to my mum and a friend of hers, who both discouraged me. Interestingly, it was a close friend, who wasn't at all averse to using terms like "Paki shop", who was completely aghast that I should be thinking along these lines. He felt really strongly that it was a bad idea and that changing my name would change something in me.'

Cynthia

Cynthia recalls that, as a mixed-race pupil with one Black and one White parent, she was 'constantly called names at school. Nothing was ever said or done about it. Interestingly, it was mainly my "friends" (boys, not girls) that called me names and I sort of accepted it. Sometimes I would cry or tell them not to. They would stop for a bit but it always started again. It was just the way it was.'

Nabeela

Nabeela's recollections of school are, in contrast, very positive:

'I was really fortunate to attend two great schools which promoted equality and respect, so I never experienced racism as a learner. My pupil experience at both primary and secondary school were incredibly positive because there was a real sense of inclusivity. There was a conscious effort to understand and celebrate the diverse school population. I certainly believe that teachers had the same expectations of me as of other students, if not higher. My secondary school exuded excellence and had really high expectations of all pupils, whether that be in behaviour, attendance or attainment. Where a pupil showed great enjoyment and perseverance towards a subject or skill, they were pointed in the right direction and presented with several opportunities. For example, I remember my English teacher encouraging me to participate in writing competitions and my form tutor motivating me to become a form rep. Staff did have knowledge and understanding of my heritage and I felt this in a number of positive interactions with them.

I recollect my heritage being reflected in the curriculum – in RE and in the study of poems such as 'Presents from my Aunt in Pakistan,' and 'Search for my Tongue' which touches upon the struggles that we might have seen first generation immigrants like our parents go through. My heritage was reflected so incredibly well in the school culture and hidden curriculum that I didn't feel the need to search for it in the curriculum. I clearly remember assemblies about Muslim figures and Islamic festivals, an option to wear shalwar kameez, a prayer room with washing facilities, an iftar event every Ramadhan – there was a real openness about the rich and diverse demographical make-up and the leaders celebrated the entire school community.

There were a number of teachers of colour in my school and many in middle or senior leadership positions. I remember speaking to my Muslim maths teacher about inspirational sayings by Prophet Muhammad (pbuh) and discussing with the deputy headteacher the racism he encountered as a Black student in the 1960s. The White teachers were just as accepting, curious and kind, but speaking to other teachers of colour who I could connect to in terms of race, religion or experiences made me feel a greater sense of belonging at the school. I didn't have to search for commonality; it was there. At the time, I don't think I realised the impact this had on me but, looking back, I think it made me subconsciously believe that race equity and inclusivity were the norm. I genuinely believed that all schools in London by default were inclusive and represented the rich diversity of the city. It's a sad reality that I have come to realise that my secondary school was a rarity and I have only seen it replicated so well in the next school my headteacher led.'

Nabeela's is an uplifting account to end this chapter with. I read her testimony with pride as I was her RE teacher and the headteacher of her secondary school. Yet I am under no illusion that not every student who passed through the school felt the same way (and neither did every parent of a pupil from a minority ethnic background). I look back on my time as a leader at the school and realise that there was far more that I and my colleagues could have done to be effective anti-racist allies. This leads us into Chapter 3, which considers the pivotal role of school leaders in creating an anti-racist culture and ethos.

Take some time to reflect on the stories told in this chapter.

How do they make you feel? What questions do they raise? What did they teach you?

Would teachers and leaders of colour in your school/trust tell similar tales of their time as school children? What are the implications for the leaders of your organisation?

Would the pupils in your school(s) tell similar stories to any of these? How do you know?

How, at your school, are people of colour encouraged and supported to share their lived experience?

What race equity issues do these testimonies raise? You might find it helpful to make a list.

We will return to the themes touched on in these accounts in the following chapters.

Before we move on, a note about asking people of colour to provide testimony of lived experience:

When I started work on this book, I wrote to a number of colleagues and asked whether they would be prepared to be interviewed by me, or complete a questionnaire, to share their experiences as educators of colour. I thought very carefully about the questions that I wanted to ask and the way in which I worded my request. I gave assurances that it was fine to just answer some parts of the questionnaire and that I would quite understand if anyone declined to participate. I offered a face-to-face interview, a zoom interview or the option to provide written responses. I ran the questionnaire and email by a close friend, seeking candid feedback as to how it might be received.

What happened next was an education for me. A few of those to whom I wrote replied almost instantly, saying that they would be very happy to provide testimony, that they thought it was really important that this book was written and that they welcomed the opportunity to play a part in it. Others agreed to participate but shared with me that the questions I had posed had caused them not inconsiderable anxiety and distress. One headteacher colleague, whom I count as a friend, said to me that when she first read the questions she felt fine and confident to answer them, but that then, over the following days, they triggered a number of deeply buried memories to surface and she started to experience disturbed sleep and distressing emotions. She told me that she briefly felt resentment towards me for having caused these long-buried feelings to re-emerge. In contrast, another colleague, whom I interviewed in person, said that she had found the discussion quite cathartic. She did, however, state that some of the testimony that she had shared with me concerned incidents that she had not told anyone about ever before. In recounting one event in particular, she paused and reflected that this incident had shaped the whole of the rest of her career and that she had never realised that before.

Notably, a small number of people to whom I sent my questions did not respond at all. I had thought carefully about which potential interviewees, from a sizeable number of possibilities, I would ask to participate in my research. I had chosen people with whom I had a positive connection and I felt would trust my good intentions and feel safe to be open with me. I now felt terrible. I was conscious that I must have caused upset or offence. I wanted to reach out to these individuals but felt that that would compound the situation. Fortunately, one of these individuals contacted me and asked to discuss how he had felt on receiving my email and the reasons for his reticence to participate. We had a very productive conversation which increased my understanding considerably. Later, I spoke to Toks Olusamokun, race equity adviser at HFL Education, about the matter and she reflected, 'When Black and Asian people are asked to speak on issues of racism, they have to confront: loss, humiliation, embarrassment, uncomfortable truths, personal failings, fear etc. It's an internal battle and I imagine that most felt conflicted: should they speak up and let it out – particularly when you're likely to meet eye-rolls or be ignored – or is it better to keep suppressing and moving on?'

This episode reinforced for me that no one knows the lived experiences of others or the memories that can be triggered by an action. It is impossible for a White person to comprehend the depths of the hurt and distress caused by being subjected to racist comments and actions. As a White, advantaged person, treading cautiously and with the utmost sensitivity is imperative. And taking responsibility for upset caused, albeit unintentionally, is essential.

A couple of my ten interviewees were not in the first tranche of colleagues I contacted but people who, as a result of discussions in the intervening months, offered to write accounts of their experiences to be included in the book.

References

Akala (2019). *Natives: Race & Class in the Ruins of Empire.* (Great Britain: Two Roads).
Kinouani, G. (2021) *Living While Black.* (London: Ebury Press).

PART TWO
Developing racial literacy

The unique and critical role of the leader

Progress occurs when courageous, skilful leaders seize the opportunity to change things for the better.

Attributed to Harry Truman

If you are a white person who would like to treat black people as equals in every way – who would like to have a set of associations with blacks that are as positive as those that you have with whites – it requires more than a simple commitment to equality. It requires that you change your life.

Malcolm Gladwell (2005:97)

A school cannot be truly anti-racist if the adults in it are not racially literate and without the staff and young people who make up the school community being effectively supported, at an age-appropriate level, to consider and talk about issues of race. And achieving racial literacy and safe spaces to talk about race starts with the leaders of the school – chairs of trust boards or governing bodies, headteachers and principals, senior leaders, middle leaders, phase leaders, subject leaders, EDI leads – anyone and everyone who leads a team of adults.

Four fundamental truths

If you are determined to make your school a truly anti-racist institution and you occupy one of the roles listed above, there are four fundamental truths that you need to embrace.

I Your role as leader is critical

It is *your* responsibility to create a culture and ethos of race equity. If you are not passionate about this mission, you will not succeed. If you do not put a commitment to eradicating race inequity at the forefront of every decision you

DOI: 10.4324/9781003275220-5

make, every action you take and your core behaviour at all times, your progress will be slow and of limited impact.

You must lead from the front in order to take everyone with you. If you are not seen by your team members and those that you lead as totally driven in your anti-racist work, you will find it difficult to take others with you. They will not appreciate the importance of this priority and make it *their* priority. They will not sense the urgency and strive to effect change for those in the school community *now*. They will not understand the moral imperative and the ways in which race equity underpins all of the school's business. And this is a problem because of the second truth …

2 An antiracist culture cannot be achieved by you alone

In fact, it will never be truly embedded unless every single individual in the school community/team is acting as an anti-racist ally. Your work will not be done until everyone in your establishment/team is working confidently and consistently to eradicate racism in all its forms. Michelle Obama said in an Instagram post of May 2020: 'Race and racism is a reality that so many of us grow up learning to just deal with. But if we ever hope to move past it, it can't just be on people of color to deal with it. It's up to all of us… to do the honest, uncomfortable work of rooting it out.'

3 Race equity requires a life-long commitment

It would be perfectly understandable if you were to be feeling somewhat daunted by this message. As Malcolm Gladwell suggests above, race equity cannot be a focus for one academic year, the theme of one training day or a strand on a school development plan that is ticked off after a few milestones have been reached. Remember that, as the old saying goes, the best way to eat an elephant is one bite at a time! But, as a leader, you know that you hold power. You can and do effect change all the time. You frequently take on audacious challenges and achieve remarkable feats. As Audre Lorde reminds us, 'There are many kinds of power, used and unused, acknowledged or otherwise' (2017:22).

4 There is nothing easy about this work

You need to be comfortable with the uncomfortable and accept that this will not be simple or straightforward. You are more than likely to face resistance, overt or unconscious. You may well bump into fears and fragilities. There are race inequities in all institutions and most people have a natural aversion to change and challenge. Rosa Parks is credited with having said that to bring about change, you must not be afraid to take the first step.

Before you read on, consider these questions:

Are you ready to make a career and life-long commitment to being an anti-racist ally?

How confident are you to lead on this agenda?

How can you increase your skill level and confidence?

Developing your racial literacy

An anti-racist culture starts at the top of the organisation and the tone is set by its leaders. So it is imperative that they are racially literate themselves. Just as the safety announcement on planes reminds you of the need, in the case of an emergency, to put your own oxygen mask on first before trying to help passengers around you, leaders need to skill themselves up around race issues in order to have the confidence, understanding and authority to develop the racial literacy of others. How should they best do that? Importantly, as with developing any skill, it requires a degree of immersion and a conscious time investment – time to read, time to think, time to listen and time to discuss.

There are lots of books about various aspects of race equity and reading lists provided by a number of organisations. At HFL Education we produced a suggested adult reading list for staff in schools to coincide with World Book Day last year and sent this to all schools, along with some vouchers for the purchase of books. Some were autobiographical stories of the experiences of people of colour, some were polemics about what is wrong with our society or our schools, some were manifestos for change and some were self-development books for anti-racism allyship. In my experience, whatever text is your gateway into the topic, you will find references and links to further reading. So, when educators ask me where they might start with their reading, I tend to say that it really doesn't matter, just as it isn't of significance which side of the pool you get into – the key thing is to dip a toe into the water, or even to dive straight in! Little by little, your understanding will grow. And then you will want to discuss your reading, your questions and your reflections, which is where setting up a staff library or reading group is a great idea. It might be that all the members of the leadership team agree to read a particular text over a holiday and then discuss it at an SLT meeting at the start of term.

Or that you choose a key reading for the governors/trustees and debate the learning and its implications for the school at a board meeting.

But remember that you will learn at least as much from listening as you will from reading and talking. It is vital that leaders find time to listen to the experiences, views, opinions and ideas of people of colour: staff, pupils, former students, parents and carers, members of the community.

This is especially important for White leaders whose privileges, conferred on them by their race, make it so hard to understand the impact of race inequality. By listening you are being educated and supported to see things from different people's perspectives. Leaders need to listen without judgement and to listen without interruption. It is important that your staff see you listening to and learning from divergent voices, because this is what you will require from them as you support them to develop their racial literacy (more of this in Chapter 5). This can be done in a myriad of different ways: through questionnaires, surveys, focus groups, group or individual interviews, informal chats. At times it might be that you are focusing on particular issues or eliciting feedback on specific matters: on other occasions it will be more a case of simply making time to hear and learn about the lived experience, in and out of school, of people of colour. Importantly, this should be natural, regular, routine and embedded into your practice.

Demonstrating your commitment

It is vital that everyone in the school community sees and feels that their leaders are fully committed to striving to make the school an anti-racist organisation. They need to be confident that their leaders will pick up and deal effectively with any incidents of racism – covert or overt, intentional or unconscious – and to feel that the school is a safe space to raise and address any issue of race equity.

There are so many ways in which leaders can show strong anti-racist leadership. Different strategies will work in different contexts and what might suit one leader's styles might not be so appropriate for or natural to another. Here are 10 suggestions:

Activity

How do you/could you demonstrate to your staff your commitment to anti-racism?

Make a list of ways in which you currently do this.

How could you do this with greater visibility and impact?

Some great ways of demonstrating to your school community your commitment to anti-racism

1. Making a public declaration and sharing personal targets that are a commitment to personal action.

2. Communicating your high expectations of all staff and all learners and striving to ensure that all staff and learners share the highest expectations of themselves and each other.

3. Giving time to ensure that every race incident is dealt with and the school's actions communicated appropriately.

4. Ensuring that the ethnicities and heritages present in the school are known by all and that key data is shared appropriately and utilised to ensure representation.

5. Leading a review of the school's policies to ensure that anti-racism is embedded within each.

6. Modelling the importance of honouring everyone's name.

7. Creating an infrastructure of roles, responsibilities and resourcing to ensure there is the capacity to generate the momentum to tackle race inequity.

8. Keeping race equity at the top of the school's agenda: on meeting agendas, in the School Improvement Plan, in appraisal objectives etc.

9. Protecting time for regular and ongoing racial literacy training, enabling staff and students to talk and learn about race issues.

10. Creating a school-wide common language around race equity.

Some of these strategies will be considered in the coming chapters. Numbers 7, 8 and 9 will be explored in Chapters 5 and 6 when we take a deeper look at developing the racial literacy of all adults in the school. Suggestion 10 gets a whole chapter to itself – Chapter 4. For now, let's take a closer look at strategies 1–6. But first …

A word about getting it wrong

It is a brave thing to do as a school leader, especially if you are White, to declare yourself as the leader of your school's anti-racism work. Not because this is a contentious priority – far from it, race equity is a fundamental safeguarding issue after all. But, because this is a complex and sensitive issue, most of us are on a steep learning curve and the potential for clumsy mistakes and unintentional upset is great. The more I delve, the more I appreciate the challenges and unpredictabilities. Making mistakes is almost an inevitability and it is important that we appreciate that, whilst far from ideal, this is OK so long as our mistakes come from well-intentioned actions, are acknowledged, owned and apologised for and we show a determination to learn from them. We have to start from not knowing. Leaders need to show their fallibility and talk about their own biases, prejudices and mistakes. Confronting and addressing these with staff and governors/trustees can be very powerful.

In her book *Just Work*, Kim Scott gives excellent advice about how to make impactful apologies. She quotes the advice of Lauren M. Bloom in Art of the Apology:

- 'Say you're sorry…sincerely

- Explain what went wrong

- Take responsibility

- Make amends

- Express appreciation

- Listen to the person's pain with patience

- Offer repair

- Request forgiveness

- Promise it won't happen again.' (2021:114–5)

Ayeesha offers the following advice to school leaders:

> This is a very sensitive issue and is very raw at the moment. Since the momentum of Black Lives Matter, I have certainly felt that I have a bigger part to play in the 'diversity' agenda. However, I still feel very uncomfortable speaking out and raising concerns about issues on race. People of colour, as with any group, are made up of all different ethnicities, genders, religions, and all have different experiences. Who am I to say how a non-Indian lapsed Muslim feels about an issue? My experience is completely different. It can be very patronising to people from ethnic minority groups when a White person attempts to talk about issues of race when they have not had any personal experience of racism or discrimination. Think about the language you use. Be open, be brave and show your vulnerability – your colleagues will respect you more.

The bottom line is that inaction is not an option. When Gary Younge came to Hertfordshire in 2020 to address the secondary headteachers, he told them very plainly that it was their job to tackle and challenge racism in their school: 'It's not a moral calling, it's your job.'

Making a public declaration and sharing personal targets that are a commitment to personal action

The words of school leaders are powerful. What you tell your school community will have enormous impact on staff, students, parents and carers. So, use that power to communicate a commitment to create an anti-racist school through your words in assemblies, staff meetings, your welcome to the school on the website, your news-letter messages, your speech at open day, your reports to governors/trustees.

Talk to people in your school community about the reading you are doing to become more racially literate, what you are learning and how it is changing your practice. You could have a picture of and link to your current reading as your email signature or on your office door.

Consider setting yourself an appraisal goal about becoming a more effective anti-racist ally. You might choose to share that goal or target with staff, parents and/or learners and update them on your progress at points during the year. By setting this example to your staff you would then be in an ideal position to suggest that everyone considers and designs an anti-racism goal for themselves on an annual basis – staff and learners. Imagine the impact that would have, especially if you shared and displayed these, allocated everyone a buddy to support them in reviewing their goal and protected time for the review activity!

Communicating your high expectations of all staff and all learners and striving to ensure that all staff and learners share the highest expectations of themselves and each other

I have written in depth in *Obstetrics for Schools* about how school leaders can create a climate and culture of the highest expectations of all, regardless of their prior attainment or performance or any barriers to success they may be struggling to overcome. The anti-racist leader appreciates that students from cer-tain ethnic backgrounds do not typically perform as well or progress as quickly as those from certain other ethnic groups. They are driven by a desire to create a culture in which all students, regardless of colour or heritage, have strong self-esteem, high aspirations, exciting dreams and a belief in their ability to break glass ceilings and achieve a great future. A key element of this is about ensuring that the curriculum is expansive and diverse and that students from all backgrounds can see themselves reflected and represented around the school – in displays, in resources, in house and room and class names. This is explored in detail in Chapters 7–9. Such leaders analyse all sorts of data sets forensically and take appropriate remedial action swiftly to ensure that there is equity of provision for and participation of all ethnic groups and no gaps between the outcomes of certain groups.

The anti-racist leader feels a responsibility to ensure that their high aspirations and expectations of all learners are shared and conveyed by all staff. And they pick up anyone whose behaviour lapses from that standard. Here a staff code of conduct can be very helpful.

Extracts from an exemplar Staff Code of Conduct:

To demonstrate belief in the potential of all students to develop the skills and character necessary to progress to higher education and/or a prestigious career and to achieve success in life.

To embrace shared accountability for the achievements of all students.

To maintain zero tolerance of any form of staff or student behaviour that runs counter to the school's stated aims and objectives: for example, disrespect, rudeness, discrimination, bullying.

To provide excellent role-modelling for students at all times.

To take responsibility for developing students' emotional wellbeing as well as nurturing their academic potential: never behaving in a discriminatory, derogatory, intimidatory, abusive or sarcastic manner towards any member of the school community.

To behave courteously, respectfully and professionally at all times.

Unconscious biases (which we will explore further in Chapter 6) can result in staff having different – lower, or higher – expectations of learners from different ethnic groups. Such behaviours require swift and direct, but proportionate intervention. Kim Scott writes, 'Any time a bias interruption takes the form of an attack on another person's morality, it's an anvil being used to pull out a screw: the wrong tool for the job, and it will cause ancillary damage' (2021:340). Instead of shaming, the best leaders focus on creating a learning environment. Having said that, the strong anti-racist leader does take firm action where incidents of bullying or racist behaviour occur against a member of staff or student.

Giving time to ensure that every racial incident is dealt with and the school's actions communicated appropriately

Teachers set the tone for their classes and leaders set the tone for the school. The headteacher is responsible for establishing and maintaining a culture where every incident of racism matters, is addressed and is resolved. Not every accusation of racism will be found to be true or proven but they all deserve to be taken seriously. It is the leader's role to establish and communicate what is acceptable and what is not. Of course, the head cannot control everything that happens in the school and will not have the capacity to deal with every incident personally. However, they need to be confident that the pastoral structures in the school are robust enough and the staff skilled enough that, whatever team or phase of the school an incident occurs in, it will be addressed and resolved consistently and equally effectively. And this practice inevitably takes considerable leadership involvement, oversight and quality assurance to establish and maintain.

Leaders must be brave. They must ensure that every complaint is dealt with. There can never be any excuses made for someone's age, background, previous 'good character' or assumed intentions, albeit that these factors will inevitably inform decisions as to the appropriate response. Leaders must never justify or 'explain away' racist behaviours. Anti-racism is about calling out and confronting racism, in every manifestation, on every occasion. This is not to say that it is about public humiliation or punishment, although it is important that the school community is informed about how high-profile incidents of racism have been dealt with and resolved.

Students need to be able to say 'This is what happens in our school when racism takes place. The headteacher takes incidents of racism really seriously and so do all the staff. This is the system. These are the sanctions. This is what anti-racism looks like here. The school takes action.' If not, there is a very real danger that pupils will not report incidents, either because they don't feel they are serious enough to pass on, or because they will not be perceived by adults as serious enough to address, or because they do not trust the adults to resolve the matter effectively, without fallout and recriminations.

And staff need to feel the faith in their headteacher that it is safe to report any incident of discrimination, stereotyping or bias without fear that they will be expected to resolve it themselves or that they are somehow causing trouble or adding to leaders' workload. In Chapter 11 we will see that, sadly, many staff of colour suffer racism in silence and there are too many stories of leaders failing to treat racism seriously or deal with it effectively. This has a direct impact on racially minoritised educators' sense of belonging and their likelihood to stay in the school and in the profession.

Through establishing a safe environment to call out racism, it is likely that the number of incidents reported will rise, and perhaps dramatically. Anti-racist leaders (heads, senior leaders, governors and trustees) are not afraid of that: they recognise that this is actually a good thing because it is only by exposing the roots and examining them carefully that the weed can be dug out fully. They examine the data forensically, learn from it and adjust their actions accordingly. They may well choose to share the figures and findings with their students, parents and the community. Far from this being a case of airing their dirty laundry in public, this is about an open acknowledgement that racism is a stubborn problem in society and that the school means business in seeking to eradicate it from the institution.

Ensuring that the ethnicities and heritages present in the school are known by all and that key data is shared appropriately and utilised to ensure representation

What is the ethnic make-up of:

a) the staff body? b) the governors/trustees? c) the pupils in your school?

What percentage are from each ethnic group?

And do you share this data regularly with all your staff and governors/trustees?

I often ask these questions (of heads, heads of subject/department, year or phase leads, chairs of governors, trustees) when I am in schools and I very rarely come across anyone who can answer with confidence. If I then follow up with the question 'So you don't carry those figures in your head but would you know where to find them?', this is also often met with uncertainty.

Why does it matter whether colleagues are aware of the backgrounds of members of the school community?

As Yasmin said to me, 'You don't run a successful business without understanding your customers.' As a head, I would regularly share key data around the ethnicity of our students and staff cohorts with staff and governors. I wanted everyone to know and understand the heritages, backgrounds and cultures present in the school. At INSET sessions at the start of the academic year we would spend time looking at the ethnicity of our students, the religions they followed and the languages they spoke and consider the implications for us as educators. Curious questions were welcomed. The expertise of staff was utilised to educate their peers. Colleagues were encouraged to delve deeper, to research heritages about which their knowledge was sketchy and resources and links were made available. This led to discussions about prayer and ablution facilities, the need for daily halal (for Muslims), non-halal (for Sikhs) and vegetarian meal options and the compilation of a list of languages spoken by staff to call on when in need of interpreters.

There was an occasion when we retendered our cleaning contract and the staff provided by the new company happened to be from a tight community of immigrants from the Islands of SaoTome and Principe, off the Western Equatorial Coast of Central Africa. I put together a fact sheet about the islands and some basic phrases in Portuguese and circulated it to all staff, along with the names of the cleaners and the areas of the school that each was covering. It was important to me that all staff members could address the cleaning staff they would come across by name, in their language and that they would know a little about their heritage to ease conversation. If I had had the same basic grounding in Sylheti Bengalis when I had started as a teacher in Tower Hamlets in the 1990s I might not have embarrassed myself in assembly in the first week by asking for Rukshana Begum to wait behind to talk to me; I would have been aware that Begum is an extremely common last name for Bangladeshi girls and Rukshana a popular first name – hence half a dozen girls staying to see me!

When I was head at Isaac Newton Academy, staff conducted a home visit to every family before each child started at the school. Part of the purpose was to get to know the background of the pupil and to check their key details (rather than relying on the previous school records which, on occasion, were incomplete or inaccurate). We would ask for confirmation of first name, last name and known name (I once taught a pupil who went his whole school career with staff calling him by his last name because his school record had his last and first names mixed up and he had not had the courage to tell anyone). The details gathered from the home visits were transferred to a data base to which staff had access so that they could get to know their tutees and those whom they taught and utilise their varied lived experiences to enrich their curriculum delivery (more of this in Part Three).

If staff are clear about the cultures and ethnicities represented amongst the school population, there is an increased likelihood that they will ensure representation (and not tokenism) in the curriculum, in visual displays and in resources used in teaching. We will look at this in greater detail in Chapter 9. Lucky reflected to me, 'The representation of different backgrounds and cultures of all the community need to be embedded in the school. If you took the children out, would you be able to tell, from what you saw in the school, the backgrounds of the children who learns there? The notion of providing a 'sense of belonging' is crucial.'

And why does it matter that staff know the percentages of different ethnic groups present in the school?

Well, I often talk to senior leaders, subject leaders, phase leaders or year leaders in schools about whether they track by ethnicity student data on: progress and per-formance outcomes, make up of pupil groupings, exclusions and other sanctions, rewards, leadership posts, student council members, prefects, progression into sixth form or on to university, NEETs, take up of extra-curricular and enrichment activities, attendance on school trips. If staff are diligent about tracking the representation of pupils from White, Black, Asian and other ethnic backgrounds in any of these data sets but don't know the overall ethnic balance in the cohort, the exercise is of limited value! An English teacher who has data showing that 20% of the students who participated in the last three Poetry Slams were Pakistani needs to have a sense of whether that broadly equates with the proportion of students in the cohort who are Pakistani. And the pastoral leader who notices that only 3% of those who have taken part in Duke of Edinburgh expedition over the last five years are Black students needs to be clear about whether that is in line with the representation of Black learners at the school or shows an under – or indeed over – representation. One of my interviewees shared with me the fact that 14% of the students in the school they worked in were Black but not one member of the pupil parliament was Black.

Anti-racist leaders equip all staff with key and powerful data around the ethnicities present in school cohorts, give time for staff to analyse and interrogate the data, encourage curious questions, provide resources to deepen understanding, expect the data to be used to assess representation, quiz colleagues about trends seen and hold them to account for smart action planning to further equity and inclusion.

Leading a review of the school's policies to ensure that anti-racism is embedded within each

One of the most effective ways of guarding against the school's anti-racism work being tokenistic, patchy or superficial is to ensure that a commitment to anti-racism is at the heart of and permeates each and every policy. The school's anti-racism policy is, of course, crucial. Sandra Smidt's book *Creating an Anti-Racist Culture in the Early Years* gives excellent advice as to what an anti-racism policy should contain and how leaders might go about creating one. She advises that co-creation with pupils, staff and parents is preferable and stresses the importance of sharing the policy produced. She says that 'Ideally the policy should be available in all the languages of the communities served by the setting...The policy should also be prominent and evident in every room of the setting.' She argues that 'The school keeper needs to see it as much as the parents; the kitchen staff as much as the teachers' and suggests that 'Every new member of staff should be given a copy and offered the opportunity to have a private session with the headteacher or head of centre or the member of staff tasked with being the leader on anti-racism' (2020:76).

Does your school have an anti-racism policy? Or is anti-racism addressed through an EDI policy?

If not, do you think there would be benefits to creating one and how might you go about this?

If you do have a policy, how well does it shape up against Smidt's exacting criteria above?

Is there a direct link to your Equality statement and Equalities Objectives?

How might you refresh and recharge your policy to ensure it is owned by all adults in the school and is driving your anti-racism work?

Most schools review their policies on a rolling cycle. Leaders who are committed to embedding a culture of anti-racism ensure that when each policy is reviewed it is considered through the lens of race equity (and that if, mid-cycle, a concern about a policy in relation to race equity is raised, it is reviewed and addressed immediately). In some schools this work is conducted by a Race Equity group. Nabeela reflected in her interview:

In my current school, we have a 'Black Excellence Group' which meets half termly and monitors progress to see how far diversity and inclusivity are promoted and embedded within the school policies, culture and curriculum. It would be great to see more teachers from a White British background join this group as currently the membership is mainly teachers of colour. The danger of only having teachers who have experienced discrimination is that they can be perceived as a bunch of people with a chip on their shoulder finding an avenue to vent. It's important to have allies from all ethnicities and background as their support and buy in would fast track the work being undertaken.

A policy that in many schools in recent years has been scrutinised and found to be wanting is the uniform policy. School uniforms are often fiercely traditional and Eurocentric (pleated kilts, starched shirts and ties). I was proud of the fact that students were given the option to wear shalwar kameez or jilbab at Walthamstow School for Girls and extended this when I designed the uniform for my new school in Ilford, Isaac Newton Academy. I was surprised to find that none of the other secular schools in the area (serving a predominantly Asian demographic with a high percentage of Pakistani heritage families) included shalwar kameez in their uniform.

Before I conduct race reviews in schools, I often take a look on their websites at what the uniform policy says about hairstyles. Here are some examples, downloaded in July 2022:

> Hairstyles should be moderate and in keeping with the school uniform. Extreme styles are not permitted, including shapes shaved into the hair. Hair should be one natural colour. 'Skin fades' or 'skin head' styles are not permitted. Facial hair is not permitted; however, students are allowed to request changes to our rule on facial hair for religious reasons.
> Children with hair past shoulder length or whose fringe is affecting their vision are required to tie it back neatly. All pupils should retain their natural hair colour and not use tints/dyes or hair decorations during term time.
> Sensible hairstyles; no extreme styles or colours are permitted.
> Hairstyles should be of professional appearance, neat and respectable.
> Hair ornaments must not be worn.

What equity issues do these rules generate?

Why might they alienate a family with Afro-textured hair?

Or a student from a Muslim or Sikh background?

Adjectives such as 'sensible,' 'respectable,' 'neat,' 'moderate,' 'professional' and 'extreme' are so value-laden and subjective and, interpreted by a White school leader with a fixed mindset, could land a student with long Afro-textured hair in trouble for simply wearing their hair naturally or having their hair braided. I heard a heart-breaking tale recently of a Year 7 pupil who spent his first day at secondary school in an isolation room because he had his hair in corn rows. Many towns do not have a hairdresser specialising in Afro-textured hair, so changing a style overnight is not an option. Do school leaders understand the ways in which Afro-textured hair is styled, protected and why hair accessories, braids, cornrows, extensions and fades are used? What role does hair play in learning and why is it so heavily scrutinised? And why should facial hair not be permitted, or a child who is required or wishes to grow facial hair as part of their religious observance be required to apply for special dispensation? Rulings like the ones above do not afford children from all ethnic backgrounds equal freedoms.

At Nicholas Breakspear School in St Albans, the student EDI representatives took a look at the school's hair rules and campaigned for changes to make them more equitable, as the following case study shows:

Nicholas Breakspear Catholic School Case Study

Review of the School Uniform Policy on Hair by the Student EDI Focus Group

Students recognised that using the term 'natural hair colour' in the policy allowed a wider range of options for white students than for students of colour. They suggested the wording should be 'colour from the human hair spectrum.' The hair policy has been updated and has become more progressive and accepting of different hair colours, acknowledging the differences in each student's hair.

The policy states that the shortest hair should be a grade one. However, the EDI Representatives wanted the school to formally recognise that this looks shorter on Afro-textured hair than European or Asian hair, because of the way the hair lies. They also requested the school look at the wording of the 'noticeable steps' regarding hair 'fades,' because if a student has curly or Afro-textured hair on top, the students felt there would be a more noticeable difference between the top and sides of the hair. This has also now been reviewed and amended.

Girls' braids often require clips to manage on Afro-textured hair. These are not decorations, but essential for keeping the braids in check. The policy was therefore changed to allow functional clips, but students accepted that these should be black/navy.

Facial Hair – Students requested that the Uniform Policy was amended to specify that boys may have beards, but only for genuine religious reasons, for example for Sikhs.

EDI Representatives, although acknowledging that these things are allowed, wanted the Uniform Policy to state specifically that religious items are acceptable to wear with the school uniform. Examples include Muslim hijab, Jewish skullcap, Sikh turban and Hindu Kautuka. They felt that specifically naming these items in the policy would ensure a feeling of inclusiveness and protect the rights of students from these religions to wear them. This has now been added.

Contrast the hair policy extracts cited earlier with this one:

> Hair must be appropriate for a smart office environment. We realise that this can be interpreted differently according to culture and ethnicity and are happy to accept and value all kinds of smart as long as these are consistent with the headteacher's final judgement. A wide range of hairstyles is permitted such as braids, locs, twists and cornrows. We follow the Halo Code.

I would suggest that a parent of a child with Afro-textured hair would feel so much more included and understood when reading these guidelines. The Halo Collective is an organisation which campaigns to end discrimination in school uniform policies against children with Afro-textured hair. On the Halo website there is a reference to a survey in which '46% of parents say their children's school uniform policy penalises afro-hair.' The action group encourages schools in the UK to sign up to a new hair code – The Halo Code – to end discrimination against children with Afro-textured hair. The code promises members of the Black community that they have the 'freedom and security to wear all afro-hairstyles without restriction or judgment.'

Edwina Omokaro, co-Founder of the Halo Collective says, 'No one should have to change their natural or protective hairstyle in order to thrive. Together, we will ensure that all Black people can learn, work, and live free from hair discrimination.'

Activity

If you have not recently reviewed your school uniform and hair policy, take a fresh look at it from a race equity perspective.

Seek the views of Black and Asian staff, students and parents, as to what might be amended to make the policy more inclusive and to afford equitable rights to all learners.

Modelling the importance of honouring everyone's name

The anti-racist leader creates and then oversees a culture where everyone knows that everyone's name is important. After all, our names are an intrinsic part of our identity. Many people's names have cultural, religious or family significance.

Leaders should expect staff to know the names of all the learners they teach. And they should endeavour to get to know the names of as many learners as they can themselves. Just as important as knowing learners by name is ensuring that names are pronounced correctly, with accurate inflection and accentuation. It is never acceptable to suggest that a name is too difficult to learn or to pronounce, or to shorten or anglicise a name. What does this say to the person about how significant they are and how much time you are prepared to invest in them? Getting people's names right is about showing respect and honouring them.

Reflecting on his own school days, Bonolo told me: 'Teachers did not have a good understanding or knowledge of my heritage. One example is my name, which is an African name and is not very difficult to pronounce. On many occasions teachers would change my name without permission and call me by an English name that I had not been consulted on because it was easier to say. If they got my name wrong on the register many would not even ask me to correct them. This clearly suggested to me that there was no desire to understand my name or my background.'

Another colleague, Jigna Patel, who is an assistant headteacher at The Hertfordshire & Essex High School and Science College, told her peers at a Great Representation seminar in December 2021 that at her school 'when it got to my name in the register, teachers would pause and then mispronounce the name and then laugh. I found it really embarrassing and stressful. But I buried the memories and didn't talk about it for years. When I look back now, I see it as a micro-aggression.'

At Herts & Essex, Jigna and her colleagues decided to take action to ensure that no student had to experience the same sort of embarrassment and stress. The following case study tells the story of their action:

Herts & Essex Case Study: Pronunciation of Names

In summer 2020, a group of minority ethnic alumni wrote an open letter to the Executive Headteacher, Headteacher and the Chair of Governors which described racist incidents that had occurred in the school when they had attended. This included testimonies from several ex-students, including mispronunciation of students' names. One member of the alumni explained that 'I constantly had to spell and pronounce my name which felt belittling … having to continuously tell the same people how to pronounce a two-syllable name was irritating and upsetting.'

On receiving the open letter and testimonials, leaders were determined to open up safe discussion about the issues raised so that they could bring the school community together to reduce and effectively address this type of incident.

Anti-racism groups were established within the school, which included members of the alumni, current students, staff, current and ex-parents and carers and governors. Initially, the meetings were focused on learning more about the experiences within school of the alumni and the current students from ethnic minority backgrounds. They quickly evolved into strategic groups which now recommend, monitor and evaluate developments in the school to tackle racism and to create an anti-racist school.

The testimonials of the Black alumni and results from the 2020 survey showed there was work to do in pronouncing students' names correctly and with sensitivity.

Therefore, a major focus for 2021–2022 was to record staff and students' names on our Management Information System (MIS) for sharing with all adults. One of the ICT technicians was given this as a responsibility within their role.

The recording of students' names has also been a powerful way in which staff have signalled and acted on a commitment to ensure all students know they belong at Herts & Essex. The recording has been undertaken on a voluntary basis and, by February 2022, 93% of the students had chosen to record their name on the MIS. It is an expectation that staff will listen to these recordings to ensure names are pronounced correctly.

The actor Uzoamaka Nwanneka Aduba, quoted by Nikesh Shukla in his book *Brown Baby*, recalls what her mother said to her when she explained that she wanted to change her name to Zoe because no one at school seemed able to pronounce Uzoamaka: 'If they can learn to say Tchaikovsky and Michelangelo and Dostoyevsky, they can learn to say Uzoamaka' (2021:181).

I would suggest that school leaders would be sending out a clear and powerful message by communicating the following:

All staff are expected to learn the names of all the learners they teach/have responsibility for. Pronouncing people's names correctly and in full is a core expectation of all staff. Suggested strategies for achieving this are:

- Communicating how important it is to you that you address people correctly and pronounce names accurately
- Asking the person to pronounce their name for you
- Spelling names out phonetically in your mark book
- Finding a synonym or mental image to remind you*
- Practising until it comes naturally

- Always referring to learners by name
- Inviting people to correct and, if necessary, recorrect
- Apologising when you mispronounce a name and never laughing, even if out of embarrassment
- Quashing any laughter from others and explaining why it is not appropriate
- Checking pronunciations with a parent/carer or colleague.

Staff can help their peers by correcting anyone whom they hear mispronouncing a name.

*One of my interviewees, Rubia, always rubs her ear to remind people how to pronounce her name!

Some pupils appreciate it when staff take an interest in the origin or meaning of their name but others don't: it can draw unwanted attention and make the learner feel hyper-visible. Here, context and the nature and depth of the relationship between the student and the adult is key.

What would you like to say to school leaders?

To close this chapter, here is some advice from four of my interviewees, given in response to the question 'What would you like to say to school leaders?'

See the school journey through the eyes of a student of every ethnicity. Look at the language, positive and negative reinforcements, the curriculum and ethos of the school. Make an effort to champion diversity as a positive thing; from student uniform to student hair, everything should be inclusive and positive. Encourage staff and students to be proud of their heritage, background and faith. Showing this off as a source of pride helps staff and students to see the positive value in identity. Train staff on the use of non-harmful language. Involve parents, the community and local organisations.

Bonolo

Have a zero-tolerance approach to racism: fewer words and more actions! Review what you are currently doing – take an honest, reflective and critical approach. Locate schools where race equity is done well and build on good practice. Consider getting an external view on your practice. Make race equity an important part of the curriculum. Use your community or any community leaders to find out what resources are available and how they can be incorporated into the curriculum. Celebrate diversity but be mindful of any tokenistic approaches. Speak to those from different ethnic backgrounds, find out more about them and celebrate. Don't worry about what is deemed right or wrong. It's okay to feel uncomfortable – this is how we learn. Be aware of and challenge unconscious bias. Share examples and scenarios so that others feel empowered too. Look for training opportunities for your staff to equip them with the knowledge and skills they need to achieve race equity.

Lucky

If you are not a person of colour, don't be scared of wanting to understand and change your school culture. Read as much as you can from different perspectives and camps and not just what's in the mainstream media. You may completely disagree with other people's interpretations but remember it is *their* interpretation and this is how *they* feel. Not you. Speak to people from your staff and student bodies and the wider community. Employ someone to help you to do this. Ensure that everybody's voice is heard; empower young people to be leaders, bring diversity to teams and raise the bar.

Ayeesha

Keep striving! No act is too small. It could be an assembly, a change in the text you teach or even just a tweet – you'll make a big difference to the self-worth of those who feel most over-looked.

Nabeela

References

Gladwell. M. (2005). *Blink: The Power of Thinking without Thinking.* (England, London: Penguin).

Lorde. A. (2017). *Your Silence Will Not Protect You.* (UK: Silver Press).

Macfarlane. R. (2021). *Obstetrics For Schools.* (Carmarthen: Crown House).

Macfarlane. R. and Catchpool. M eds. (2022) *Great Representation. Collection of School Case Studies.* (Hertfordshire: Herts For Learning Ltd).

Scott. K. (2021). *Just Work: Get it Done, Fast and Fair* (London: Macmillan).

Shukla. N. (2021). *Brown Baby: A Memoir of Race, Family and Home.* (London: Pan Macmillan).

Smidt. S. (2020). *Creating an Anti-Racist Culture in the Early Years.* (London: Routledge).

The power of language

Words, so innocent and powerless as they are, as standing in a dictionary, how potent for good and evil they become in the hands of one who knows how to combine them.

Attributed to Nathaniel Hawthorne

There is no such thing as race. None. There is just a human race – scientifically, anthropologically.

Toni Morrison

This chapter explores the language around race. It examines the complexities, nuances, messages and meanings conveyed by the words that we use. It acknowledges the indisputable power of language to do good and to cause harm, to challenge assumptions and to address misconceptions but also to reinforce stereotypes and perpetuate myths. In a racially literate school, much attention is given to the language used by members of the school community.

Creating a common language around race equity

When I had the unique and golden opportunity of designing a new school from scratch, of the one hundred or so policies that I wrote, I would say that the Language for Learning Policy was one of the five most crucial: it was central to the ethos and culture of the school. It included language of growth mindset, language of learning power and language of honour, respect and inclusion.

DOI: 10.4324/9781003275220-6

Extract from INA Language for Learning Policy

Language of honour, respect and inclusion

At Isaac Newton Academy, the school community is made up of people from a wide range of backgrounds, beliefs and cultures. It is vital that the language used by all members of the school community conveys respect to and of all. Language that is discriminatory in any way is not tolerated and it is an expectation of everyone that they challenge any such incidence appropriately.

There is an agreed set of terminology that we use at Isaac Newton Academy…

Does your school have a language for learning policy?

Do you have an agreed set of race terminology that all members of the community use?

What might be the benefits of creating a common language around race equity?

I would suggest that there are three key benefits:

Firstly, the process of creating a common lexicon of language is, in itself, an educative process and provides crucial staff training and a common understanding amongst all the adults working in the school.

Secondly, by creating a glossary of words that are used (and therefore clarity about words and phrases that are NOT used and why), staff will feel more secure and confident in talking about race. My co-lead on the Great Representation programme, Dr Michael Catchpool, reminded me several years ago that 'people often have a fear of "saying the wrong thing" or of appearing to be on the wrong side of the argument, and can end up retreating and disengaging, because they feel vulnerable. If people are to be helped on their journey, they need to feel safe in taking the steps.' Providing guidance about the language that is acceptable and not acceptable to use in discussing race is a good way to do this.

Thirdly, once you have a language policy and glossary of language that everyone has co-created and accepted should be used by all, you can legitimately challenge any language that deviates from what has been agreed.

So how might you go about designing a glossary of terminology and definitions? Well, this will depend on your school, your context and the staffing capacity you have to lead on this work. There is a plethora of excellent exemplar glossaries available online and in many of the texts cited in this book (e.g. Choudry, Sarpong, Boakye, Kinouani, Saad) which provide a good starting point for discussion. If you have an EDI Officer, they might take the lead. If you have a Race Equity Forum or student Race Equity reps, you will want to involve them. Ideally staff, governors/trustees, students and parents/carers would all play a part in fashioning the glossary. It is essential that people of colour in the school community are listened to, consulted and involved. People of colour need to tell White people the terms they feel comfortable being used.

Key words, terms and concepts to unpick, discuss and define

A great place to start is with the concept of 'race' itself. As Toni Morrison says in the quote at the start of this chapter, race is an artificial social construct. Hirsch tells us it was designed 'to distinguish between members of the same biological species' (2018:24). Sarpong reminds us that 'We really are all one, and that oneness began in Africa' (2020:32).

There are lots of different definitions of race. It would be a powerful CPD activity to discuss some of the various offerings and decide on one that your school community feels comfortable to adopt and can acquiesce around.

Here are two examples:

- 'Race is a social construct, an agreed-on myth that has empirical grit because of its effect, not its essence.' Michael Eric Dyson in foreword of Robin Diangelo's *White Fragility* (2019:ix)

- 'Race is an evolving social idea that was created to legitimize racial inequality and protect white advantage.' Robin Diangelo (2019:17)

What do you think of these definitions?

How are they different?

Could you see either being adopted in your glossary?

If so, why? If not, why not?

Ta-Nehisi Coates interestingly describes race as 'the child of racism, not the father' (2015:8).

It is important that the adults (and older learners) in your school understand the difference between race and ethnicity. Jeffrey Boakye explains this well in *Black, Listed*: '*Ethnicity* relates to human groupings according to any number of subjective (often cultural) factors: geography, language and religion to name three. *Race*, as we now understand it, pertains to supposedly scientific ideas of racial difference, marked by physical and biological indicators' (2019:15).

The Law Society also gives useful definitions: 'Race is a categorisation that is based mainly on physical attributes or traits, assigning people to a specific race simply by having similar appearances or skin colour (for example, Black or White). The categorisation is rooted in White supremacy and efforts to prove biological superiority and maintain dominance over others. It's now widely accepted that race is a social construct.' 'Ethnicity is broader than race and has usually been used to refer to long shared cultural experiences, religious practices, traditions, ancestry, language, dialect or national origins (for example, African-Caribbean, Indian, Irish).'

You will agree on your own wording that works for your school and your context.

From 'race', a logical next step is to 'racism' and 'racist' and 'anti-racism' and 'anti-racist'. Again, you will find lots of alternative definitions to consider and discuss but starting with McPherson's definition is a sound idea: 'conduct or words or practices which disadvantage or advantage people because of their colour, culture, or ethnic origin'. The Collins English Dictionary, quoted by Sarpong (2020:1) has the following definition: 'Racism is the belief that people of some races are inferior to others, and the behaviour that is the result of this belief. Racism also refers to the aspects of a society which prevent people of some racial groups from having the same privileges and opportunities as people from other races.' Wellman, quoted by Beverly Daniel Tatum, defines racism as 'A system of advantage based on race' (2021:86). Ibram X. Kendi says there 'is no neutrality in the racism struggle. The opposite of "racist" isn't "not racist". It is "anti-racist". ...The claim of "not racist" neutrality is a mask for racism' (2019:9).

Do you agree with Kendi?

Why/why not?

With whom might you debate this in your school?

Also important is to define the difference between systemic, structural and institutional racism and to ensure that everyone is clear about what constitutes examples of each.

'Equity' and 'Equality' should also feature in any good glossary and, again, all adults and older learners should be clear about the distinction between the two and when and in what scenarios the school is striving for each. Sameena Choudry gives clear definitions of each: Equality 'means treating everybody the same by giving everyone the same tools and assistance' (2021:17). 'Equity on the other hand refers to treating people fairly and impartially according to their needs' (2021:18). Bennie Kara reflects: 'The former teaches that everyone is the same. The latter acknowledges different starting points and asks society to create better stepping stones to successful futures' (2021:10).

Next, I would propose a number of terms that should feature in your glossary not just because they are important concepts but also because the discussion of them will help to develop the racial literacy of your school community and the understanding of them will better enable your staff to provide a truly equitable education. They are 'microaggressions', 'unconscious bias', 'white privilege' and 'white fragility'. We will explore these in more detail in Chapter 5 and return to micro-aggressions in Chapter 11.

Psychologist Derald Wing Sue, quoted by Tatum, defines microaggressions as 'the brief and commonplace daily verbal, behavioral, and environmental indignities, whether intentional or unintentional, that communicate hostility, derogatory, or negative racial... slights and insults to the target person or group...They can occur at any moment of the day, a constant potential source of stress' (2021:51). Discussing and defining microaggressions helps colleagues and learners who are not likely to experience racism themselves to understand the degrees and myriad manifestations of prejudice and discrimination and its invidious impact. (You might also include definitions of prejudice and discrimination.)

Unconscious or implicit biases are defined by Pragya Agarwal in *Sway* as 'biases that exist without our conscious knowledge, the ones that manifest themselves in our actions and reactions often without us realising it, rearing their heads when we least expect it and sometimes taking us by surprise' (2020:16). She reminds us that 'Each of us form and carry unconscious biases of some sort. It's not only the behaviour of bigoted, racist or sexist people but of everyone.' She says, 'The answer is to go to the roots, to understand the processes that shape us, to be aware, to acknowledge that we are all biased – to a certain degree – and that we all discriminate. We judge, we exclude people, we stereotype' (2020:22). Accepting this uncomfortable truth is, of course, a prerequisite to being open to personal development in terms of racial literacy.

Reni Eddo Lodge defines White Privilege as 'an absence of the consequences of racism (2017:86); the fact that if you're white, your race will almost certainly positively impact your life's trajectory in some way. And you probably won't even notice it' (2017:87). We will look at ways to explore this with staff and students in the next chapter, particularly in light of the DfE's guidance on what it sees as politically controversial terminology and comments by Ofsted's Chief HMI, Amanda Spielman, in June 2022.

Robin Diangelo's book *White Fragility* is a useful read on this concept. She reflects that 'pointing out white advantage will often trigger patterns of confusion, defensiveness and righteous indignation. These responses enable defenders to protect their moral character against a perceived attack while rejecting any culpability. Focusing on restoring their moral standing through these tactics, whites are able to avoid the challenge.' We will look at her excellent advice on how to avoid generating white fragility, and how to deal with it when it is encountered, in Chapter 5.

Three other terms that I would strongly suggest it would be useful to include in a glossary are 'normalising,' 'usualising' and 'othering'.

Normalising (normalisation) is a term that reduces patterns, experiences and behaviours to two alternatives – normal or not normal/abnormal.

Usualising (a term credited to Sue Sanders) is a useful alternative to normalising. Kara suggests that, 'Using "usualise" rather than "normalize" allows us to convey the idea that there is an everyday-ness to diversity. It is not an add-on; it is the day-to-day reality of the world we live in' (2021:64).

Othering (otherism) describes the exclusion or marginalisation of a person, group or demographic within society. Sarpong explains that

> Otherism happens when our brains make incredibly quick judgements and assessments of people and situations, often without us realising. Our prejudices are influenced by our background, culture and personal experiences. Without us actively exploring and challenging our limiting beliefs we can be inadvertently complicit in fuelling inequality.
>
> *2020:2*

A comprehensive understanding of these will support staff in their work on diversifying the curriculum and ensuring true and impactful representation of people of colour in the school, avoiding the traps of tokenism or marginalisation.

What other words might you include in your school glossary?

How will you go about creating it?

Who will take the lead?

How will you ensure that the voices of all groups in the community are heard and reflected?

How will you navigate disagreement?

How frequently will you revisit and refresh the glossary?

Naming ethnic groups

Perhaps of all the discussions that you, your staff, your governors/trustees and your learners will have, the most sensitive and potentially divisive might be around the adjectives used to describe different ethnic groups. Here Beverly Daniel Tatum helps by reminding us that 'The language we use to categorise each other racially is imperfect. These categories are still evolving... The original creation of racial categories was in the service of oppression.' She says that 'Some may argue that to continue to use them is to continue that oppression...yet it is difficult to talk about what is essentially a flawed and problematic social construct without using language that is itself problematic' (2021:97).

In schools it is important that we track and monitor performance, progress, opportunity and participation of all students, and sometimes by ethnic group. At times we will want granular detail: at INA, where around 70% of the pupils were of Asian heritage, it was important that we analysed the GLD, SATs, GCSE and A level performance of Pakistani, Indian, Sri Lankan and Bangladeshi students by subgroup. When looking at exclusion rates, we know that nationally the over-representation of Black Caribbean pupils is greater than for Black African learners, so an analysis by Black sub-groups is again useful. In other situations, we might want to compare the data for White learners against all others; for example, in a school with a 95% White cohort when looking at the allocation of merits to pupils over a term.

Before we go on, let's just remind ourselves that there is, of course, no such thing as racial Whiteness. Picking up on this fact, Ta-Nehisi Coates uses the wonderful terminology of people 'believing themselves white'. That withstanding, it is useful for educators at times to have a term to describe all learners other than those who categorise themselves as White. But what that term should be is the topic of much debate.

Options include (although this is not an exhaustive list and is ever-changing):

Non-White. This is a problematic and, for many, an offensive term. Who wants to be classed as non-anything or defined by what they are not?

BAME (Black, Asian and Minority Ethnic). This is problematic and indeed offensive to many people. It groups so many ethnic groups together. Boakye (2019:55) says 'Anyone who isn't White, all us brown-skinned immigrants from Far Far Away, we all get lumped together.' If said as BAME (rhyming with 'game') it can sound lazy and sloppy. Spelt out as four initials it is arguably less offensive. It doesn't explicitly include Gypsy, Roma and Traveller people.

BME (Black and Minority Ethnic). This is arguably even more problematic than BAME in that, as Boakye argues (2019:56), it is seen as 'throwing the odds and ends of British society into an untidy drawer' but without acknowledging Asians which are a sizeable ethnic group in the UK.

Minority Ethnic. This might be factually accurate in many UK schools and indeed in UK society but it is not true for the world where Whites are a minority group. Hence many people's preference for the next term.

(Note, there is a subtle difference between **Ethnic Minority** and **Minority Ethnic.** Some people prefer the former as it acknowledges the fact that we all have an ethnic group, including White British people.)

Global Majority. This term is far more empowering and uplifting. It does not describe the fact, however, that in our country and our education system, people of colour are under-represented and too frequently receive an inequitable provision.

Minoritised people. This term is often used to describe people who have been pushed to the margins. The Law Society says 'It recognises that individuals have been minoritised through social processes of power and domination rather than just existing in distinct statistical minorities. It also better reflects the fact that ethnic groups that are minorities in the UK are majorities in the global population.' It has more of a political message to it.

Racially Minoritised. This term applies specifically to those minoritised due to their 'race'.

People of Colour. This term was coined in the USA but has become increasingly adopted in the UK. It does not recognise, however, minority ethnic groups that are White, for example many Jews.

Black, Indigenous and people of colour (BIPOC). This definition highlights indigenous peoples as an acknowledgement that not all people of colour (POC) may face the same levels of injustice.

Black and Brown. The adjective Black is now commonly used, and sometimes to describe everyone other than White people. But the adjective Brown is heard less. You might want to debate why this is amongst your staff. But again, what about races that are White but not White British?

Melanin-Rich. A relatively new entrant to the glossary list.

I will stop there. You can see how rich, complex and nuanced the language is.

There are some adjectives that were commonly used decades ago but would be highly offensive today. An obvious example is 'coloured'. Nikesh Shukla is helpful on articulating the difference between 'coloured' and 'of colour', in case you ever need to explain this to anyone in your school community: 'Words are not free of history. Coloured, historically, was a slur…The word "coloured" was always used to own us. Language is often about ownership…But we own the words "people of colour" and while it may be an imperfect term, it still belongs to us in a way that "coloured" does not' (2021:56–58).

Lots of white people do not know how to describe people from East Asia. They wonder, can they use the term oriental? Or yellow? Vera Chok, in her essay *Yellow* in *The Good Immigrant* is helpful on this matter. She says, 'I use the word "yellow", offensive as many find it, because this how I believe I'm seen.' She also advises that 'In the UK, "East Asian" is replacing the word "oriental" as the politically correct way to refer to people from the countries in that region' (2016:37).

The terminology used to describe Jews is also sensitive. In *Jews Don't Count*, David Baddiel reflects that 'those concerned about offence tend to say "Jewish people" rather than "Jew". Because even though it is the correct word, and not a slang word coined by racists, the deep burial of it in a bad place in the Christian unconscious means that it feels insulting anyway' (2021:33).

In all the above cases, my advice would be the same: ask the person concerned how they describe themselves and the terminology they would wish you to use to describe and refer to them.

The wise leader will devote significant time for members of the school community to discuss, reflect, argue (sensitively) and debate around the terminology that is right for the school. There will, without doubt, be a divergence of views. This is a regularly changing landscape and everyone's lived experience is different, leading to personal views and preferences. Some will prefer 'mixed heritage' to 'mixed race', others will argue for 'dual heritage' or 'bi-racial'. It is important to seek and invite the views of all those in the school who do not classify themselves as White British. Everyone's voice should be heard and we should endeavour to use the language that people feel most accurately describes them. And that can sometimes be challenging; from time to time, school leaders may come across a child who has been ethnically classified by parents as White when they present as Brown or Black and I recently heard of a case whereby two full siblings in the same school had been coded differently from each other by their parents.

In this book you will notice that I have chosen to predominantly use the terms 'People of Colour', 'racially minoritised' and 'minority ethnic groups.' You will see the terms BAME, and sometimes BME, when I am quoting others. I have chosen to capitalise the adjectives Black, Brown and White but, again, not everyone I quote does so. I apologise in advance to anyone who might be irritated or offended by my choice of terminology. I sincerely hope that it does not detract from the messages of the book.

Once you have agreed your school glossary one thing is for certain, your staff and learners will feel a sense of empowerment and a greater confidence to talk about race without causing unintentional offence.

Equipping staff with the language to be confident to challenge racism

In her article 'How do I talk about race with children in the Early Years setting?' Liz Pemberton says, 'Do not let your fear of getting things wrong silence you into not having conversations about race, because it is the most dangerous thing to do, especially when it comes to addressing racist incidents.' She says, 'Whether that be with co-workers or between the children, you cannot afford to turn a blind eye because you're scared of getting it wrong' (2020).

Racism happens – both direct and indirect, unconscious and unconscious, in school as well as out of school, amongst adults as well as children. It should never go unchallenged. Not speaking up and addressing racism is a form of racism in itself. Denying or explaining it away or making excuses for what has happened (they're a nice person, they didn't mean it, it's their generation, it's because they're from a different cultural background, that's their religious belief, I wouldn't want to hurt their feelings or affect the dynamic) is always unacceptable. Kim Scott reminds us that 'When you notice injustice, whether its small or large, you have a responsibility to take action. And you have an obligation to notice it' (2021:25).

Would the adults in your school community all have the confidence, language and strategies to call out racism that they witnessed from other adults – staff, governors/trustees, parents?

How do you know?

What training have they had?

Is there a shared understanding that this is an expectation of them?

(Might it be a good idea to add a definition of an anti-racist ally to your glossary?)

Staff training in this area might take many forms. I would suggest:

1. starting by clearly communicating your expectation that all staff challenge any racism that they encounter from other adults and why this is so important

2. discussing various scenarios and how they might be tackled

3. providing (or, even better, co-constructing) phrases/sentence starters/techniques/ a framework of ways of addressing racism.

In *Just Work*, Kim Scott usefully advises that it is important to distinguish between bias, prejudice and discrimination and to respond to each differently (2021:21).

Scott states that bias is often unintentional and unconscious stereotyping. She advises 'interrupting it' and making the person aware of their behaviour or words, using 'I statements' and 'holding up a mirror'. Examples might be phrases like 'I'd like to check what you meant by…', 'I'm sure you didn't mean to imply…', 'I'm not sure what you meant by that' and 'I'm sure you didn't intend to…' These challenges allow the person to review their words or actions and correct themselves. They also allow you to flush out whether the racism was indeed unintentional.

Prejudice, Scott suggests, is intentional and for this it is necessary to 'hold up a shield'. Here your staff code of conduct will be invaluable. Scott advises the use of 'It statements' to tackle prejudice – phrases such as 'It is racist to…', 'It is against our anti-racism policy to…' 'It is a violation of our values to…' or 'It is illegal to…'

Jay Smooth in his Youtube video '*How to tell someone they sound racist*' offers similar advice to tackle racist comments. He says to focus on what the person did (their words and actions) rather than who they are. He argues that saying 'That thing you said was racist' (an 'It statement') is hard to deny. In contrast, if you were to say to someone 'You are a racist,' they can derail you and deny it: it's hard to prove, it lets them off too easily. He reminds us that your ultimate goal is to hold the person to account for the impact of their actions.

Scott describes discrimination as intentional and desiring to cause harm: 'what happens when people have enough power to put their bias or prejudice in to action' (2021:59). In the case of discrimination, Scott advises the use of 'You statements' to tackle discrimination. Examples might include, 'You need to stop doing that', 'You are stereotyping', 'You said something offensive', 'You can't do that', 'You are being racist', 'You need to understand that…' Here direct language is required and the fact that there are consequences to the person's words or actions needs to be spelt out.

Activity

Consider each of the following scenarios.

For each one, decide whether it constitutes bias, prejudice or discrimination. How would you respond to each?

Try this exercise with a group of staff, governors or trustees.

What is the learning that comes from this activity?

A: A lunchtime supervisor asks you for help with the lunch queue, saying 'It's all the Black boys. They keep pushing in.'

B: A traveller pupil speaks to the teacher and says that she heard another pupil's parent refer to her at the school gate as 'that pikey'.

C: In a governing body meeting, one governor queries why the students are discussing the Black Lives Matter movement in PSHE, saying 'Don't White lives matter anymore?'

D: At a time of a rise in hostilities in the Israeli-Palestinian conflict, a member of staff displays a PLO flag in their classroom and tells their tutees that the Jews have no claim to Palestine.

E: A Year 2 teacher is heard in the staffroom saying 'I love it when I get lots of Indian children in my class. They're always so well behaved and their parents really value education!'

The strategies proposed above (clarity of expectations, discussing scenarios and practising language and strategies to use) can also be used to empower staff to address racist language and behaviour from children. You will recall from Chapter 2 the experience that Bonolo had as a pupil when he reported to a teacher that another child had said his skin was 'dirty' and the teacher had avoided the racism in the comment, telling Bonolo that it was probably said because he was playing outside and maybe the boy was being inquisitive. We have to eliminate incidents like this and the long-term damage that they cause. The more that leaders protect regular training time for groups of staff and governors to reflect on historical cases of racism and how well they were dealt with, as well as pre-empt possible future scenarios and agree best responses, the better.

Helping children to develop the language to talk about race and to call out and challenge racism

Pragya Agarwal's book *Wish We Knew What To Say* is a great resource for skilling adults to talk to children of all ages about race. Agarwal explains that children notice colour and they assimilate messages from the media. She warns that if educators don't proactively discuss race with children, from a young age, they will form their own theories and come to their own conclusions and these may be problematic. Because children see that difference exists, we need to help them understand that this should not be the basis for inequality. She argues powerfully that 'We need to help our children build a strong vocabulary around race and racism' (2020:19). She advises that we 'use explicit, proactive language' (2020:156).

Agarwal's book pre-empts the type of inquisitive questions around race that children typically ask at various ages, starting with the Early Years. For example:

- Early Years: 'Why is she so brown?' 'Why can't I have blonde hair?'

- Age 4–6: 'Why are people's skin colours different?' 'If my friend is Black then why isn't his mum?'

- Age 7–9: 'Why can't I use the N word?' 'Why are people still racist?'

By reading and discussing this text and the implications of Agarwal's messages for them, educators in schools would be well-equipped to respond positively to any question or comment, making a learnable moment from it, rather than a scarring memory.

Ensuring that our children can recognise racism and have the confidence and language to report it to adults around them is key to making a school more racially equitable. By equipping children with the words and techniques to talk about how people are different and similar in a safe, curious and non-judgemental setting, we can assist them in becoming increasingly able to independently address any bias, prejudice or discrimination they may witness or experience.

Reflections

How sure are you that children of all ages in your school are confident about the language to use to refer to people from different ethnic groups and to talk sensitively and respectfully about issues of race equity?

How sure are you that children of all ages in your school are confident about the language to use to call out racial bias, prejudice and discrimination when they witness it or experience it?

What steps will you take to increase your degree of certainty?

References

Agarwal. P. (2020). *Sway: Unravelling Unconscious Bias*. (London: Bloomsbury).

Agarwal. P. (2020). *Wish We Knew What To Say*. (Great Britain, London: Dialogue Books).

Baddiel. D. (2021). *Jews Don't Count*. (London: TLS Books).

Boakye. J. (2019). *Black, Listed*. (Great Britain, London: Dialogue Books).

Chok. V. *Yellow* in Shukla. N. ed. (2017). The Good Immigrant. (London: Unbound)

Choudry. S. (2021). *Equitable Education*. (St Albans: Critical Publishing).

Coates. T. (2015). *Between The World And Me*. (Melbourne: Text Publishing).

Diangelo. R. (2019). *White Fragility*. (Great Britain, London: Penguin).

Eddo-Lodge. Reni (2017). *Why I'm No Longer Talking To White People About Race*. (London: Bloomsbury).

Hirsch. A. (2018). *Brit(ish): On Race, Identity and Belonging*. (London: Vintage).

Kara. B. (2021). *Diversity In Schools*. (London: Corwin).

Kendi. I. X (2019). *How To Be An Anti-Racist*. (London: The Bodley Head).

Morrison. T. (2014). Interview with Stephen Colbert. Available at: www.huffingtonpost.co.uk/entry/toni-morrison-colbert_n_6199402

Pemberton. L. (2020). *How do I talk about race with children in the Early Years setting?* Foundation Stage Forum. Available at: https://eyfs.info/articles.html/teaching-and-learning/how-do-i-talk-about-race-with-children-in-the-early-years-setting-r332/

Sarpong. J. (2020). *The Power Of Privilege: How White People Can Challenge Racism*. (London: HQ).

Scott. K. (2021). *Just Work: Get it Done, Fast and Fair*. (London: Macmillan).

Smooth. J. *How To Tell Someone They Sound Racist*. (You tube). Available at: www.youtube.com/watch?v=b0Ti-gkJiXc

Tatum. B. D. (2021) *Why Are All The Black Kids Sitting Together In The Cafeteria?* (Great Britain, Dublin: Penguin).

5 Confronting assumptions, biases and privileges

> Erroneous and deep-seated notions about race persist because we are scared to discuss misconceptions about colour and race in our classrooms and boardrooms. Racism is probably humanity's single biggest impediment to human achievement.
>
> Nina Jablonski (quoted by Sarpong (2020:52))

> What hurts the victim the most is not the cruelty of the oppressor, but the silence of the bystander.
>
> Elie Wiesel (quoted by Scott (2021:73))

This chapter considers why there is a need to engage staff in training around race and to develop their racial literacy. It explores the assumptions and biases that we all have and which impact our thoughts and actions. It examines the concept of White Privilege and suggests some practical activities that can be undertaken with adults to explore unconscious bias and privilege. It also offers advice, through case studies and personal testimony, on creating safe spaces for adults and young people to talk about race. It provides guidance on dealing with race incidents, from micro-aggressions to less covert forms of racism.

Why is there a need for staff training on racial literacy?

As we saw in Chapter 1, we have a situation in English schools where only around 14% of the teaching force are people of colour, whilst around a third of the pupils are. We need to get greater diversity in the profession (and Chapter 10 looks at how we might do that), but whilst we have an under-representation of minority ethnic adults in schools, we must upskill White staff to be more racially literate and confident to talk about race to their learners.

We know that currently many teachers don't feel equipped to address matters of race: in February 2021 the House of Commons Petitions committee considered a petition in which a quarter of teachers said they lacked confidence, and 88% of primary and 85% of secondary teachers said they felt they would benefit from specialist training.

This should not come as a surprise as many White people have no connection with people of colour. They have very limited understanding of what it means to experience race inequity in the UK. As an illustration of the impact of this, I was presenting to a senior board of executives recently about the anti-racism work that my organisation carries out and the White chair challenged me on some data I was showing about stop and search race inequalities. He argued that the disproportionate number of young Black men searched did not imply any race bias on behalf of officers and that Black people would not be searched without reasonable grounds for suspicion. A Black colleague at the meeting then gave several harrowing examples of times when her son had been stopped and searched with absolutely no grounds for suspicion. The chair looked genuinely surprised and said he had never heard anything like this before. The colleague asked him politely whether he mixed in friendship circles that included people of colour and he accepted that no, he only saw and heard about the world through a White lens.

What is truly shocking is that, at the current time, there is no requirement in England for race equity or racial literacy training to form part of teacher-training courses. A Runnymede Trust report reported that the Department for Education's Newly Qualified Teachers' Survey of 2018, found that almost half of respondents did not feel that their ITE course prepared them to teach 'across all ethnic backgrounds' and only 39 per cent felt prepared to 'teach EAL (English as an Additional Language) pupils.' (2021:35) Most of my interviewees reflected that they had never been taught how to address matters of race or incidents of racism when they trained. Rubia said that not only was there no focus on race on her PCGE course (in multi-racial London) but, worse, that 'a colleague of mine who is four years out of training was told during her training that "black students underachieve and can be challenging".'

We would be horrified to hear of a PGCE course that did not include training on how to safeguard children, yet racial trauma is a safeguarding matter. We expect our training institutions to shape trainees into teachers who have the highest expectations of, and meet the needs of, all learners and enable them to achieve great outcomes, and yet we are not addressing explicitly how teachers might do this for pupils from ethnic groups, such as gypsy, Roma and traveller children, who perennially underperform. Our teachers' standards talk explicitly about demonstrating good subject and curriculum knowledge, yet we are not preparing our future class teachers and tutors to discuss race equity confidently with their students.

How many of your teachers were given anti-racism training as part of their ITT?

Have you surveyed your staff (teaching and operational) on their level of confidence in discussing race issues with colleagues/learners?

If yes, what do the findings tell you and how have you used them to support you in planned CPD?

If no, what questions might you ask in order to design a CPD programme that would meet staff needs?

Until anti-racism education is made mandatory in ITT, PGCE and ECT courses, the responsibility sits with Multi Academy Trust (MAT) CEOs and headteachers to ensure that staff have comprehensive and ongoing race equity training. In my local authority, schools have access to HFL's team of race equity advisors: they provide training for educators and support leaders to run their own CPD, to grow confidence and capacity. But this provision and support is not replicated across all LAs. School leaders need to ensure that they have created the infrastructure to meet the needs of staff. This would typically involve the appointment and training of an EDI or race equity leader, ideally with access to supervisions or coaching. In many schools, the EDI leader is supported by an EDI or inclusion or race equity forum/working party.

In her blog '*Do you understand what it's like to be a black student in a UK school?*,' Amanda Wilson asks, 'what can we do to adequately prepare those teachers who have no prior knowledge, to understand what it's like to be a black child attending school in the United Kingdom? How do school leaders ensure that early career teachers understand what cultural diversity actually means and what it looks like in their school?' Of course, we are not just talking about ECTs and not just teaching staff.

Creating the space and conditions to talk about race and the lived experiences of people of colour

A good starting point for developing the racial literacy of staff is to create opportunities for staff to talk about race together, for colleagues of colour to share their lived experiences, for White staff to listen, learn and develop understanding and for all to consider the implications for their school community. This is essential but not straightforward, as leaders of many schools have found. One Inner London secondary school headteacher, Mariella Ardron, told me recently:

We started on our EDI journey in the summer of 2021 with discussion within the Leadership Team. We duly arranged for a highly-rated EDI trainer who had led a thought-provoking session with us to facilitate the launch of a year-long focus on EDI with staff. It was agreed that the trainer would deliver three whole-staff sessions across the academic year with inter-sessional work to be completed by staff groups in the intervening time. Despite having completed due diligence and the fact that the trainer had led some excellent sessions with our sixth formers back in the spring of 2021, nothing prepared us for the fall out after the first staff session in September. There followed a very traumatic and unsettling month where I wondered if we had made a massive mistake even starting this much-needed conversation. Staff were triggered by past experiences of racism, by their colleagues' insensitive and, at times, racist responses. There was also a feeling from Asian staff that the focus was too heavily skewed towards the experiences of Black colleagues. As a Leadership Team we had not thought through the implications of such a session and the need to provide a proper debriefing structure and space straight after the first session.

Fast forward a year and we have now come to a better place where we have worked through many of these issues. We have all read a lot more and dug deep to consider what the issues are, as well as taken the time to learn from our mistakes – the first of which was not to have involved more of our Black and Asian colleagues from the very beginning. We have reviewed and amended our uniform policy, held our first (brilliant) student-led Cultural Day and are ready to start some exciting work on an anti-racist policy.

Before you read on, take a minute to reflect on this testimony.

What learning do you take from it?

What are the pros and cons of using external trainers to facilitate discussions on race with your staff?

What structures do you have in your school to support staff of colour with wellbeing, mental health and racial trauma?

At Laurance Haines Primary School in Watford, leaders set up a staff forum which meets regularly to discuss matters of race.

Laurance Haines Primary School Case Study: Creating a safe and brave space to talk about race matters

The murder of George Floyd highlighted the need for a forum to be created, where staff could share their own experiences, personal reflections on, and feelings about, the tragic event.

Following consultation with some members of staff, school leaders circulated a written response to the Black Lives Matter movement. In this letter, a commitment to creating safe spaces for conversation around race, equality, diversity and inclusion was set out to the wider community. This became a starting point for school improvement work dedicated to creating a safe and brave forum. Although the commitment to the wider community set out plans to invite all community members to be a part of this conversation, it transpired that the school needed to begin the journey with its own staff, building confidence before inviting children and parents into the conversation.

The conversations throughout the forum sessions were shaped around the curriculum, the children's experiences, staff diversity across the trust, lack of representation in the leadership teams and recruitment. A defining moment within the conversation was when the topic of honesty was raised. Staff reflected on the challenges of being able to speak honestly, as well as the fear of saying the wrong thing. The themes of bias and stereotyping were brought forward. At this stage, only a small number of individuals were confident to address these areas and there was discomfort felt by others.

Barriers such as confidence, a lack of subject knowledge, not having a shared understanding between staff around culture, ethnicity and identity, as well as a lack of teaching resources that represented the community were all brought forward. The question, 'How do we overcome these barriers?' was asked. Staff responded with ideas around an extension of the safe space that had been created in the forum to the children, encouraging staff and children to be brave and remove the fear of getting things wrong.

Staff discussed the need for key principles to support staff to overcome the barriers. This resulted in the following being agreed:

- No judgement: be brave and speak freely.
- Acknowledge we all have sub-conscious bias and different cultural experiences.
- It is safe to speak up.
- All have a responsibility to be a part of the conversation: be a voice.
- Recognise that certain topics may evoke certain emotions.
- Call people out (choose to challenge) or call people in (support them to understand, with compassion and patience).

Christine Callender shared some wise advice at a Great Representation seminar in January 2022 about how to create the right conditions for discussing race. She stressed the need for all participants to be alert, to read the mood of the room, to watch for visual and non-verbal cues, to be aware of gasps, reactions, when someone is getting upset – which could be at any moment or triggered by anything. She advised that facilitators ensure that colleagues know they can take a break and leave the room if they need to – prioritising self-care. She spoke about honouring confidentiality, welcoming and respecting the diversity of voices and paying particular attention to those voices that may be under-represented. She stressed the need to be mindful of the impact of what we say, to give and receive caring feedback, to notice and be curious about physical and emotional, as well as intellectual, responses.

If you have facilitated sessions for staff to discuss matter of race, how did they go?

To what extent were they structured?

If you have not done so yet, what will you need to consider when planning the first session?

Who will be involved?

Making time for ongoing and purposefully planned staff training

Establishing spaces for staff to speak openly and without fear is very powerful. For staff of colour, giving permission to talk candidly about matters of race equity is crucial. Too often, in society, people of colour are made to feel guilty for highlighting inequities. In his essay in *The Good Immigrant*, Daniel York Loh says, 'the Golden Rule that all "minority ethnic" people learn when we're growing up in Britain is that we're simply not supposed to get angry about any of this' (2017:49). Gary Younge told Hertfordshire secondary heads in 2020 that by the time a Black person raises an issue of race, they will have chewed over it several times.

However, staff of all ethnicities need to feel that they are being protected through clear protocols in a safe space, and that there is serious and long-term commitment to improving race literacy in the school, in order to engage willingly and not through coercion. The dangers of a one off, three-line-whip CPD session is that at best it is unlikely to be anything more than surface level and tokenistic, and at worst it can lead to resentment, cynicism and merely lip service engagement. This is perhaps why so much unconscious bias training does not lead to long term change – it is simply a tick box exercise, arguably assuaging the conscience of the organiser. 'Many of the current training schemes are simply too brief to have the desired effect' says David Robson in a 25 April 2021 *Guardian* article on what unconscious bias training needs to be like to have an impact.

Arguably, only consensual, interactive and embedded activities stand a chance of leading to a change of hearts and minds. So, I would suggest, the smart school leader will be doing some or all of the following:

- planning successive training events,

- considering how issues arising at whole staff training might be picked up via line management or small team meetings,

- ensuring that there is protected time for review and revision of schemes of learning,

- working out how to facilitate co-planning and co-delivery of lessons related to race literacy,

- thinking about how to get feedback from participants on what they found useful and what they need next to develop their racial literacy,

- supporting all staff to create and work towards anti-racism goals.

Activity

Using the Laurance Haines case study, Christine Callender's advice and your own experience, you might like to devise a staff protocol or behaviour code for use by adults in your school when discussing race.

Supporting staff to consider their assumptions, biases and privileges

In her 5 February 2021 article *Why white teachers must learn to talk about race in schools: the problem unpacked*, Claire Stewart-Hall writes: 'Questioning one's own assumptions and staying curious about race is a critical part of being able to manage conversations about race professionally. The role of white teachers comes with tremendous institutional power and learning how to handle talking about race carefully and with humility takes expertise, professional reflection and new learning.' She continues, 'Most teachers live outside of the communities in which they work. Unless teachers have taken the time to reflect on race and identity work themselves, neither the sector nor institutions are currently providing it, leaving teachers and leaders pretty exposed.'

We all have biases and if we are not careful they can become prejudices: staff need to be supported with skill and sensitivity to examine their biases and assumptions. Pragya Agarwal explains this in her book *Sway*: 'Each of us form and carry unconscious biases. It's not only the behaviour of bigoted, racist or sexist people but of everyone, including you and me' (2020:22). Equally inevitably, all White educators exhibit certain racist tropes – we have been brought up in a social context based on assumed White superiority. But it is hard to accept that we have racial biases.

As Sophie Williams points out, 'The conversation around racism that most of us have heard since childhood is usually pretty one-dimensional. Very black and white. Racism is bad. People who are racist are bad people. And you are a good person, so you are not a racist.' She continues, 'Since childhood we have been building up our personal mental images of "a racist" – someone who is uncaring violent, dangerous, hateful. You'd know one if you saw one and you'd definitely never be one. But it doesn't quite work like that in practice.' Williams concludes that 'this good/bad, black/white binary has made it really difficult for us to find the grey when we come to examine our own lives, actions and the systems that have benefited us along the way' (2020:15).

Gary Younge reminded Hertfordshire headteachers in a talk in 2020 that 'People take this topic personally. They retreat into a mindset of indignation and hurt.' And this is problematic for the impact of racial literacy training. David Robson suggests that unconscious bias courses 'often fail to bring about change because people become too defensive about the very idea that they may be prejudiced. Without excusing the biases, the courses might benefit from explaining how easily stereotypes can be absorbed – even by good, well-intentioned people – while also emphasising the individual responsibility to take action' (2021).

Diangelo urges White people not to feel guilty about the inevitable race biases they have, but instead to take responsibility for them and seek to understand and educate themselves to be anti-racist: 'I was socialized as White in a racism-based society, I have a racist world view, deep racial bias, racist patterns and investment in the racist system that has elevated me...I didn't choose this socialization, and it could not be avoided. But I am responsible for my role in it' (2019:149).

White Privilege

To understand this more deeply, staff need to have an awareness of what White Privilege is and what it is like to live without it.

Peggy McIntosh famously described White Privilege as 'like an invisible weightless knapsack of special provisions, maps, passports, codebooks, visas, clothes, tools and blank checks' (1989). She said that 'As a white person, I realized I had been taught about racism as something which puts others at a disadvantage, but had been taught not to see one of its corollary aspects, white privilege, which puts me at an advantage' (1989). Michael Holding gives some powerful examples of White Privilege in his book *Why We Kneel, How We Rise*: 'If you are white, for example, and you stand in a residential street for a couple of minutes, it's highly unlikely someone's going to call the police because they think you're going to steal a car. If you're a white barrister you're not going to be mistaken for the accused.' He tells the story of Black Barrister Alexandra Wilson who, in September 2020 'was mistaken for the defendant three times on the same day in London' (2021:39).

In her knapsack essay, McIntosh lists 50 advantages that she has as a White person over people of colour. These include:

- being able, if she so wishes, to 'arrange to be in the company of people of my race most of the time'

- being able to 'turn on the television or open to the front page of the paper and see people of my race widely represented'

- being shown, when 'told about our national heritage or about "civilization", ... that people of my color made it what it is'

- being sure that her children 'will be given curricular materials that testify to the existence of their race'

- being able 'to go into a music shop and count on finding the music of my race represented, into a supermarket and find the staple foods which fit with my cultural traditions, into a hairdresser's shop and find someone who can cut my hair'

- never being 'asked to speak for all the people of my racial group'

- being 'pretty sure that if I ask to talk to "the person in charge", I will be facing a person of my race'

- being sure that, if pulled over by traffic cop or having her tax return audited, 'I haven't been singled out because of my race'

- finding it easy to 'buy posters, postcards, picture books, greeting cards, dolls, toys, and children's magazines featuring people of my race.' (1989)

Activity

Discuss the Peggy McIntosh essay with your staff (you could give it them to read in advance of a training session).

Invite them to identify

a. the privileges that they recognise

b. those they had not considered before but can now see exist

c. any that they do not feel exist in the UK in 2022

d. any that they feel exist but are not in McIntosh's list

e. the implications for the school

f. ways in which the school community could mitigate any of these inequities.*

---

* Dr Matt Jacobs, in Thomas's Representation Matters, gives helpful advice as to what White people can do in response to their White Privilege (2022: 90–92). In summary, his actions are:

- Take responsibility

- Challenge your perspective

- Be intentionally conscious

- Learn critical questioning

- Be active as a White anti–racist

- Be visible as a White anti-racist

- Call out Whiteness and make it visible

- Be mindful of the pitfalls of allyship.

The last point is an interesting one and is explored in more detail in the conclusion of this book.

The penultimate point is worthy of a staff CPD session or PSHE lesson discussion. As Whites are a majority in the UK, the adjective 'White' is rarely used in descriptions of people: how often do you hear 'the White police officer,' 'that White judge' or 'the White cashier at the supermarket'? In contrast you will likely have heard descriptions like: 'my Asian friend,' 'that Chinese stallholder' or 'the Black doctor.' This has the effect of highlighting the race of minority ethnic people but not White people, so putting Whites at the centre, normalising Whiteness. Allan G. Johnson, quoted by Sarpong (2020:7), suggests that this 'also encourages whites to be unaware of themselves as White, as if they didn't have a race at all. It also encourages whites to be unaware of white privilege.' Furthermore, this practice has the effect of implying that any other race is unusual, or of note. This is especially problematic when the race identification is applied to people in positions of power, suggesting that it is remarkable or exceptional to see that person in that role. This was applied a lot to Barack Obama, who was routinely described as 'the Black President.'

Some White people find it very difficult to accept the validity of the concept of White privilege. The denials often cite the disadvantages of other groups due to socio-economic status, gender, disability, or other protected characteristics. The disadvantages faced by many White working-class people are often used to refute the suggestion that being White is a privilege. But the concept of White Privilege does not suggest that all White people are more privileged overall than all people of colour; it is simply saying that White people, whatever other challenges or disadvantages they might face, have race as an advantage. As Aisha Thomas explains, there is a 'politicised misrepresentation (of the concept of White Privilege) that seeks to conflate race privilege and class privilege in a process that weaponises class against Black, Asian and minoritised people' (2022: 89). Some government ministers have made unhelpful comments on this subject, for example Kemi Badenock who said that she did not want White children being taught about 'white privilege and their inherited racial guilt' (Guardian Jessica Murray 20 October 2020). The DfE response to the Education Committee report *The forgotten: how White working-class pupils have been let down, and how to change it of Oct 2021* – 'Schools should consider whether the promotion of politically controversial terminology, including White Privilege, is consistent with their duties under the Equality Act 2010' – also led to many educators feeling unclear as to how to address race equity training. However, in June 2022, Ofsted's Chief HMI, Amanda Spielman, said the following in her speech at the Festival of Education: 'We need intellectual openness in the young. The willingness to listen to alternative opinions, the ability to conduct reasoned debate, and the tact to offer constructive criticism are more important now than ever.' This should, I believe, be seen as giving the green light to having an open and balanced discussion of this concept with adults and learners; no educator should feel unable to explore and debate the concept of White Privilege, in an age-appropriate way, with learners provided they do not present it as a universally accepted reality and allow space to examine the position of those who find it problematic.

Activities

A: One way to discuss White Privilege alongside other advantages and disadvantages is to look at various 'pairs' of hypothetical people and consider which might be more or less advantaged in our society and why. Pairs could include the following, but you might want to create your own examples. This activity needs to be facilitated with sensitivity and, I would suggest, with colleagues who know each other well, but it leads to powerful and illuminating discussion.

- A British Indian law graduate or a White British working-class single mother

- A Hijabi-wearing Muslim Bangladeshi school girl in London or a Traveller school girl in Knowsley

- A Chinese female GP or a male Black Caribbean surgeon

- A White British rabbi or a White British imam

- A White working class boy attending a low performing state school or an Asian middle class boy attending a top independent school.

B: Another effective activity to explore structural advantages and disadvantages with adults (or older students) is to invite them to list the privileges or advantages that they feel they have and any disadvantages they feel they have and then to discuss this with a trusted colleague.

C: A suggested activity for a PSHE lesson or a tutorial activity is to take a data set like the following one, cited by Agarwal in *Sway* (although you may choose one that is more recent or geographically local to you), and ask students What might be the possible reasons for this inequality? This should include consideration of the validity and reliability of the source and the data in it. It could lead smoothly into a debate about the concept of White Privilege:

'In December 2018, a survey for the Guardian of 1,000 people from minority ethnic backgrounds found that they were consistently more likely to have faced negative everyday experiences…than white people… The survey found that 43% of those from a minority ethnic background had been overlooked for a work promotion in a way that felt unfair in the last five years – more than twice the proportion of white people (18%) who reported the same experience. The results also showed that minority ethnic individuals are three times as likely to have been thrown out of or denied entrance to a restaurant, bar or club, and 38% of respondents from minority ethnic backgrounds said they had been wrongly suspected of shoplifting, compared with 14% of white people' (2020:253).

Ensuring that all staff have the skills and confidence to deal with racist incidents involving learners

Racist incidents occur in every school and setting. Under the Education and Inspections Act 2006, headteachers have a duty to identify and implement measures to promote good behaviour, respect for others, and self-discipline among pupils, and to prevent all forms of bullying. This includes the prevention of bullying around race, religion and culture. The Equality Act of 2010 requires schools

- to eliminate unlawful discrimination, harrassment and victimisation and

● to advance equality of opportunity between people from different (equality) groups and

● to foster good relations between people from different (equality) groups.

It is vital that all staff recognise racist incidents when they see them or when they are reported to them and respond to them consistently and effectively. The only way to ensure this is through regular and comprehensive training, covering what constitutes racism and how to respond to it, so that the recipient feels supported and the perpetrator is educated and/or sanctioned.

Schools which have developed great practice in this area have done so through a great deal of conscious practice and a culture of open discussion, reflection and dialogue. Using real life or fictitious scenarios, unpicking them and considering the pros and cons of various responses is an effective way of involving all staff in practical training. Below are some examples, devised by my colleagues Karin Hutchinson and Toks Olusamokun for school leaders on the Great Representation programme that you could adapt for your school context.

Activities

1. With the staff, devise a full and comprehensive list of all the types of behaviour that constitute racist incidents

2. Read each of the following scenarios. These are incidents that could take place in a school. They are not held up as examples of good practice, simply realistic scenarios. In your group, discuss the following:

   • Is this a racist incident (as defined by the Stephen Lawrence Inquiry Report definition: 'A racist incident is any incident which is perceived to be racist by the victim, or any other person')?

   • How well was the incident dealt with?

   • How could the action taken have been improved?

Scenario A:

In a predominantly white primary school, a reception class child, Thomas, asked his friend Ben, 'Why do you have brown skin?' Ben was upset and began to cry. The class teacher took the boys to one side and listened to Ben explaining that he was upset because Thomas had been nasty about his skin colour. She said she was very sorry that he was upset and asked Thomas to also say what happened. Thomas was clearly surprised and upset that Ben had been offended. The class teacher asked Thomas if he had meant to upset Ben and he said no. She then reinforced that it had been a very good question as there are many different skin colours and it would be good to learn why Ben's was brown and Thomas' was creamy pink. She reassured both children.

The incident was recorded and both sets of parents were informed of what had happened and how it had been dealt with, so that they could provide any further support to the boys at home. The teacher followed up the incident with some work on how we look different and how we look the same.

Scenario B:

Jasminder and Sophie are in Year 5 and were both playing in the playground with different groups of friends. When the games began to merge, the girls had a disagreement. The girls started to argue about who would be the leader in the new game and started name-calling. During this argument Jasminder called Sophie 'fat' and 'spotty.' Sophie called Jasminder 'dirty' and said she 'stinks of curry.' Supervisors come over to the girls, separated them and, on hearing their accounts and that of witnesses, they took the children involved to the headteacher.

The headteacher interviewed Jasminder and Sophie and took statements from six other children involved in the game and argument. She discovered that on numerous occasions Jasminder had called Sophie unpleasant names. The headteacher informed both sets of parents. Both sets of parents were upset about the behaviour of their children and Sophie's parents were shocked about their child's language. The head explained to Sophie's parents that the incident would be recorded as a racial incident and Sophie's class teacher would be exploring the views and language she expressed. She tells Jasminder's parents that she will miss a playtime and will start seeing the 'Place2Be' mentor once a week.

Scenario C:

Amelia is a dual-heritage child in Year 1. Whilst she is handing out invitations for her birthday, she tells Khadijah (who is Black) that she cannot come to her party because she is too dark. Khadijah tells her teacher. The teacher tries to reassure Khadijah and says some kind words to her. Amelia is told to sit on the 'red spot' for being unkind. After a short time, Amelia apologises to Khadijah and they carry on with the day.

The teacher is uncertain about how she handled the situation and speaks to her colleague at lunchtime who advises her that she should speak to both parents at pick-up. Unfortunately, Khadijah's parents are not at pick-up on that day and so the teacher is unable to speak to them. Amelia's dad is in a rush and reacts badly.

The following day, Khadijah's mum asks to speak with the teacher following a report from her daughter and Amelia's dad complains to the headteacher. The teacher is reprimanded for not contacting home or following the anti-bullying procedure.

Scenario D:

As a part of the curriculum within a Year 9 English lesson, a supply teacher was reading the text 'Of Mice and Men' aloud to the class. As she was reading, she came across the 'n word' and said the word aloud. Several pupils in the class were shocked that the teacher had used the word and a handful of Black students immediately accused the teacher of racism. The teacher became distressed and subsequently lost control of the class. She employed the school's behavioural policy and two students were removed until they calmed down. No further action was taken with the students.

In a subsequent conversation with the head of department, the teacher felt that she was justified in using the 'n word' as it had been written in the book. Both the head of department and the supply teacher spoke with the class; the teacher apologised for any upset that had been caused. The teacher also recognised that she hadn't previously thought that using the 'n word' was controversial if it was written in a book.

Scenario E:

Whilst lining up in the lunch queue Abdi heard the 'p word' whispered. He was not able to distinguish exactly who had said it or whether it was directed at him. It upset him as it had happened before in other parts of the school, and he has never been able to identify exactly who is saying it. He felt powerless.

When Abdi got home, he told his older sister who told his mum. His mum contacted the school and was directed to the Head of Year. The Head of Year was busy teaching but contacted the mum the following day. She made a note of the parent's complaint but explained that there was nothing she could do about it. She told Abdi's mother to encourage Abdi to make another report directly to her if something happens again.

Scenario F:

Ryan and Rotimi are in the same class in school. They have been friends since primary school and often tease one another and use accents that reflect one another's families. They have been warned in the past that their jokes might cause upset. During a science lesson on the food chain Rotimi and Ryan are bored and start to flick through the textbook. Ryan likens Rotimi to a monkey, makes a few monkey sounds and teases him about how much he likes bananas. The teaching assistant, who is sitting close by (as she supports Ryan with his autism), hears this and reports it to the teacher.

Later that day, both boys write an account and are interviewed by the headteacher. Rotimi insists that he was not offended or upset and that he and Ryan were joking around. Ryan thinks the whole thing is ridiculous and does not accept his words and behaviour might have caused offence. The headteacher informs both sets of parents about the incident. Given Ryan's lack of contrition, the headteacher decides Ryan needs one day in isolation. Ryan's mum disagrees with this punishment and supports Ryan in not attending school. After three days, Ryan returns to school and the matter is dropped.

Scenario G:

Faye, a 15 year old White girl, has started using Tik Tok and Insta to make videos. She is part of a group of girls in her school who are in the same Whatsapp group and socials online. Faye has been producing make-up and hair tutorials; she also choreographs short dance routines.

In one of her earlier videos, Faye is demonstrating a make-up technique. She has a towel on, drying her wet hair and says something vague about the towel looking like a hijab.

Following an assembly in school about racism, girls in Faye's group of friends tell her to take the video down because of the hijab comment. Faye isn't sure exactly why, but she agrees to. Other students in the year group overhear the conversation and inform staff. By lunchtime, several students have made complaints to a variety of teachers. Faye is upset and is called in to speak to her Head of Year. Her parents are informed that her video is inappropriate and offensive, and Faye is sent to the removal unit for the rest of the day as a sanction.

Understanding, noticing and addressing microaggressions and 'hidden' racism

Some forms of racism are more covert than others. In the last chapter, we touched on microaggressions. By definition, microaggressions are often difficult to prove and this in itself makes their effect pernicious. The person subjected to the microaggression cannot be sure of the motive of the perpetrator and this is psychologically unsettling. In her blog *Do This, Not That*, Jaya Hiranandani says 'When I was sidelined, ignored or marginalised, the younger me was left wondering – Was it me, them or the situation? Am I being too sensitive? Did I do something wrong? Is it just an individual personality trait or is there something bigger here?' Her questions continue, 'Is this person incapable of trusting me just because I am different from them? Am I being sidelined because I am not interesting enough, or is the other person just having a bad day? Is this person not interested in knowing me because they think they already "know" how I am from their experiences with other people of my ethnicity?' (2022).

It is virtually impossible for a White, advantaged person like me to understand what being subjected to racist microaggressions must feel like. The nearest I have got to being able to experience such a microaggression was perhaps an incident in a French boulangerie in autumn 2021. Hard as I work on both my language and pronunciation, it is always obvious to a French shop assistant that I am English (I sometimes sense that they have worked this out long before I even open my mouth!). On this particular occasion, I waited in the queue until my turn came to be served, by which time I was the only customer remaining, but as I stood forward and asked for a baguette, the assistant turned from the counter and started a conversation with her colleague at the back of the shop. I waited patiently for several minutes until she had finished and turned back to me. She took my order, gave me my baguette and told me how much I owed her. As I went to put the money in her hand, she turned away again and resumed the conversation with her colleague, leaving me standing, arm outstretched at the counter. It was at least another two minutes before she came back to take my money. I was left wondering why she had not given me the same quality of service as afforded to everyone else before me, why she had not saved her conversation until after serving me (there was no one else in the queue by then) and why she had left me waiting to finish the transaction when she could clearly see I was offering her my coins. Was it because I was English? Was the woman who served me consciously or unconsciously biased against me as an English woman (post Brexit, at a time when COVID infections were 10 times higher in the UK than in France and the Prime Minister had insensitively told Macron to 'man up' over the French losing out to the UK on a nuclear submarine deal)? It's impossible to know. This was one trivial incident. I was in no hurry. It didn't really matter at all that I was held up. It was an isolated occurrence. And if it had been fuelled by a conscious or unconscious anti-English sentiment, frankly I could have understood. The fact is, I don't normally experience treatment like this in France or elsewhere abroad and certainly not in the UK, due to White privilege. But it gave me a taste of what living with regular microaggressions must feel like.

It is worth noting that the term and concept 'microaggression' is problematic for many people of colour. In *How to be an Anti-Racist*, Ibram X. Kendi states powerfully 'What other people call racial microaggressions I call racist abuse…I do not use "microaggression" any more… A persistent daily low hum of racist abuse is not minor' (2019:47). Jaya Hiranandani uses the term 'covert racism' instead of 'microaggression.'

Although many adults and students are conscious of what might constitute covert racism or microaggressions, others will benefit from support and training on recognising and addressing them. Bennie Kara gives some great examples in *Diversity In Schools* (2021:57), including asking people of colour where they are from, touching Black people's hair or commenting on its texture or adjusting a Muslim's hijab (or a Sikh's turban).

Staff training should also cover so-called 'hidden' racisms, such as racism against white people, for example Jews, Gypsies or Russians. Some adults mistakenly separate anti-Semitism from racism, considering it to be religious rather than racial hatred. But as David Baddiel says in *Jews Don't Count*, 'I am an atheist and yet the Gestapo would shoot me tomorrow. Racists who don't like Jews never ask the Jew they are abusing how often they go to synagogue.' (2021:41) Adults need to know how to deal with anti-Semitism when it surfaces, such as in literary texts or at times of Palestinian-Israeli unrest.

Guidance for dealing with race incidents in school

Does your school have a clear set of protocols for dealing with race incidents?

Read the following advice and consider how closely this reflects your school's practice.

Can you improve on it?

Dealing with race incidents

1. Ensure that all pupils understand what racism, discrimination and prejudice are and what racial incidents look like in a school

2. Ensure that all pupils understand the expectation that all incidents of racism should be reported and know how to report racist incidents in your school

3. Ensure that all pupils know how racist incidents will be dealt with

4. Address significant incidents publicly (e.g. in form time or assembly). This is not about naming and shaming or embarrassing pupils but demonstrating publicly the school's strong anti-racist stance and taking opportunities to educate and teach pupils.

5. Listen to the pupil(s) who were the target of the racism, as well as any witnesses, and provide the appropriate support

6. Educate and address the language/behaviour/attitude of the perpetrator(s)

7. Support meaningful reparations and ensure an apology

8. Enforce consequences in line with the school's agreed policy.

9. Record the incident internally

10. Inform the parents/carers of both parties

11. Follow up and review with the pupil(s) targeted (including parents/carers if appropriate)

12. Maintain records for governors/trustees

13. Ensure that serious incidents are referred to the police should they constitute a hate crime

14. Be sensitive to the impact for all involved.

Making time to talk about topical race incidents with students

One of the indicators of a racially literate staff body is evidence of skilfully facilitated conversations and debates with learners about topical race issues in tutor time, in circle time, in PSHE lessons, even in dining halls. In the last year or two there have been numerous news stories that would merit discussion in such forums: the Yorkshire Cricket Club race scandal, footballers taking the knee, Meghan Markle's treatment by the press, Nadhim Zahawi's comments about 'cultural vandalism' in relation to OCR refreshing its set poems at GCSE, Lady Sarah Hussey's questions to charity leader Ngozi Fulani and Rupa Huq's comment about Kwasi Kwarteng to name but a few.

At St Albans Girls' School (STAGS), leaders formalised opportunities for students to discuss such incidents through a programme called STAGS Talks.

Reflection

Once you have read the following case study, you might like to consider what it would take to set up something similar in your school or setting.

St Albans Girls' School Case Study: STAGS Talks

The current generation has access to much information and many voices from across the world in a majority social media setting. Misconceptions, misinformation and fake news cause rifts in society. It is the role and responsibility of educators to give students the cultural capital needed to ensure that they are prepared for the wider world and are able to be active participating citizens in society. Leaders recognised the importance of the school's role in facilitating conversations between staff and students on the topic of race.

The aims were

- to create a safe and positive space for students to explore, talk about and discuss challenging issues, including race equality, within and beyond the classroom and

- to support staff in facilitating such conversations in a productive and inclusive manner.

The means was a weekly discussion space and a bi-weekly form time with a focus on EDI – fora for discussions on equality diversity and inclusivity. The initiative became known as STAGS Talks.

The Israeli-Palestinian conflict in May 2021 was a trigger for the school's intent to enhance diversity and equity dialogue and actions. Many of the school population were personally and culturally affected by this international crisis. This manifested in some negative activities that took place across the school: propaganda leaflets, Israeli flags being crossed out on world flags maps in geography rooms and an aggressive outburst between two students. It was clear that many of the students felt passionate, upset and frustrated at the situation and, as a result of lockdown, had not had the chance to air and consider their views in a healthy way. Students wanted to discuss the crisis with members of the school community and wanted to speak with staff members about their frustrations. In some cases, students felt shut down and not heard as, due to the sensitive nature of the situation, some staff were nervous about opening up discussion and perhaps 'saying the wrong thing' or igniting the situation further.

Leaders agreed a plan to outline both sides of the debate by presenting the facts of the conflict in terms of the history and context of the situation. It was decided to engage Social Action Leaders in the sixth form to lead an assembly, providing the whole school community of students and staff with an educational understanding of the crisis. A follow-on discussion club would be set up and promoted by the Social Action Leaders on the day of the live assembly for all students who felt passionate and wanted their voice to be heard to come together with key staff to discuss the conflict.

The inaugural meeting of the club took place with over 100 students coming together to talk about the Arab-Israeli crisis. It was an emotional and powerful session and the KS5 leaders led the discussion with support from senior staff. The now weekly *STAGS Talks About* club is promoted to all students across the school and has gained huge momentum from staff and students alike, with the ebb and flow of content in the media.

STAGS Talks (a weekly dedicated time to consider the importance of EDI in all areas of the school by ensuring a centralised place for world and current affairs to be discussed) was then set up in the new academic year to complement the STAGS Talks About club. STAGS Talks would ensure that the pastoral curriculum provided the time and space to be inclusive of all. Leaders created an annual plan of events that was published to all staff. Staff were offered the opportunity to contribute to this. Themed sessions were then centralised and delivered to all students across the school. The calendar of sessions was created to represent world events such as Black History Month, Diwali, Hanukkah, Human Rights Week and Pride Month. In addition to world events, there would be bi-weekly sessions on current affairs. Topics included, 'If it wasn't for mobile phones being able to record video would race be the discussion point it is today?' Discussion points were differentiated by key stage to ensure age appropriate content. In addition to this fixed calendar, it was important that the programme provided flexibility to make sure that any important new issues that arose could be added and discussed with all students. Leaders supported staff by providing materials and facilitating initial educational prompts on discussions. STAGS Talks discussions fed into the next STAGS Talks About club session – students could come and continue the discussion further with members of staff who were comfortable with facilitating in depth debates on topics. STAGS Talks About club is promoted at the end of every STAGS Talks form time session.

STAGS Talks has given students the confidence to take inclusivity and diversity further into the school community. Thirty students who come to STAGS Talks About have become Global Ambassador leaders; they are helping staff lead a Personal Development Day on diversity for the whole community. It has also developed the racial literacy of the staff body.

References

Agarwal. P. (2020). *Sway: Unravelling Unconscious Bias.* (London: Bloomsbury).

Baddiel. D. (2021). *Jews Don't Count.* (London: TLS Books).

Diangelo. R. (2019). *White Fragility.* (Great Britain: Penguin).

Hiranandani. J. (2022). *Do This, Not That.* (Diverse Educators). Available at: www.diverseeducators.co.uk/do-this-not-that/

Holding. M. (2021). *Why We Kneel, How We Rise.* (London: Simon & Schuster).

Kara, B. (2021). *Diversity In Schools.* (London: Corwin).

Kendi. I. X. (2019). *How To Be An Anti-Racist.* (London: The Bodley Head).

MacIntosh. P. (1989). *White Privilege: Unpacking the Invisible Knapsack.* Available at: www.bing.com/search?q=peggy+mcintosh+1989&cvid=ec86084ff2f946869cd4b9c61586348c&aqs=edge.0.0l2j69i11004.5101j0j4&FORM=ANAB01&DAF0=1&PC=U531

Macfarlane. R. and Catchpool. M eds. (2022) *Great Representation. Collection of School Case Studies.* (Hertfordshire: Herts For Learning Ltd).

Murray. J. (2020). *Teaching white privilege as uncontested fact is illegal, minister says.* (The Guardian). Available at: www.theguardian.com/world/2020/oct/20/teaching-white-privilege-is-a-fact-breaks-the-law-minister-says

Robson. D. (2021). *What Unconscious Bias Training Gets Wrong And How To Fix It.* (The Guardian). Available at: www.theguardian.com/science/2021/apr/25/what-unconscious-bias-training-gets-wrong-and-how-to-fix-it

Sarpong, J. (2020). *The Power Of Privilege: How White People Can Challenge Racism.* (London: HQ).

Scott. K. (2021). *Just Work: Get it Done, Fast and Fair.* (London: Macmillan).

Stewart-Hall. C. (2021). *Why white teachers must learn to talk about race in schools: the problem unpacked.* (Equitable Coaching). Available at: https://equitablecoaching.com/why-white-teachers-must-learn-to-talk-about-race-in-schools-the-problem-unpacked/

The Runnymede Trust (2021). *Civil Society Report To The United Nations CERD.* Available at: www.runnymedetrust.org/publications/civil-society-report-to-united-nations-cerd

Thomas. A. (2021). *Representation Matters.* (London: Bloomsbury).

Williams. S. (2020). *Anti Racist Ally.* (Great Britain, Dublin: Harper Collins).

Wilson. A. (2021). *Do you understand what it's like to be a black student in a UK school?* (Understanding Black Students). Available at: https://amandawilson.coach/2021/08/07/do-you-understand-what-its-like-to-be-a-black-student-in-a-uk-school/

Yoh, D. Y. *Kendo Nagasaki and Me* in Shukla. N. ed (2017) *The Good Immigrant* (London: Unbound).

6 Addressing the effects of stereotyping

It is never too late to give up our prejudices.

Henry David Thoreau (quoted by Scott (2021:102)

Blanket denial is one of the main reasons why Black people find it difficult living in the UK.

David Harewood (2021:227)

This chapter further explores the nature and inevitability of prejudice. It then considers racial stereotyping and the hyper-vigilance and adultification of some racial groups. It examines the many negative ways in which racial stereotyping impacts children of colour and encourages the reader to consider ways of addressing and countering these consequences. It closes with the reflections of a school leader on personal learning from the school's work to develop the racial literacy of the staff.

The inevitability of prejudice

Staff racial literacy training should at some point, ideally quite early on, address the fact that all humans stereotype and therefore have racial prejudices. Beverly Daniel Tatum is helpful on this: 'Prejudice is one of the inescapable consequences of living in a racist society. Cultural racism – the cultural images and messages that affirm the assumed superiority of Whites and the assumed inferiority of people of colour – is like smog in the air' (2021:86). 'When we claim to be free of prejudice, perhaps what we are really saying is that we are not hatemongers. But none of us is completely innocent. Prejudice is an integral part of our socialization and it is not our fault' (2021:86). These quotes alone would make a great provocation for a staff or governor/trustee discussion.

This brings us onto an important question: Can people of colour be racist? There are many views on this matter, largely because definitions of racism vary so much. Again, Tatum shows clarity on this question:

DOI: 10.4324/9781003275220-8

'If one defines racism as racial prejudice, the answer is yes. People of colour can and do have racial prejudices. However, if one defines racism as a system of advantage based on race, the answer is no. People of colour are not racist because they do not systematically benefit from racism' (2021:90).

And, logically, a further question that it is important to address is: Are all White people therefore racist? Let's defer to Tatum once more:

'All White people, intentionally or unintentionally, do benefit from racism' but 'not all Whites are actively racist. Many are passively racist. Some, though not enough, are actively antiracist. The relevant question is not whether all Whites are racist but how we can move on' (2021:91).

Questions

How could you use these quotes with staff or governors/trustees to generate debate and reflection?

Do they have implications for the definition of racism that you use in your glossary of terminology?

How do you respond to racism from learners from minority ethnic backgrounds? In the same way or differently to racism from White learners? Why?

The dangers of stereotyping

Just as we each have prejudices, we all have a tendency to stereotype people, based on the groups they belong to. In *Sway*, Pragya Agarwal reminds us that 'In essence, stereotypes of any sort are bad – even if they are positive – because they lead to group-based biases, and they give out the message that people can purport to know everything about an individual based on their group' (2020:139).

When I first started my current job in Hertfordshire, colleagues in my organisation and leaders of schools across the county inevitably showed an interest in what I had done previously and the school that I had led most recently. The pupils at Isaac Newton Academy performed very well in public exams. I remember vividly one person saying to me 'Well of course it's much easier to get great exam results in a school like that with a high proportion of Asian children.' She was displaying the stereotype of Asian children being hard-working, well-behaved, supplicant to teachers and backed by supportive parents and extended families, set on their child becoming a doctor or engineer. The reality was, of course, that every one of the 180 students in each cohort was an individual with strengths and weaknesses, advantages and challenges. The Asians who represented around 80% of the pupil population comprised Indians, Pakistanis, Bangladeshis, Sri Lankans, Mauritians; Muslims, Sikhs, Hindus; some first generation, some with families well established in London; some with one parent, some with two, some with none; some with parents who had never attended school themselves and spoke limited English, some from highly educated families; some living in dire poverty and others enjoying economic comfort. And then, of course, there were White and Black students.

It is important that leaders support their staff in educating themselves about the culture and heritage of different ethnic groups represented in the school, to enhance cultural awareness and understanding. But it is equally important to emphasise and appreciate differences within groups and not to treat all those in a racial group as one.

Educators can easily fall into the trap of categorising and stereotyping learners and this is highly dangerous. It leads to the setting of different expectations for different groups of students and it is quickly detected by children, affecting their attitudes and behaviours. We will return to this a bit later in the chapter.

It is vital that leaders are attuned to their own biases and the biases of their staff, vigilant in spotting evidence of stereotyping and the assumptions that results from them and quick to interrupt and challenge them. It is also important that they provide training to help staff, governors and trustees to spot their own stereotyping behaviours and address them. This is not easy; it requires discipline, effort and self-awareness to question and challenge our assumptions and biases.

Prevalent negative racial stereotypes

Louise Archer's research paper *The Impossibility of Minority Ethnic Educational "Success"? An Examination of the Discourses of Teachers and Pupils in British Secondary Schools* references a wide range of research studies that show the negative stereotyping of certain groups of pupils in schools. She found that 'Black pupils (but particularly those of Caribbean origin) were frequently constructed as 'problem' pupils within schools. However, the increase in Islamophobia in the United Kingdom – and the cleavage between Asian 'achievers' and Muslim 'believers' within the popular imagination – also positioned Muslim boys within this category to an extent.' Stereotypes associated with 'demonised' minority ethnic pupils 'were organised around notions of rebellion/insubordination, loudness and inappropriate (hyper)heterosexuality. These combined with historical racist discourses to position these pupils as "naturally" unambitious and unacademic due to their ethnic/cultural backgrounds' (2008:94).

Archer found that this 'notion of aggressive and confrontational behaviour has been particularly associated with Black boys...yet it was also strongly linked with teachers' perceptions of Black girls too'... 'Black femininity was identified as problematically loud (visibly and audibly) and hence was seen as challenging within classrooms and schools. Furthermore, this "loudness" was associated with a lack of educational motivation or application' (2008:95).

Archer argues that there are

> popular racist discourses and constructions of Black/minority ethnic families as 'culture poor'...and historical racist discourses which position Black people as being of lower intelligence... Hence, Black pupils are positioned as 'naturally' unambitious and unacademic due to their location within 'unacademic' families and cultures. Thus, dominant education policy discourse effectively silences other competing explanations and accounts of minority ethnic underachievement – such as the role that structural inequalities and racism might play in producing the tail-off in achievement that has been noted within many Black pupils' school careers.
>
> *2008:97*

In other words, negative stereotypes result in educators failing to question or feel sufficiently accountable for the higher exclusion rates and lower academic scores of some Black groups.

Hyper-vigilance and adultification

David Gillborn believes that poorer academic outcomes and higher exclusions for Black boys are to do with teachers' lower expectations of black pupils and hypervigilance over their behaviour, which leads to harsher discipline. Cited by Irena Barker in the *TES* on 6 August 2021, he argues that 'the overwhelming majority of work suggests that black students, especially boys, are subjected to more surveillance. They're watched more closely.'

Why might this be? Well, if teachers (consciously or unconsciously) hold negative stereotypes of certain groups, they will be anticipating poorer behaviour from them and therefore on the look-out for it. Holding suggests that 'The teacher thinks the pupil is a problem, so the pupil becomes a problem' (2021:158). He goes on to address what he suggests is a key taboo that people don't like to talk about, admit to or recognise, namely that 'White people are generally afraid of Black people' (2021: 161). In *Whistling Vivialdi*, Claude M. Steele talks of the fear that Brent Staples, a *New York Times* columnist, saw on the faces of White people on the streets of Chicago when he walked past them at night: 'People who were carrying on conversations went mute and stared straight ahead, as though avoiding my eyes would save them... I'd been a fool. I'd been walking the streets grinning good evening at people who were frightened to death of me. I did violence to them just by being' (2011: 6). By developing the racial literacy of staff, it is less likely that White teachers will feel nervous about, threatened by or fearful of challenging behaviour from Black students.

A further reason for hypervigilance of certain racially minoritised groups might be adultification. This is the practice of perceiving and treating someone as older than they are and expecting a level of maturity from them beyond their years. This is often felt by Black children. If minority ethnic children are sub-consciously adultified by White teachers, it is easy to see how this could result in tension and resentment. Similarly, if a Black student feels hyper-visible and under greater teacher scrutiny than their White peers, it is likely that this frustration might manifest in poor behaviour, creating a vicious cycle.

What follows are the reflections of Bonolo on this matter:

'I have witnessed plenty of examples of poor racial literacy amongst staff in the schools where I have worked but the most disturbing and most prevalent is when teachers have conversations about black students in a negative way. The conversations often involve the adultification of black boys and girls. Some members of staff are quick to judge and treat black students differently by expecting them to act much older than their age. Often when students are taller, there is an expectation that they are not children and not entitled to be talked to or treated as a child. Some staff members use certain adjectives and phrases such as 'intimidating,' 'aggressive,' 'giving attitude,' 'little madam,' 'part of a gang of students' or 'loud' when describing black students. I have noticed that some adults are quick to use these terms and will use them with the students or when having discussions in meetings. On one occasion, a cover teacher accused a high attaining shy black girl of having an 'attitude' because he asked her a question and she said that 'she didn't know' the answer. The teacher insisted that the student did know and that the student withheld her answer as an act of defiance towards him. The student in question was so hurt by the words said by the teacher and was upset by the detention given. As a result, the student refused to go to break and chose to sit in her form room the rest of the week, just in case she crossed paths with that teacher.

I often have to highlight and challenge the negative impact of adultification and stereotyping of black students when having conversations with staff. Often students are compared to each other just because of their ethnicity. Teachers often pick out a black boy, for example, and make comments like 'Oh he is good, not like X – he is so rude.' This bias does not serve either student well as the 'good' student is never talked about without reference to a badly behaved student. There is a lack of understanding that all black students are unique and require an individual approach, just like every other student.'

The impact of negative stereotyping, hypervigilance and adultification – stereotype threat

Albert Adeyemi, in his essay *Labelling of Black Students In Schools in Diverse Educators: A Manifesto*, argues that there is an element of 'self-fulfilling prophecy which highlights the potential effect of labelling for students' (2022:274). Akala reflects on the issue of White educators underestimating Black children's attainment and potential. He argues that 'If a fair proportion of your teachers or even just a couple of them constantly assume you are way less clever than you actually are simply because you are black, and treat you accordingly, you are going to resent them and it will naturally affect your self-esteem and grades' (2018:81).

Agarwal tells us that 'The more one is aware of the fear of being stereotyped and facing biases, the more one is keen to avoid any confirmation of these, and the more one is responsive to any cues that hint towards rejection or performance errors.' She says that 'One way that individuals often deal with stereotype threat is by reaffirming their own individual self-identity and disengaging from the larger stereotyped group' (2020:144–5).

When I joined Walthamstow School For Girls as headteacher in 2002, one of my early priorities was to tighten up on student adherence to school rules. After a period of time without a substantive head, some of the girls were taking liberties with the uniform policy – rolling up their skirts, wearing big gold hoop earrings and trainers rather than shoes. There was also a laxness about getting to lessons on time and some students were regularly found after the lesson bell joking and messing about by the toilets or in corridors. The school had a sizeable cohort of Black Caribbean and Black African girls (around 15%), some of the worst offenders were Black girls and many of the Black girls socialised together. It became apparent as I worked with the staff to tighten up on adherence to the school rules that colleagues were uncomfortable about what they saw as 'big groups of Black girls behaving loudly and flouting the uniform rules.' They were hesitant about addressing them, partly nervous of being challenged back and partly sensitive to the fact that they were targeting the black girls rather than their Asian or White peers. More than once I heard colleagues reflect that 'It would be so much better if the Black students integrated more socially. It's such a shame that they all stick together.' I was questioned on a similar point when conducting a race equity review at a majority White boys' school recently. The headteacher took me to one side and said, 'I really don't think that we have a problem with students of different races getting along together in the school, but at break and lunchtimes you always see all the Black students together, they're never with the White boys. What should we do about that?'

I directed the headteacher to Tatum's useful book, *Why Are All The Black Kids Sitting Together In The Cafeteria?* Tatum points out that we tend to socialise with people who are like us – who speak the same language, listen to the same music, eat the same foods at home, worship at the same mosque/church/temple/gurdwara/synagogue. Therefore, it is totally natural that members of an ethnic group should gravitate towards each other in the lunch hall and at break times – they have more in common to talk about. She points out that educators don't bat an eyelid at White students mixing with other White students!

However, the same phenomenon does not manifest as noticeably with younger children. Isaac Newton Academy is an all-through school and there it was noticeable that the children in the primary tended to play with peers from a mix of ethnic groups but the secondary students socialised in slightly less integrated groups. Tatum says that this is natural too: as puberty hits us we become more conscious of our identity and, for children of colour in a White majority society, race is a significant part of identity. She explains: 'Why do Black youths, in particular, think about themselves in terms of race? Because that is how the rest of the world thinks of them' (2021: 133). She tells a story of her son who, if asked when aged seven to describe himself, would have talked about his interests, his family and perhaps his height. As an adolescent, however, one of the first adjectives her son would use to describe himself was 'Black.'

Activity

As part of your racial literacy training, you might like to try this activity of Tatum's:

Ask your staff to complete this sentence in 60 seconds: 'Who am I?' They can use as many descriptors as they like. Then compare the way that people have described themselves. Usually it is the case that White adults tend not to describe their ethnicity but people of colour do. If this is the case for your staff/governors/trustees, encourage a discussion about why this might be. Tatum suggests that the parts of our identity that we notice tend to be the parts that others notice and reflect back to us. (2021:101–2)

When one adds into the mix that children of colour are likely to experience covert or overt racism, and perhaps within the school environment, it is sadly totally understandable that they should seek the support and solace of those who will empathise and identify with such experiences: 'racial grouping is a developmental process in response to an environmental stressor, racism' (2021:144). So rather than feeling uncomfortable or even threatened by Black kids sitting together, educators should appreciate that 'it is immensely beneficial to be able to share one's experiences with others who have lived them' (2021: 154) and perhaps to consider what in the school environment might be contributing to Black children's sense that they need the emotional support of others in their ethnic group.

Activity

The following extract from Tatum's book *Why Do All The Black Kids Sit Together In The Cafeteria?* might make a good provocation for discussion with the adults in your school:

'When the Black people are sitting together, the White people notice and become self-conscious about being White in a way that they were not before…What does it say about the White people if the Black people are all sitting together?' (2021:180)

On the question of certain racially minoritised groups perhaps seeming to push uniform expectations more than others, Archer has some useful insights. She talks about the 'style' that groups develop – typified by the wearing of branded clothes and 'bling.' She says that this enables 'the young people to generate a sense of value and self-worth' and 'status and value within their peer groups.' But, of course, 'these practices also brought pupils into conflict with schools in several ways. For instance, many of them got into trouble regularly for contravening school policies on uniform. Moreover, the young people's interest in, and attachment to, these performances of "style" were interpreted negatively by teachers, as demonstrating an "anti-school" attitude' (2008:95).

Are your staff hypervigilant of pupils in certain racially minoritised groups? If so, how can you address this?

Does adultification of certain students happen in your school. How do you know?

The impact of negative stereotyping on academic performance

Steele's research at American universities, described in *Whistling Vivaldi*, showed the negative effects of marginalisation and worry about belonging on the attainment of black students. But more than that, he revealed the impact of negative stereotyping on Black learners at inner-city high schools: what was depressing their performance was 'the pressure of the negative stereotype – the risk of confirming it, or of being seen to confirm it' (2011:58). The irony was that what put these students at risk of stereotype pressure was their academic strength and their high expectations which made them particularly sensitive to the negative stereotyping and determined not to let themselves and others in their racial group down by proving the stereotype to have credibility. Steele concluded that classrooms and exam halls, 'though seemingly the same for everybody, are, in fact, different places for different people' (2011: 60). We pick up on this in more detail in the second section of this book, where we look at the curriculum and teaching practice. One further effect of negative stereotyping that Steele identified through his research was the tendency of Black students 'to protectively isolate themselves and to over commit to self-sufficiency – strategies that might help them avoid people who they worried might stereotype them, but that would also isolate them from the help they needed.'

The impact of racial trauma

Yasmin shared with me a harrowing story of a little Nigerian boy in her school whom she found one day in distress; he was clawing at his skin and crying 'I hate the colour of my skin.' As Yasmin considered the emotional trauma her pupil was exhibiting, she reflected: 'How is he in a place to learn?'

I was a headteacher in Walthamstow at the time of the 7/7 bombing. Many of my students travelled to school by tube. After the attack, some would arrive distressed. They told staff that when they got into a carriage with their school bag, commuters would look at them, note their ethnicity and their backpacks and register fear, display aggression, mutter or even exit the carriage. How were these teenagers in a place to learn when they walked through the school gates?

In her essay *Not Just A Black Muslim Woman in It's Not About The Burka*, Rafia Rafiq writes about arriving in England from Zanzibar and trying to fit in: 'According to my teachers I was "loud", "disruptive" and "sassy"' (2020:200). She naturally gravitated towards the Black girls 'realising I would neither understand nor be understood by the white girls' (2019:200). She reflected that she had felt normal in Zanzibar but now didn't. 'The whole thing was exhausting and ultimately, the small decisions I made as a child to ensure I fitted into the different places I found myself actually meant that I had no place, no intersection that I could call home' (2019:203). How was she in a place to learn?

Nigel described to me his experiences of living in North Hertfordshire as a teenager:

> There were now some racist views in the community. Some older people would shout racist things. It was the Enoch Powell era; the National Front were active. It was the time of the Hitchin marches. My Dad always wanted to know who I was with when I went out. I was kept on a tight rein; I felt quite resentful. My dad had spoken to me and my brother about how we needed to handle ourselves; we should never be in a group of more than 2 people and never out after dark. We should be polite and never put ourselves in a position where we were likely to be stopped by the police.

Despite this advice, on one evening Nigel had what he describes as a 'Stephen Lawrence moment.' He was out alone. A car with three men in it drove by. The men shouted racist abuse out of the window. The car stopped, the men got out and one punched Nigel. He ran and dived into a nearby restaurant. A man in the restaurant tried to push Nigel outside. The attackers came in. They were violent and caused damage. Finally, the police arrived. When Nigel returned to school the next day, how was he in a place to learn?

Nigel reflected that 'Every young male Black person has a Stephen Lawrence moment at some point.' Michael Holding agrees; he reflects that 'At some stage in their life, most Black people have metaphorically felt that knee on their neck' (2021:72). Do their teachers know? Are they aware of the impact of such an incident?

Ta-Nehisi Coates, in his letter to his son – *Between The World And Me* – recalls all the emotional load that he carried with him as a boy on his walk to school each day: 'To survive the neighbourhoods and shield my body, I learned another language consisting of a basic complement of head nods and handshakes. I memorised a list of prohibited blocks. I learned the smell and feel of fighting weather.' He continues, 'I recall learning these laws clearer than I recall learning my colours and shapes, because these laws were essential to the security of my body.' Coates tells his son, 'When I was about your age, each day, fully one-third of my brain was concerned with who I was walking to school with, our precise number, the manner of our walk, the number of times I smiled, who or what I smiled at, who offered a pound and who did not.' He concludes, 'I practised the culture of the streets, a culture concerned chiefly with securing the body' (2015:23–4). How was the young Coates in a place to learn?

Akala describes his first memory of being racially abused by a peer as a five-year-old, when he was called a 'Chinese Black nigger bastard.' 'This is my earliest memory of a racist insult directed at me; there were countless more to come, of course. The overriding feeling that I remember from the numerous instances of verbal racial abuse growing up was a sense of shame.' He says, 'Racial insults leave you feeling dirty because, even at five years old, we already know on some level that, in this society at least, we are indeed lesser citizens with all the baggage of racialised history following us ghost-like about our days' (2018:38–9). How was he in a place to learn?

Reflecting on the disturbing testimony above, how are incidents such as these likely to impact children of colour?

What might the manifestations of racial trauma be for learners?

How might their self-confidence, self-identity, mental health, attitudes, behaviour and educational performance be impacted?

White staff need to hear about the ways that racism impacts their pupils. Ideally, they should hear it first hand, from the mouths of people of colour. But the next best way is through reading accounts.

Impact on behaviour

In *Natives*, Akala speaks of how he learnt to throw punches but that that was not really in his nature: 'I was naturally a soft-hearted boy and would often cry when I got home even if I had won the fight because I didn't like hurting people' (2018:40). Barrister Hashi Mohamed, in *People Like Us*, reflects: 'I was badly behaved, aggressive and not interested in taking up the opportunities offered to me. I disrupted the education of other children, preventing them from taking up opportunities themselves. But there were reasons for my behaviour: I was grieving, confused, alienated and very, very lonely' (2020:105).

Impact on attitude to education

Sarpong says, 'The sense of never fully being accepted doesn't go away, especially as it is reinforced daily, which continuously erodes a sense of belonging and self-worth.' She continues that 'For some black men in particular this can result in the rejection of education and the world of work, and lead to the pursuit of validation from a sub-culture where material possessions are valued above those things deemed further out of reach, such as employment and schooling' (2020:33).

Impact on identity and socialisation

Ta-Nehisi Coates recalls in his letter to his son, 'When I was your age the only people I knew were black and all of them were powerfully, adamantly, dangerously afraid. I had seen this fear all my young life, though I had not always recognised it as such.' He says 'The fear lived on in their practical bop, their slouching denim, their big T shirts, the calculated angle of their baseball caps, a catalogue of behaviours and garments enlisted to inspire the belief that these boys were in firm possession of everything that they desired' (2015:14).

Impact on mental health

In his autobiography *Maybe I Don't Belong Here*, actor David Harewood links a psychotic breakdown in his twenties to his first direct experience of racist abuse: 'That single encounter shattered my perception of myself, splitting my identity in two' (2021:3). 'There is now a Black half and an English half and I could feel myself slowly coming apart. At times in my life I've been able to fuse these two halves together, but occasionally the gap between them is too big and I struggle' (2021: 11). 'Since that fateful day when the man on the street told me to get the fuck out of his country, I have felt boundless in a sense. I have the feeling that I don't quite belong to the ground beneath my feet and it still makes me feel unsettled' (2021: 228).

Many of our learners of colour are experiencing degrees of racial trauma. In *Living While Black*, Kinouani describes racial trauma as 'a long-lasting sense of overwhelm, unsafeness and distress' (2021: 37). She explains that racial trauma can be caused by experiencing direct racism but also by indirect exposure to racism, such as witnessing an incident of racism, hearing about a close friend or relative's experience of racism or 'being repeatedly exposed to graphic details of a stressor/traumatic event' (2021: 36). Many people of colour in schools (or in lockdown) were, we know, struggling to cope in 2020 after witnessing the murder of George Floyd on their TVs or phones.

In *Representation Matters*, Aisha Thomas provides a useful checklist for educators to use in supporting learners who are experiencing racial trauma. This includes

- Giving children 'time to heal'

- Equipping 'all staff with a basic understanding of racial trauma'

- Having 'named staff who are trained with trauma-informed approaches that are racism specific'

- Supporting 'children to talk to those they trust'

- Giving 'children opportunities to talk about race and access to other children who may have shared lived experiences'

- Building 'links with the school's local community'

- Ensuring 'that children have access to culturally sensitive healing and therapeutic support from a professional'

- Providing 'supervision for pastoral support staff'

- Building 'a culture of openness'

- Understanding 'that racial trauma may also impact staff from Black, Brown and racially minoritised communities.' (2022:77)

Take some time to consider the list of action that Thomas recommends.

How many can you say with confidence happen consistently at your school?

Are there any you might add?

What further actions might you take?

I would add to Thomas's list being aware of the impact of racial trauma on parents, carers and family members, both in terms of relationships in the home and in terms of relationship with the school. Archer reflects that 'a number of Black parents and pupils across the studies recounted feeling uncomfortable and dissuaded from attending parents' evenings or engaging with home-school activities due to previous negative experiences.' (2008:97) Kinouani discusses the fact that racial trauma can affect family functioning, saying 'It can affect closeness, patience and availability. In some cases, chronic stress in parents can even lead to abuse and neglect.' (2021:103) Parents of colour may not feel confident about how to address racism with their own children and might have a fear of re-visiting trauma, or indeed creating trauma, by doing so.

When children (and adults) experience trauma, they need access to counselling, or at the very least an adult with whom they enjoy a good relationship to talk to. At Walthamstow School For Girls we arranged access to one-to-one counselling for pupils who showed signs of being, or disclosed that they had been, particularly impacted by the Islamophobia and racism that manifested in London after 7/7. We also arranged for workshops to explore the issues that arose and held assemblies around the theme of 'Not In My Name.' However, when I reflect on my headships, I am not for a minute suggesting that I facilitated counselling, mentoring and the appropriate support for all those learners who were struggling due to racial trauma. Sometimes this failure would have been because traumas were well-hidden and sometimes because my colleagues and I were not sufficiently skilled or attuned to recognising them. I also see now that I did not sufficiently understand racial trauma and its impact. I was, at times, too concerned about consistent practice and striving to treat everyone equally, to ensure that the school's practice was always equitable – that everyone got access to what they required.

As a school leader I was, of course, aware of the statistics around Black boys being disproportionally excluded. I had always been determined that that should not be the case at the schools I led and I felt the pain of the suspension of Black students especially keenly. My staff and I tracked rewards and sanctions closely by ethnicity and looked to see whether they were roughly in proportion with the representation in the school. We treated each child as a person, not a number, and we avoided crudely measuring by statistics alone, especially when figures for certain groups might be so small as to be of questionable validity but, still, we saw the data as a useful indicator. My governors, rightly, required me to explain the suspension of a Black child in particular detail but if you had asked me ten years ago to articulate exactly why, I would not have been able to explain it as I can now because I didn't have the depth of racial literacy that I do now.

The case of Michael (name changed) is one that I think of often; it is a tragic story and I frequently consider what I might have done differently and whether the outcome could have been an alternative one.

Michael's story

I first met Michael in the summer term of 2012, when I conducted his home visit. I remember meeting a cheerful, lively little boy, who seemed quite young for his age, albeit sociable and easy going. After about half an hour of talking to Michael and his mum together to get to know them, to familiarise them with the school systems and transition procedures and to get a sense of Michael's educational journey so far, his mum asked for a word with me on her own. She explained to me that she was excited about her son coming to the new school, that she was passionate about his doing well and that she and her husband recognised the power of education. She then said that they were determined that Michael should not become a casualty and go the way of so many Black boys, succumbing to pressure to join a gang, making poor life choices and taking decisions with irreversible consequences. She intimated that he was quite impressionable and that he had got into a spot of trouble at his primary school. I remember this conversation as clearly as if it was yesterday. I assured her that we would work closely with the family and that her high expectations were echoed by all the staff appointed to work at the school.

On returning to school, I wrote up my notes from the visit as I did for all home visits, recording that we needed to think carefully about how we best supported him.

I thought carefully about which would be the most appropriate tutor group to place Michael in. I decided to put him with our great new head of PE, as Michael was sporty and loved football and the head of PE was an experienced teacher with great pastoral and behaviour management skills. He would be with a number of other sport-loving boys.

Sadly, Michael got involved in several fights and verbal confrontations in Year 7 and Year 8. Ongoing incidents were dealt with by pastoral staff and he received a number of detentions, internal exclusions and short suspensions. Staff used mediation and worked with Michael and his parents to avoid more serious exclusions. He was given a police link worker, himself a young Black Caribbean man.

In Year 9 Michael brought a knife into school. He claimed that it was to protect him from boys out of school. I decided not to permanently exclude him for this incident, to the surprise of certain staff and parents. It was my belief that he had not intended any harm to any member of the school community and did not pose a health and safety threat. We involved the police and Michael was interviewed and referred to the Youth Offending Team. At his readmission it was made very clear to him and his parents that he was being given another chance at the school and was very lucky not to have been permanently excluded. This was also communicated to the school community.

A few weeks later, Michael got involved in a minor physical altercation with another student and, due to his inappropriate reaction, was fixed term excluded again. Then he took part in a very serious incident at the end of a school day, involving him going with four out-of-school friends to threaten, hit and punch a boy not known to him who attended another school. The event was a public and shocking one and undeniably brought the school into disrepute. It led me to believe that Michael had not learnt from earlier incidents or adapted his behaviour following his previous exclusion. I decided to permanently exclude him. It was the end of Year 9 and he was the first student to be permanently excluded from the school since it opened three years earlier.

Michael never attended mainstream school again. Sadly, his mother's fears came to realisation; he got involved in drugs and crime. I heard recently that he had been convicted of murder and was starting a prison term just as his peers were graduating from university.

Did I do all that I could for Michael? Did my staff and I work as hard as we possibly could to understand his needs fully? To what extent was his behaviour the response to racial trauma in or out of school? Did I get the balance right between his interests and those of the rest of the school (and local) community? I was aware that some staff thought that I had been very (over?) understanding of his past transgressions. They felt that the school should be taking a firm and consistent line; that as a new institution, still establishing its reputation, it was important that we set down a clear marker about what standards of behaviour were and were not acceptable, that we needed to be protecting the learning environment for all our students and staff and that that might on occasion mean sacrificing the individual for the collective. They were additionally concerned for the physical safety of the students. I was also aware that a number of staff felt that if I excluded Michael I would be failing him. I was conscious of his likely ongoing educational prospects (limited), I was aware of the impact that exclusion was likely to have on his life chances. I did consider the influence of peer pressure and undesirable out-of-school influences.

But I did not consider sufficiently the impact of growing up as a Black boy in that part of London, with what would have likely been regular incidents of racist name calling, abuse and prejudice directed towards him, how this would have affected his behaviour, his focus, his coping mechanisms, his choices. And I didn't therefore impress that on my staff or governors.

And what of the impact of his exclusion on others? I appreciate now that I did not consider as deeply as I should have what the impact on the Black community would be from the fact that the first permanent exclusion from the school was of a Black boy. I did not work extra hard to engage the Black parents in the aftermath. It was only a couple of years later, when I was having a very candid conversation with a mother of another pupil and she raised it, that I considered how this action may have dented the faith of some members of the school community in my commitment to inclusion and anti-racism. In retrospect, I feel I was fortunate that this did not lead to a degree of parental disengagement.

Perhaps, had I had an empowered EDI group at the school, with student, staff, governor/trustee and parental representation, to question the handling of the Michael situation at each step of the way, everyone in the school community would have felt assured that the level of support and challenge was as robust as it could be.

To draw this section of the book to a close, here are the reflections of an inner London headteacher on her learning from the process of striving to develop the racial literacy of herself and her staff.

Reflections of a headteacher on the complexity of racial literacy training

This testimony brings to mind a metaphor used by one of my interviewees, Rubia. She said to me, 'When you rip off the plaster, you have to be prepared for the blood to flow.'

My deputy and I had had endless conversations about the underachievement of our Caribbean students and the behavioural issues we had with a particular group of these students. Anecdotally, it had become very clear to us that some families were not comfortable engaging with us and we really wanted to unpick this. Of course, this led us straight into colonialism, the legacy of slavery, structural racism in the UK and the lived experiences of these communities in London since Windrush. We were also working in a borough that was trying to address the disproportionality around young black men, school exclusion and criminality. We were therefore involved in lots of borough-wide discussions and initiatives addressing permanent exclusions, inclusion, behaviour policies and cultural competency.

We were addressing in-school issues around low-level disruption and corridor behaviour. In observing these issues in action – watching staff on corridors and the playground – we were concerned that there seemed to be an anticipation of aggression and anger from taller/bigger black girls or groups of black girls – and that many staff avoided these students or barked at them. This reflected some of the informal feedback we gathered from students. This worried us a lot.

So we began by informing ourselves as an SLT, attending training on cultural competency and unconscious bias and then sharing this with the rest of SLT. This in itself was illuminating; not everyone was as on-board as I would have liked.

Alongside this we were talking to staff and to students, to get their lived experience. This included inviting one of our curriculum leads, who was often sought out by students to discuss concerns and who was of Black Caribbean heritage, to speak to SLT about her own observations and experience and what the students had shared and told her.

One of our LSAs, also of Black Caribbean heritage, worked with a group of students and shared feedback with us. This was challenging as it created a desire for change and a sense from these students and staff that we were not doing enough – the proverbial can of worms was opened and we were not yet ready to take action! I was accused of not addressing the issues that the LSA shared with us. With hindsight I would have attempted to manage expectations a little better; however, doing that could have easily been seen as diminishing the importance of the issue.

My deputy and I read extensively and realised that we had educated ourselves in a way that the rest of the staff hadn't. That took us some time to understand; in our reading we had re-educated ourselves and had started to take some things as 'read' that the rest of the staff just did not get. We started with *Why I Am No Longer Talking To White People About Race* by Reni Eddo Lodge and then, between us, moved onto a variety of different books, including *Natives*, by Akala. *White Fragility* by Robin Diangelo was a real turning point for us, as we could see ourselves in it and realised how much we were relying on BAME staff to sort out our problems for us. This book was really helpful; every time I thought it was too difficult, too challenging, too impossible, there were words and stories from that book that reminded me to stop being so fragile!

Our anti-racism work included the following:

- Cultural Competency training for members of SLT

- SLT reading

- Informal discussion with staff and students

- Unconscious Bias training for staff (this highlighted the importance of trigger warnings, which was not handled particularly well on this occasion)

- Anti-racist working group (staff and students)

- Anti-racism included as part of our curriculum intent

- Staff and student reading lists

- Including an 'anti-racist' lens and a focus on representation within the curriculum in curriculum reviews

- Staff training on being an ally

- Student assemblies on anti-racism

Staff, students and parents all responded very differently – both positively and negatively. We rarely kept many of the people happy at any given time. That was quite a shock. I spent a lot of time apologising as we were seen to not be doing enough, fast enough. Debates around hair and clothing became complex – simplistic views about creating an inclusive hair code brought out issues around wearing scarves, bonnets, weaves and braids that started to unpick preferences and opinions within separate BAME cultures and heritages. We had to think a lot more deeply than we had originally thought.

After reading the reflections of this headteacher, what are the key learning points for you?

Do any of her reflections chime with experiences that you have had?

What do you take from it that will support you in your anti-racism work?

Questions and activity

Having read and reflected on Chapters 4, 5 and 6, how comfortable and confident do you feel your staff are to talk about race?

Do they do so only when time is set aside for this or do they create their own opportunities?

Do they support each other actively? Are they reactive or proactive?

Do all staff see it as their responsibility to support the school to become an anti-racist organisation or is there a danger that colleagues from racially minoritised groups (often comprising very small numbers) are burdened with being the mouthpiece for EDI matters? (The more that the racial literacy of all staff is developed, the less of an issue this becomes.)

Take some time to design an action plan for developing racial literacy in your school. Think carefully about the success criteria. How will you know when the staff body is confident and comfortable talking about race?

Might you ask the students?

In Chapters 4, 5 and 6 we have looked in detail at how you might go about developing your racial literacy and that of your staff and learners. In the next section of the book, Part Three, we will turn our attention to the curriculum.

References

Adeyemi. A. *Labelling of Black Students in Schools* in Wilson. H. and Kara. B. ed. (2022). *Diverse Educators: A Manifesto.* (London: University of Buckingham Press). p 273–276.

Agarwal. P. (2020). *Sway: Unravelling Unconscious Bias.* (London: Bloomsbury).

Akala (2019). *Natives: Race & Class in the Ruins of Empire.* (Great Britain, London: Two Roads).

Archer. L. (2008). *The Impossibility of Minority Ethnic Educational 'Success'? An Examination of the Discourses of Teachers and Pupils in British Secondary Schools.* (EERJ Vol 7 No 1). Available at: https://journals.sagepub.com/doi/10.2304/eerj.2008.7.1.89

Barker. I. (2021). *Racial Bias and Attainment.* (TES). Available at: www.theguardian.com/education/2021/sep/23/black-girls-in-england-twice-as-likely-to-be-excluded-from-schools-as-white-girls

Coates. T. (2015). *Between The World And Me.* (Melbourne: Text Publishing).

Harewood. D. (2021). *Maybe I Don't Belong Here: A Memoir of Race, Identity, Breakdown and Recovery.* (London: Bluebird).

Holding. M. (2021). *Why We Kneel, How We Rise.* (London: Simon & Schuster).

Kinouani, G. (2021). *Living While Black.* (London: Ebury Press).

Mohamed. H. (2020). *People Like Us* (London: Profile).

Rafiq. R. *Not Just a Black Muslim Woman* in Khan. M. ed. (2020). *It's Not About The Burka.* (London: Picador). p 199–208.

Sarpong. J. (2020). *The Power Of Privilege: How White People Can Challenge Racism.* (London: HQ).

Scott. K. (2021). *Just Work: Get it Done, Fast and Fair.* (London: Macmillan).

Steele, C. M. (2011). *Whistling Vivaldi.* (New York: Norton).

Tatum. B. D. (2021). *Why Are All The Black Kids Sitting Together In The Cafeteria?* (Great Britain, Dublin: Penguin).

Thomas. A. (2021). *Representation Matters.* (London: Bloomsbury).

PART THREE
The curriculum

Getting ready to diversify and decolonise the curriculum

You cannot be what you cannot see.

Attributed to Marian Wright Edelman

You may write me down in history
With your bitter, twisted lies,
You may trod me in the very dirt
But still, like dust, I'll rise.

Maya Angelou

This is the first of three chapters which explore the vital role of the curriculum in creating an anti-racist school. This chapter considers the concepts of 'diversifying' and 'decolonising' the curriculum and clarifies the difference between the two. It then presents arguments for why both activities are so vital and encourages the reader to prepare the ground with staff and governors/trustees to ensure buy-in to both activities.

Two Annas

I trained to teach in 1988 at the University of Oxford's Department of Education. Here I was lucky to be taught by the best teacher I had ever met – Anna Pendry. She opened my eyes to what great teaching could look like. She role modelled and showcased exceptional practice (for example, in our lectures she dissected video extracts of teachers skilfully leading discussions and handling challenging behaviour) and she practically demonstrated how to create vibrant learning spaces (designing and filling the walls of her teaching room with inspiring examples of history-related displays). She encouraged her students to be creative and imaginative with curriculum design; I trained in the year before the National Curriculum was introduced and was very aware of the fact that the curriculum freedoms that teachers enjoyed in the department in which I was undertaking my teaching

DOI: 10.4324/9781003275220-10

practice were about to come to an end! I was interned for the year at a school in Didcot with another history student, Katherine, and we worked closely together.

Katherine had lived in South Africa between finishing university and training to teach and her partner had been active in the anti-apartheid movement. With the blessing of our teaching practice school, she and I decided that we would design and teach a unit on the history of apartheid in South Africa. This was so well received by the pupils that I began to find ways of showcasing the effects of colonialism elsewhere, to tell the inspiring stories of people fighting race inequality across the world and to prioritise developing the skills of questioning evidence and critical thinking. (I was recently reacquainted with a pupil I taught thirty years ago who reflected in an email to me, 'You'll be pleased to know I'm still a keen historian today and remember a lot of the lessons I had with you. I remember being particularly moved when learning about the Ku Klux Klan, but also just loving learning how to interrogate sources and argue a point.')

When I started my first teaching post in the London Borough of Enfield, I was quickly introduced to the Authority's Teachers' Centre, a treasure trove of research and loanable resources for all ages, stages and curriculum areas, home to an impressive team of education advisers and a space where teachers came for training courses, conferences and to network and share ideas. I regularly attended twilight sessions run by the history adviser and, through her, made connections with the borough's race equality adviser – Anna Salnow. Anna was a source of great inspiration and, like the other Anna, a charismatic teacher. Through her I discovered seminal texts such as Peter Fryer's *Staying Power: The History of Black People in Britain* and Rozina Visram's *Ayahs, Lascars and Princes: The Story of Indians in Britain 1700–1947*. With her support and encouragement, and empowered by twilight courses she ran, I crafted lessons for my classes that featured the stories and achievements of Black and Brown people in Roman, Tudor and Victorian Britain to diversify the newly designed National Curriculum materials which told only the history of White people in these eras.

Influenced by Anna, I applied for an Equal Opportunities lead role at my school and, when I became Head of Humanities at a school in nearby Barnet, took on the EO Coordinator role. Barnet also had a vibrant Teachers' Centre, from which I borrowed a multitude of resources to diversify the curriculum, and another great EO adviser, Chris Henshaw. Chris supported me to run a range of events at my school, including an EDI drop down day involving a range of community groups.

Younger readers will likely be amazed to read of bygone days of local authority EO and race equality advisers providing loanable resources and ongoing, often fully funded, EDI training for teachers. In fact, just to make you more incredulous, I should mention that Enfield also had a gender equality adviser!

Sadly, in current times many LAs struggle to fund even core subject curriculum advisers and most MATs are not of a size to sustain a wide central team of curriculum leads. Teachers new to the profession tell me that they are not taught how to diversify the curriculum on their training courses. They are keen to ensure that they are teaching in an inclusive manner and that the curriculum they teach is diverse, but they are unsure of the language to use, where they might find examples of inspiring people of colour to add into units they are teaching or resources from around the world to use and how to go about decolonising the curriculum. I am fortunate to work for one of the largest school improvement companies in the country, with a team of nearly 100 advisers and consultants supporting early years, primary, secondary and special school teachers. When I joined the organisation in 2018 we had a small team of specialists who provided EDI training to schools. In 2021 we secured the funding to employ an adviser dedicated solely to race equity. Within weeks, her diary was packed with consultancy engagements in schools. The demand for support was so great that, six months later, we took the decision to appoint a second race equity adviser.

'Diversifying' and 'decolonising'

What do we mean when we talk about diversifying and decolonising the curriculum, and what's the difference?

Diversifying the curriculum is about ensuring that what we teach is life from across the globe, representing and giving voice to a broad cross section of people: women as well as men, people of all socio-economic backgrounds, all sexualities, ages, religions, those with and without disabilities.

Decolonising the curriculum refers more specifically to the lens through which we view, interpret and teach knowledge and is more specifically about 'creating spaces and resources for ... all cultures and knowledge systems in the curriculum' Esther Wilkinson (2021). It is well explained by the educationalist Sofia Akel who says: 'Decolonisation typically refers to the withdrawal of political, military and governmental rule of a colonised land by its invaders. Decolonising education ... is... the process in which we rethink, reframe and reconstruct the curricula and research that preserve the Europe-centred, colonial lens' (2020).

In her book *Brit(ish)* Afua Hirsch reflects on how 'we celebrate Britain's role in abolition but forget Britain's role in the creation of the slave trade in the first place' (2018:59). Decolonising the curriculum involves seeking a more balanced and holistic coverage. So, for example, a secondary school wishing to decolonise its unit of history teaching the Trans-Atlantic Slave Trade would ensure that the narrative included foci on

- The origins of imperialism and the motivations and attitudes that enabled the West to embark on the slave trade

- African leaders resisting the capture and sale of their people into slavery

- Mutinies and uprisings on slave ships

- Slave rebellions and resistance in the Caribbean

- The role of Black people (enslaved and free) in achieving abolition

- The lasting legacy of the slave trade and the question of reparations (highlighting the compensation paid to slave owners and the mark that this has left on modern society).

In a blog of 26 April 2021, Louise Holyoak explains that decolonisation is about 'giving voice to the knowledge of marginalised peoples.' She says that decolonisation of the curriculum concerns 'redressing often longstanding factors that have, sometimes deliberately and consciously, ensured that curriculum, pedagogy and assessment protect the interests of a dominant group whilst marginalising others by portraying them as inferior (sometimes by not portraying them at all).' She concludes that 'Decolonisation of the curriculum, therefore, requires us to be cognisant of where unequal power relations between groups have established structures where the ways of knowing and being of one group are held as a norm while others are found to be in deficit according to those norms.'

Akel states that decolonisation is distinct from diversification, 'as diversity can still exist within this western bias. Decolonisation goes further and deeper in challenging the institutional hierarchy and monopoly on knowledge, moving out of a western framework' (2020).

In the autumn of 2022, at a training session on political impartiality, it was suggested to Ofsted inspectors that the term 'decolonising the curriculum' was a politically partial one and should be viewed with caution. In the sense that it is important for young people to have access to knowledge from a range of civilisations and cultures in order to achieve balance, rather than simply being presented with a Western colonial perspective, it is hard to see how this is the case. And any good historian would want their students to interrogate both the benevolent and malevolent aspects of a regime, system, society or world leader without partiality. It is important that the curriculum is both diversified and decolonised, that staff in schools are clear about the distinction and, most importantly, that they understand and can articulate the moral imperative for both.

Why is it important to diversify and decolonise the curriculum?

What we choose to teach conveys clear and powerful messages about what we value.

Worryingly, the National Curriculum (NC) which all maintained schools are required to teach and most academies tend to follow in order to ensure that they meet the Ofsted requirement that their curriculum is at least as broad, balanced and ambitious as the national curriculum, is based in all curriculum areas on a canon of knowledge dominated by Western civilisations. Sticking to the example of the history curriculum, Moncrieffe, in an article for *Impact* magazine, points out the dominance of White British history at key stages 1 and 2, with a focus on 'Britain's settlement by Anglo Saxons and Scots' and 'Viking and Anglo-Saxon struggle for the Kingdom of England' (DfE 2013 p5). He states, 'The primary school history curriculum is totally absent in giving any teaching and learning starting points on the migration and settlement to the British Isles by non-White ethnic groups or their cross-cultural engagements with inhabitants' (2022).

Critics would say that there is nothing to stop teachers from adding to and augmenting the content laid out in the NC documentation. Indeed, the view of the DfE is that 'teachers should be able to use their own knowledge and expertise to determine how they teach their pupils, and to make choices about what they teach' (UK Parliament 2020). But most primary teachers are White and are not history specialists. The history they were taught at school was from a highly colonised perspective. The resources they turn to have been designed to complement a NC with a colonial view of history. In a powerful article for The Guardian on 12 October 2021, Built on the bodies of slaves: how Africa was erased from the history of the modern world, Howard W French reminds us of the problematic bias of our historical perspective:

'Traditional accounts have accorded a primacy to Europe's 15th-century Age of Discovery, and to the maritime connection it established between west and east.' He argues that the famous feats of explorers like Vasco da Gama, Ferdinand Magellan and Cristopher Columbus 'dominate the popular imagination, they obscure the true beginnings of the story of how the globe became permanently stitched together and thus became "modern". If we look more closely at the evidence, it will become clear that Africa played a central role in this history.' He says that 'By miscasting the role of Africa, generations have been taught a profoundly misleading story about the origins of modernity' and goes one to argue that 'The elision of these three pivotal decades is merely one example of a centuries-long process of diminishment, trivialisation and erasure of Africans and people of African descent from the story of the modern world. It is not that the basic facts are unknown: it is that they have been siloed, overlooked or swept into dark corners.'

What French is describing is what the author Chimamanda Ngosi Adichie calls, in her powerful TED talk of the same title, 'The danger of the Single Story.' She reflects that it is power that 'determines the definitive story.' In the case of Africa, she says, the single story is one of catastrophe, with 'no possibility of a connection as human equals.' The single story 'shows a people as one thing, only one thing, over and over again.' It creates dangerous stereotypes, biases and prejudices by telling incomplete stories. 'It robs people of dignity. It emphasises how we are different, rather than how we are similar.' Adichie concludes that 'we need a balance of stories.'

Darbar and Greenfield agree in their article of 2022: 'The texts, sources and voices we choose to include in our curriculums create a culture that can elevate certain value and belief systems, often at the expense of others…In our experience, history in UK schools has been more about identifying with a national story of progress and achievements.' Racially minoritised children do not see themselves in this story and the worry is that they therefore don't identify with the past. David Olusoga, in an article in the *Guardian* which is quoted by June Sarpong, asserted that students 'are being taught a whitewashed, sanitised version of the British past. One in which their stories, those that make sense of who they are and how they and their families came to be here and how they came to be British, have been largely omitted' (2020:83).

It is not just the curriculum in history that is dominated by knowledge from a White and European canon. The constrictions placed on set text choice in English at GCSE have led many teachers to voice concerns about a lack of diversity and relevance to today's society. In July 2021 a report from the University of Oxford in collaboration with Penguin Random House UK and The Runnymede Trust, *Literature in Colour*, examined the diversity – in terms of the ethnicity of authors and characters – in English literature teaching from key stages 2 to 5 in England. The study's most stark finding was that fewer than 1% of 2019s GCSE English literature candidates answered a question on a novel by an author of colour. The KS3 science programme of study is based firmly on Western science. It references several White Europeans' laws and theories (such as Newton's law of gravity and Einstein's theory of relativity) and requires students to learn about just seven scientists specifically – all White, dead Europeans and almost exclusively men (Watson, Crick, Wilkins and Franklin (DNA), Mendeleev (Periodic Table), Dalton (atoms) and Hooke (elasticity). The KS3 programme of study in music references 'the works of the great composers,' as if there could be no debate as to who the great composers were!

All children need a sense of belonging and to see themselves represented and reflected in the curriculum. As Bennie Kara write so eloquently in *Diversity In Schools*, 'The curriculum we deliver is the foundation of student knowledge. If that curriculum is limited to the thoughts, experiences, histories and achievements of white, western Europe, we are not allowing all students the chance to view the truth of the world they live in.' She continues 'We are not allowing them to build a wide enough schema to know they are citizens of the world and all of its history. Nor are we allowing them all to belong' (2021:41). This diversity of knowledge and perspective is as important for White learners as it is for children of colour. All children need to see outside of themselves as well as to see themselves. Through the curriculum they need to see into British and global society. Yet, as Bim Adewunmi reflects in an essay for *The Good Immigrant*, 'Whiteness…exists as the basic template' (2017:209).

In Chapter 1, I presented stark data showing the underachievement of certain ethnic minority groups in school assessments. We reflected in Chapter 6 on the part that stereotype pressure and the emotional load of coping with covert racism and more direct discrimination plays on the performance of some children of colour. Now we can see that, if the curriculum that minority ethnic children are studying in school seems to have little relevance to them, if they cannot see themselves featured in the stories of achievements, discoveries and developments, they are likely to feel further marginalised, devalued and disconnected from education. If the societies and individuals showcased and revered by their teachers are over-whelmingly White and European, children of Asian and African descent are likely to find it harder to connect with their educators.

Michael Holding, in *Why We Kneel, How We Rise*, reflects on the damage caused by the whitewashing of the curriculum. He cites numerous examples of inventions and discoveries that are typically attributed to White men which were, in fact, the work of Black men: the smallpox vaccine (for which Jenner, rather than Onesimus, is credited), the lightbulb (attributed to Edison when Lewis Howard Latimer invented the carbon filament), the discovery of the North Pole (credited to Robert Peary when Matthew Henson, his Black teammate, got there first). About the last of these examples, Holding comments that children are 'being taught a lie con-venient to the status quo, to reaffirm white supremacy. It just would not do that a Black man was equal to a white man in extraordinary feats' (2020:196). He asks, 'What precisely, is wrong about championing and remembering black achievers?' (2020:198). He implies that the erasure from our established and taught version of history of so many of the atrocities committed by Whites on Blacks over the centuries is in no small part responsible for the distrust of authority felt by many Black British people today, linking this to relatively low uptake amongst the Black community to the Covid vaccine (2020:110).

In the TV documentary *Where's My History?* screened on 23 May 2022, foot-baller Troy Deeney interviewed several of his colleagues about the impact that seeing Black people feature in their school history lessons as slaves and subjugated people had on them. Anthony Joshua responded: 'You feel dehumanised' and Mica Richards reflected, 'We're taught self-hate from the start.'

Lastly, if we fail to diversify our curriculum, there is a danger that our children will, consciously or unconsciously, mask or hide their identities when asked to give personal responses or engage in activities which require or invite them to record or share their lived experiences. Yasmin attended a large primary school in London with predominantly Punjabi Indian pupils, but the school's curriculum was very anglicised and there were only two Asian staff members. She recalls how she became aware that she was 'not "proper English".' On one occasion the pupils were asked to keep a diary of the food that they had eaten for a week. She felt confused about the task as she was conscious that her teacher would probably not know what chapati and dhal were and she did not know how to spell them in English. So she fabricated the diary and made up a range of English foods that she had supposedly eaten! She was ashamed to record the Asian foods her family ate, feeling that they were not as legitimate as Western meals and wondering what her teacher would think if she revealed her family's diet: 'What would they say?' After a brief pause, Yasmin reflected, 'I've never spoken about that to anyone before.'

Who controls the curriculum at your school? Who decides what knowledge and skills are taught?

What messages does your school curriculum convey about what knowledge is valued and whose stories are important?

Does your curriculum represent all of your pupils? How do you know? How diverse is it?

Are there places in your school curriculum where single stories are told? If so, what might be the consequences?

Is there a danger that on occasions teachers design activities that leave their racially minoritised pupils feeling uncomfortable and could lead to them masking their identities? If so, what could you do to rectify this?

How open are you and your staff to diversifying and decolonising the curriculum?

In my experience, most teachers and leaders agree in theory that the curriculum should be inclusive, equitable and diverse. But in practice there are several significant barriers that can get in the way of taking action:

- Time and cost
- Fear or nervousness
- Lack of direction.

Let's look at each in turn and consider some responses and practical suggestions for overcoming them.

Time and cost

'We've already revised the curriculum since the introduction of the new Education Inspection Framework; we don't have time to do it again. There is no space in an already packed curriculum for more content and, anyway, we can't afford more resources!'

In schools up and down the country, staff have taken a fresh look at their curriculum in preparation for, and since the introduction of, the 2019 Ofsted framework. In many institutions, as part of this curriculum review, teachers have seized the opportunity to look at what is taught and how it is delivered through an EDI lens and have diversified content wherever possible. However, in other schools the curriculum, whilst revised, is still largely representative of only the White pupils and reflects a broadly imperialistic perspective.

In such instances, leaders are required to show conviction in leading staff though a further curriculum review. What is important here is to convey the moral imperative to diversify and decolonise the curriculum. The key first step is to win hearts and minds, so gaining staff support. Staff need to understand why you are asking them to make further changes to their programmes of study. The rationale given earlier in this chapter could be used to start a discussion with staff.

A very common concern of teachers who are trying to diversify their curriculum is that their schemes of learning are already very full; the NC stipulates that key content must be covered and exam syllabi seem to get ever more content-laden. Teachers are conscious that the knowledge they teach is often Eurocentric but there is insufficient time and space to add in more content, especially if it will not be assessed or impact on test and exam outcomes. They are time-poor professionals and it is easier to use the resources provided in the standard text books and schemes than to seek out or create bespoke and more representative teaching materials and aids. And financial constraint would not allow for a whole new set of class readers or textbooks, so even if a secondary school English department decided, for example, that *Of Mice And Men* was no longer an appropriate text to be using, they could not replace it with a less problematic novel.

Here are some of the responses I offer when I encounter these kinds of barriers:

- Our primary responsibility as educators is to prepare all our children to move into and thrive in a diverse world, so the curriculum needs to be diversified.

- Students from a racially minoritised background (as well as those with any protected characteristic) will engage more fully with a diversified and decolonised curriculum and are therefore more likely to perform better when assessed.

- Ofsted inspectors assess the extent to which the curriculum is ambitious for all pupils and the attitude to learning of students. How can a curriculum show ambition for pupils if they cannot see themselves in it? And why would they demonstrate a thirst for knowledge if the knowledge taught was of limited relevance to them?

• Diversifying the curriculum does not require seismic change. It is not necessary to throw out entire schemes of learning. Kara says, wryly, 'We don't have to take things out or replace Shakespeare with Stormzy.' It is fine to start small, one unit at a time, by injecting just a few examples from different cultures, parts of the world or under-represented groups and then build up (more of this in the next chapter).

• By showing respect for, interest in, getting to know and celebrating the lived experiences of your pupils, you will find that you have all manner of diverse experiences that can be shared, without financial cost, with others in the school community. Adults and children can contribute as expert witnesses to lessons about all manner of topics: the habitat, climate, cuisine, customs, religious practices, lifestyles, costume, economy of various places across the globe. As a humanities teacher I would invite, by arrangement, pupils to share experiences of, for example, seeing a tiger in the wild, surviving an earthquake, living in Hong Kong, preparing for Bar Mitzvah and going on Hajj.

• Decolonising the curriculum can be partly achieved by investing just a few minutes in a lesson to acknowledging and name-checking similar stories, achievements, inventions and discoveries from other cultures to those from the Western tradition being studied for examination. This allows teachers to make global comparisons and showcase the sophistication of different cultures.

• Independent learning and homework tasks can focus on curriculum exploration. For example, while studying Ancient Roman heating systems and bath houses, pupils could also explore Ancient Indian equivalents or whilst learning about food storage and preservation systems in the West, students could examine systems across the globe from Aboriginal people to the Inuit. It is important, however, to ensure that achieving diversity is not solely seen as an out of class or independent task: we will return to this in the next chapter.

• Decolonisation is partly about encouraging critical thinking and curious questioning. It involves inviting students to notice whose stories are not being told and which groups are not represented. Returning to our science example from earlier in the chapter, Steve Rollet in an article for the CST says, 'decolonisation of the science curriculum does not necessitate the rejection of scientific principles.' He stresses that we must ask 'important questions, such as "who's science story are we not telling?" "Who is being silenced within science?"'(2021:6) He continues, 'Perhaps we might help pupils to understand some of the social context of science; to help them to know why, for example, historic privileges have meant that many scientific discoveries are credited to men rather than women, and White rather than ethnic minority people.' He concludes that 'more can be done to strengthen the representation within the curriculum of key scientific knowers from ethnic minority backgrounds. Incorporating this thinking within the curriculum might help more children to see themselves within the curriculum, or at least to understand some of the social factors that have limited the representation of particular groups within science' (2021:6).

- If it is not possible to update class sets of textbooks, then it is important to encourage pupils to look critically at the resources that are available. For example, if all the pictures in a geography textbook are of White people – on beaches, on mountains, in shopping centres – then this should be discussed and acknowledged. It can also be rectified by ensuring better representation in classroom displays.

And finally, a word about *Of Mice and Men*.

Of Mice and Men has long been a staple on the English curriculum. For years it was a GCSE set text for several exam boards (and still is for CCEA and WJEC). Its disappearance from set text lists for some of the larger exam boards has resulted in it now being taught at KS3 in many schools.

There is no doubt that John Steinbeck was a great novelist of his time. However, the portrayal of Black Americans (and also women) in *Of Mice and Men* is problematic. Many educators would argue that it is not a suitable novel to teach to adolescent audiences, especially to 11–14 year olds, in modern times. For those schools that do choose to continue to teach the novel, placing this work in its historical and societal context is essential and extreme sensitivity is needed.

One of the major difficulties with *Of Mice and Men* is the appearance of the 'N' word. Over recent years, my work colleagues and I have been approached by a number of English teachers seeking advice about how to 'deal' with the 'N' word when they are reading the text with classes. I strongly advise them not to use the word themselves or to allow their students to use the word, but instead to say 'the N word' when it appears. I also advise that they create time for an open discussion about why it is not appropriate to use the word. Such a discussion can be aided by use of a text such as Jeffrey Boakye's *Black, Listed*, which has a 13-page mini essay on the word, it's history, what it represents, how it has been appropriated and why it is such a charged and highly offensive term (2019:130–43).

During the COVID lockdown periods, several schools I work with received complaints from Black students and parents about the fact that they were being taught the novel. Indeed, in one instance a group of students refused to engage in online lessons related to the text. They found it offensive and upsetting. And this was no surprise at all. How could the book be taught in context and with the required sensitivity when lessons were remote and teachers and pupils could not even see each other, let along engage in safe and nuanced discussion? This highlighted for me the very real problems associated with choosing such a text to be the focus of a whole unit of work with, despite the best planning and preparation on the part of the class teacher, the potential for a learner to feel uncomfortable, or distressed when reading a passage alone or for homework or when discussion does not go quite as planned in, for example, a cover lesson. The same issues apply to a number of examination set texts or class readers.

Fear or nervousness

'We don't want to teach topics badly or in a way that could cause upset or offence. We don't want to be tokenistic or shoehorn topics in for the sake of it. And the government has told us that we shouldn't teach Critical Race Theory.'

Let's firstly address any uncertainty around what teachers can and cannot, should and should not be teaching around issues of race. During Black History Month in October 2020, Kemi Badenoch, the UK's Equalities Minister, gave a speech in the House of Commons in which she declared Critical Race Theory (CRT) to be a 'dangerous trend in race relations.' She suggested that the curriculum did not need to be decolonised, for the simple reason that it is not colonised. She described moves to decolonise disciplines in UK universities as a 'fad.' She said, 'The curriculum, by its very nature, is limited; there are a finite number of hours to teach any subject' and added 'We do not want teachers to teach their white pupils about white privilege and inherited racial guilt. Let me be clear that any school that teaches those elements of critical race theory as fact, …without offering a balanced treatment of opposing views, is breaking the law.'

This understandably caused confusion, uncertainty and concern amongst many teachers. However, in amongst a good degree of emotive personal opinion, was reference to the fact that the promotion of partisan political views in class has been unlawful since 1966 under the Education Act of this year. Put simply, this means that where teachers present controversial political views in a lesson, they must offer a balanced overview of opposing views. It does not mean that teachers cannot discuss or teach about CRT.

In February 2022, a Political Impartiality in Schools guidance document was published by the Department for Education. This advises teachers to think carefully when planning lessons and choosing class materials. It urges teachers not to offer their own political views in lessons and to teach sensitive issues in an unbiased way. It aims to help teachers address complex topics, such as the history of the British Empire or the Israeli-Palestinian conflict, without pushing one political view over another. It draws a distinction between subject areas which may be part of the formal curriculum, such as racism or colonialism, and promoting support for campaigning groups, such as Black Lives Matter. The then Secretary of State for Education, Nadhim Zahawi, declared in the guidance that no subject should be off limits, but that teaching must be impartial.

The point about teaching emotive topics with sensitivity is an important one. Teachers can become desensitised when they have taught topics several times over and must always be minded of the likely, and possible, emotional impact of the resources they use. It is always wise to run resources of a sensitive nature by a race equity or EDI lead in the school before using them in class and to prepare students (and even parents) for the nature of material to be studied and/or the rationale for curriculum choices, in advance. Bonolo reflected in his interview with me,

> I remember completing the slave trade unit over the space of two weeks during our history lessons. During that topic, I remember a student saying to me 'This is your history now.' I recall feeling embarrassed because there were images of people without clothes on and I thought that all my friends would be thinking that my family dressed like that. If there had been more opportunities to study the positive impact of individuals in black history, I may have felt less embarrassed and more interested when looking at the slave trade.

Balanced against the need to be politically neutral in class is the legal duty that teachers have towards all their pupils, as addressed in

- the UN convention on the Rights of the Child (in which article 13 gives children the right to freedom of expression and article 30 gives them the right to learn the language, customs and religion of their family)

- The Equalities Act of 2021, which provides protection against discrimination and harassment for all against the 9 protected characteristics, including race

and the expectation in the DfE's Teachers' Standards (2013) that teachers will

- Adapt teaching to respond to the strengths and needs of all pupils and

- Have a secure understanding of how a range of factors can inhibit pupils' ability to learn, and how best to overcome these.

Another legitimate fear that teachers may have when teaching about cultures and heritages different from their own is unintentionally stereotyping or getting things wrong and thus attracting criticism or causing offence. Let's face it, this happens routinely in the media and in films and TV so it is inevitable that it happens from time to time in our classrooms. In *The Good Immigrant*, Nikesh Shukla speaks of the video game 'Call of Duty' setting a level in the city of Karachi but making the elementary error of writing all the street signs in Arabic rather than Urdu (2017:7). In another essay in the same collection, Wei Ming Kam addresses the stereotyping of East Asians in the media, concluding 'We're not seen as human, because we never get to be complex individuals' (2017:95). And David Baddiel agrees in *Jews Don't Count*; he talks of how it was not until well into his teens that he saw 'the Anglo-Jewish experience accurately portrayed anywhere in British culture' (2021:10). We're back to the single story.

Leaders committed to creating an anti-racist curriculum in their schools must support staff by providing time, resources and training to feel confident in teaching out of their comfort zone and beyond their lived experiences. And they have to accept that on occasions, hopefully only very rarely, mistakes will be made. One of my colleagues had to intervene recently to address understandable offence caused by an image of 'ethnically diverse' cartoon characters of early years pupils on a slide used in a training session which depicted an East Asian child wearing a coolie hat. It was a painful experience, but the individuals concerned learnt from it.

There are a huge number of resources and organisations that can support with reference and teaching materials, CPD and training around diversifying and decolonising the curriculum. Sameena Choudry's book *Equitable Education* contains an excellent summary list (2021:103–110).

We have to avoid superficial representation of racially minoritised groups as we strive to diversify the curriculum. My heart sinks when I have reason to look at the music curriculum for a school and I see the appearance of a single, solitary unit on 'African music,' as if there were such a thing as a single style or type of music that represented the entire continent and 57 countries of Africa! Even for a tiny country like England it would be laughable to suggest that there is such a thing as English music: would it be Elgar, or Elton John, Purcell or The Police? In his book *Between The World And Me*, Ta-Nehisi Coates recalls history books from his childhood which 'spoke of black people only as sentimental "firsts" – first black five-star general, first black congressman, first black mayor' (2015:43). Likewise, shoe-horning minority ethnic poets, musicians, mathematicians and scientists into the curriculum can feel tokenistic. A music teacher at a school in which I conducted a race review said to me that he tried to find examples of great Black classical musicians to spotlight in his lessons but that he always felt awkward, especially when there might be just one Black student in the class, in case it came across as if he was expressing surprise that a Black man or woman could be a great classical musician. We need to be aware of tokenism (and I shall return to this in the next chapter) but this is not a good enough reason not to start somewhere.

And lastly, teachers who are diversifying their curriculum can feel nervous when first teaching material with which they are not very familiar. They may be anxious about the types of questions that could arise and how they would answer them. My advice here would be to welcome questions, to explore them with the class, to demonstrate your interest and be comfortable with curiosity, to be open when not sure of the answer and to invite learners to help to find it together. Nothing is more disappointing to observe than a teacher closing down a question and overlooking an opportunity for exploring cultural connections. I saw an example of this recently in a music lesson about virtuosity. Pupils were asked to research one of a number of musicians who were known for their virtuosity. Amongst the options was Freddie Mercury, the lead singer of Queen. One of the pupils asked the teacher where Freddie Mercury was from. She gave a very closed response – 'He was British' – and moved on. I couldn't help thinking what rich discussion could have developed from considering his unique cultural heritage (born in Zanzibar to Parsi-Indian parents) and the impact of this on his musical influences and style.

Lack of direction

'It's all very well to diversify the English and history curriculum but how do you go about doing that in maths or science?'
It is important that Black and Brown students and learners from all ethnic backgrounds see themselves reflected in all parts of the curriculum, but there is no doubt that resources and materials are more plentiful and easier to come by in certain subject disciplines than others. Having said that, diversifying the curriculum in the 2020s, with a growing number of EDI fora, education organisations and websites and the internet, is a much easier task than it was for those of us who trained in the 1980s!

A while ago, when conducting a race review in a secondary school, the Head of Maths said to me in all seriousness that 'diversity doesn't really apply to Maths.' Presumably he had never heard of great mathematicians such as Elbert Cox (African American who was the first person in the world to get a PhD in Maths), Euclid (ancient Greek founder of geometry), Katherine Johnson (who, in 1962, provided the orbital entry and launch window calculations that enabled John Glenn's orbit around the moon and then provided calculations that coordinated the Apollo moon landing), Fibonacci (twelfth century Italian who introduced the Indo-Arabic numbering system that we use today), Al Kashi (fourteenth century Iranian famed for his use of decimal fractions), Shiing-Shen Chern (awarded the Wolf prize for his immense number of mathematical contributions), Srinivasa Ramanujan (famed for his work on the partition of numbers), Shakuntala Devi (Indian Mathematician known as the human computer for her ability to solve complex calculations without a calculator) or thought that it might be powerful and inspirational to tell his pupils the stories of great mathematicians of colour and from all parts of the globe!

The school leader's role is to listen to and show understanding for colleagues like this (who are most likely the product of a whitewashed education and were never trained how to build diversity into their planning and delivery) but then to communicate an expectation, and support them, to upskill their own depth and breadth of knowledge and to revisit and diversify their schemes of learning. And a degree of challenge is important too. In my discussion with this head of maths we explored:

- Where he could look for examples of cultural connections and resources with greater representation

- How he could use his colleagues and peers for support

- How he could set up a discussion with his classes about why there is absence of diversity in the maths text books

- Writing to publishers (or getting the students to) to highlight the need for greater ethnic representation in their resources

- Naming the school's maths classes after diverse mathematicians (male and female) from around the world.

This last suggestion was taken from my last school, Isaac Newton Academy, which was a new school I set up from scratch with a founding staff team in 2011. We decided from the outset that we would name each teaching set in every subject after an influential practitioner from the discipline. The heads of subject were given the lovely task of coming up with group names to reflect diversity – in terms of ethnicity, gender and other protected characteristics. So, for example, science groups were named Anning, Curie, Descartes, Pascal and Garrett and the English groups included Angelou, Bronte, Chaucer, Duffy and Tagore. One of the first independent learning activities for pupils joining a group was to find out about the person the class was named after. Not only was this a more inclusive and imaginative way of distinguishing groups than using the teacher's cypher or a numerical system but it also avoided groups being seen as ranked from highest to lowest in subjects that set by attainment.

In the next chapter we will look at the steps that you might take towards creating an anti-racist curriculum and consider some case studies from schools which are some way down the line, in order to glean practical advice and learn transferable lessons.

Activity

How committed are you to diversifying and decolonising the curriculum?

What concerns do you have? What barriers stand in your way? How can you overcome them?

How open are your staff to making this change? How do you know?

Which of the obstacles addressed above stand in their way?

And how can you work to remove them?

References

Adewunmi. B. *What We Talk About When We Talk About Tokenism* in Shukla. N. ed. (2017). The Good Immigrant. (London: Unbound). p 208–212.

Adichie. C. N. (2009) *The Danger of the Single Story* (TED talk). Available at: www.bing. com/search?q=Chimamanda+Ngozi+Adichie+The+Danger+of+the+single+story+TED+talk&cvid=2e1bcb7319514e96a78b73ff657cc694&aqs=edge..69i57j69i11004.4723j0j4&FORM=ANAB01&DAF0=1&PC=U531

Akel. S. (2020) *What Decolonising The Curriculum Really Means.* Available at: https:// eachother.org.uk/decolonising-the-curriculum-what-it-really-means/?msclkid=3a91e4e6b3c511eca67107ae6188c443

Angelou. M. (1986). *Still I Rise.* (Random House).

Baddiel. D. (2021). *Jews Don't Count.* (London: TLS Books).

Boakye. J. (2019). *Black, Listed.* (Great Britain: Dialogue Books). p 130–142.

Choudry. S. (2021). *Equitable Education.* (St Albans: Critical Publishing).

Coates. T. (2015). *Between The World And Me.* (Melbourne: Text Publishing).

Darbar. S. and Greenfield. A. (2022). *Multidirectional narratives: diversifying the English and history curriculums.* (CCT Impact Magazine) Available at: https://my.chartered.college/impact_article/multidirectional-narratives-diversifying-the-english-and-history-curriculums/

Department For Education (2022). *Political Impartiality In Schools.* Available at: www.gov.uk/government/publications/political-impartiality-in-schools

Elliott. V., Nelson-Addy. L., Chantiluke. R. and Courtney. M. (2021). *Lit In Colour: Diversity in Literature in English Schools.* (Penguin Books and The Runnymede Trust). Available at: https://litincolour.penguin.co.uk/

French. H. W. (2021). *Built on the bodies of slaves.* (The Guardian). Available at: www.theguardian.com/news/2021/oct/12/africa-slaves-erased-from-history-modern-world?CMP=Share_AndroidApp_Other

Hirsch. A. (2018). *Brit(ish): On Race, Identity and Belonging.* (London: Vintage).

Holyoak. L. (2021). *Developing An Anti-Racist Curriculum* Blog. Available at: https://bigeducation.org/blogs/

Holding. M. (2021). *Why We Kneel, How We Rise.* (London: Simon & Schuster).

Kam. W. M. *Beyond 'Good' Immigrants* in Shukla. N. ed. (2017). *The Good Immigrant.* (London: Unbound).

Kara, B. (2021). *Diversity In Schools.* (London: Corwin).

Moncrieffe. M. L. (2022). *Challenging, decolonising and transforming primary school history curriculum knowledge.* (CCT Impact Magazine) Available at: https://my.chartered.college/impact_article/challenging-decolonising-and-transforming-primary-school-history-curriculum-knowledge/

Rollett. S. (2021). *Curriculum decolonisation as a disciplinary process.* (Confederation of School Trusts) Available at: https://cstuk.org.uk/assets/CST-Publications/CST_Bridge_ Decolonisation...

Sarpong, J. (2020). *The Power Of Privilege: How White People Can Challenge Racism.* (London: HQ).

Shukla. N. *Namaste* in Shukla. N. ed. (2017). *The Good Immigrant.* (London: Unbound).

Troy Deeney: Where's My History. Channel 4 documentary. Available at: www.channel4. com/programmes/troy-deeney-wheres-my-history

Wilkinson. E. (2021) *What is decolonisation?* (University of Essex). Available at: https:// library.essex.ac.uk/edi/whatisdecolonisation?msclkid=3a929adcb3c511ec9905c8970 1b93107

8 Taking steps towards an anti-racist curriculum

Building a curriculum that embraces, celebrates, highlights and foregrounds diversity is an act of equity and allyship.

Bennie Kara

Our curriculum should whisper to our children, 'You belong. You do not come from nowhere. You are one of us.'

Ben Newmark

Chapter 7 articulated the case for change – why it is so vital for all learners, regardless of their ethnicity, that the taught curriculum is both diversified and decolonised. In it we looked at the barriers that school leaders are likely to face in implementing an anti-racist curriculum and started to consider how to prepare for the task. Chapter 8 is designed to offer some practical steps and advice around how to progress. However, what follows is not a step-by-step approach or a 'how to' manual. Every school is different in its composition and context. And every school is at a different point with its anti-racism work, with unique strengths, opportunities and challenges. The optimal mix of ingredients and the precise recipe for one school will be slightly different to that required for another. My advice would be to read the chapter, reflect on it and then have an honest and candid discussion with colleagues (senior and middle leaders, governors or trustees) about what, for your school, would be the best approach, involving which precise steps, in what order and over what time period.

Taking a comprehensive and honest look at the current curriculum

The logical starting point is to assess the status quo by asking, and seeking answers to, some broad and open questions, such as:

DOI: 10.4324/9781003275220-11

- Who, and what, features in the curriculum currently in each year group and curriculum area?

- Whose stories are being foregrounded? What features at the centre of the curriculum and what is more peripheral?

- How are different civilisations, nations, societies and people in them being depicted? (as heroes? as villains? as oppressors? as the oppressed? as dominant? as marginalised? as ordinary people?)

Why these questions? How might you answer them and from whom might you seek responses? Let's pick this a bit.

Who, and what, features in the curriculum currently in each year group and curriculum area?

This question is clearly about representation and diversity. The obvious starting point is an examination of schemes of learning/curriculum plans. Ideally, senior leaders and middle leaders should examine these together and track the civilisations, societies and individuals that feature in them in each learning/subject area for each year group and across the entire curriculum journey – in Early Years in nursery schools, from Reception to Year 6 in primary schools, Years 7 to 13 in secondary schools and for the entire 14-year learning journey for all-through schools. This exercise can be replicated with learners, especially where schools have designed student versions of the learning journey or knowledge-organisers, which summarise the programme of study for the year or key stage. It may well throw up some subject strengths which can be held up as shining examples, and even in less diversified curriculum areas there could be gems of great practice on which to build. However, in my experience of working with schools to conduct this exercise, leaders have sometimes been shocked to see that pupils can go a whole year or more without encountering any black or brown people of note in the curriculum or learning about anywhere beyond the Western world.

Looking at the curriculum design is, of course, just the starting point. Examining what is actually delivered and in what depth is more significant. Here book looks and discussions with groups of learners about what they have been taught and what they remember from certain units is really illuminating. This leads us neatly into the second set of questions.

Whose stories are being foregrounded? What features at the centre of the curriculum and what is more peripheral?

Steve Rollett, in his CST article, says 'Some calls for decolonisation articulate the need to recentre the curriculum...this includes challenging the tendency in history curricula to start with the history of another people but only as a means then of tying it back to Western history. This has the effect of positioning other histories as being only a form of prelude for the arrival of Westerners onto the scene.' He continues, 'Decolonisation is about more than re-shaping the national curriculum; it is also about how teachers bring their students to knowledge and how knowledges are brought into relation with each other' (2021:10).

Bennie Kara, in a powerful talk to school leaders in Hertfordshire, drew on the work of Christine Counsell around the 'core' curriculum – basic knowledge and facts to be learnt and retained – and the 'hinterland' – supplementary knowledge that broadens the learner's schema. She argued that the core is typically presented as White, Western and European and that it is often in the hinterland that we encounter diversity and parallel stories from other cultures, societies and parts of the world.

To get a true sense of whose knowledge and stories are valued and the impressions being projected, it is essential to talk to the consumers of our curriculum. By conducting regular pupil voice activities with learners across a range of ages and attainment levels, leaders can get an informed and nuanced understanding of the curriculum that is received and learnt, as opposed to that which has been planned and taught.

Many secondary school leaders across the UK were contacted by current and ex-students at the time that the Black Lives Matters movement gained momentum in the UK who expressed frustration at lack of representation or foregrounding of people of colour in the curriculum they had been taught. Ex-pupils are a great source of feedback, in that they can look back on a seven or even 14-year curriculum journey and comment on their diet in its entirety. Schools that are really serious about achieving an anti-racist curriculum also make a point of seeking feedback from parents of students of colour about their perceptions of the diversity of the curriculum taught to their children.

Setting up pupil voice discussions about representation is a great opportunity to ask students about whether they have opportunities to contribute knowledge from their lived experience to lessons and what they would like added to the curriculum and highlighted more (I saw a consultation along these lines recently where pupils were asked who they would like to see featured in their assemblies). But there are limits to this line of enquiry: lots of young people are so conditioned by hearing single stories that they are unaware of the range of stories that exist! Another issue that merits discussion with learners is tokenism. In my experience, learners give very astute feedback as to areas of the curriculum where they see diversity and the telling of multiple stories as well embedded and those where people of colour pop up only occasionally and in a way that does not feel integrated or natural.

Questions about visual representation in resources and displays and the impact of this are also informative. I often see beautiful displays showcasing the achievements of people of colour in different disciplines when I visit schools. However, unless these are integrated into teachers' lessons and used to generate discussion, the time and effort spent on creating them can be wasted. I recently conducted a review of science lessons which started with some lesson observations and then involved meetings with groups of students. I noticed two fabulous displays celebrating Black and Asian scientists – one outside and one in the classroom where Year 7s were being taught. When I spoke to a handful of pupils from the class after the lesson, they could not name me one person of colour involved in science in the past or present that they had learnt about and none of them had noticed either display!

Activity

From whom would it be most useful for you to get feedback regarding the diversity of the curriculum at the current time? Staff? Pupils in a particular subject area or year group? A range of students? Ex pupils? Parents? Ex parents?

How will you select/construct your feedback group members?

What questions will you ask? Will you vary the questions according to the make-up of the group?

Who will ask the questions?

Let's consider the practicalities of conducting staff/pupil/parent voice activities. From time to time I am asked by schools to support them in auditing the curriculum experience by meeting with groups of students or staff to discuss race representation. I have come to the conclusion that these activities are most effective and the conversation most fruitful when the group size is between four and six people: any more and a few individuals tend to dominate, any fewer and it is possible that individuals may feel pressured to answer when they might rather 'pass' to the next question. I always start my discussions by saying that some of the questions I will ask might feel a little personal and that if anyone would rather decline to answer a particular question that is absolutely fine. I also request staff putting together discussion groups of pupils to choose students who they believe will be comfortable talking about the subject matter and to bear in mind that it tends to work best when the students are of a similar age to each other. When seeking feedback from parents and ex-parents, again it is advisable to look for volunteers; some schools do this via the newsletter or by using parent governors to seek parents to participate.

Parent voice activities are a great way to engage and work positively with parents who have concerns that they or their children have felt about some aspect of equity in the past. The ethnic make-up of pupil, staff and parent voice groups will likely be determined by the line of enquiry most relevant to the school at the time but, in my experience, people of colour often find it easier to open up to discuss issues related to race when in a group of other people of colour. As for who is best placed to conduct interviews, the key factor is that the participants feel that they are in a safe space to talk openly and candidly. Sometimes this is best achieved by an adult with whom the participants already enjoy a positive relationship but, conversely, people can sometimes feel more comfortable talking to an outsider about what they would like to see changed or improved as they are not having to negotiate the sensitivities of appearing critical of the establishment of which the interviewer is a part.

How are different civilisations, nations, societies and people in them being depicted? (as heroes? as villains? as oppressors? as the oppressed? as dominant? as marginalised? as ordinary people?)

It is vital that people of colour are encountered in the curriculum as leaders, achievers, as powerful and in control, as well as, sadly frequently, victims and discriminated against. Here language is powerful. Using the term 'enslaved Africans' conveys a very different message to the noun 'slave.' But not all people of colour in history and in the world today are heroes or victims! Most were and are ordinary people doing ordinary things. Bim Adewunmi, in his essay in *The Good Immigrant*, argues that 'if white people do not see ordinary people of colour doing ordinary things, they cannot see them as anything more than two dimensional' (2017:212). Sue Sanders argues that we need to *usualise* people of colour in our curriculum. She is referring both to the frequency of encountering people of colour and the activities that people of colour are seen engaging in. Again, language is important here. The concept of 'usualising' is so much more positive than that of 'normalising': 'normal' in comparison to what?

Asking specific questions like the ones above about how people of colour are portrayed through the curriculum can be highly illuminating and thought-provoking. But the impact of the feedback gained from student, ex-student and parent voice activities and the auditing of schemes of learning, knowledge organisers and curriculum maps is, of course, maximised by ensuring that time is provided to share the messages with all teaching staff, that safe spaces are created for discussion about the implications and that support is put in place for smart action planning from the findings.

We will come back to action planning later in the chapter. But first, let's look at the varied approaches taken by a few schools with whom I have worked where staff were determined to improve representation across the curriculum.

A variety of approaches to diversifying and decolonising the curriculum

The approach taken at Thomas Alleyne Academy in Stevenage was both 'top down' (directed by SLT) and 'bottom up' (taking regular and comprehensive soundings from the students and acting on their feedback):

Thomas Alleyne Academy Case Study

The emotions that swept across the world in the spring of 2020, following the murder of George Floyd, were a powerful motivation for change. The first step was to gather the senior leadership team and discuss the events occurring in the UK and in our community. Our concern was how our staff and students would be affected and how we could support them as a school both in the present and in the future.

In May 2021, the curriculum was reviewed in depth to identify areas for improvement. Across the school, each department was encouraged to review their content and resources and to take action to adapt the curriculum. The clear message was that the revised curriculum should reflect diverse narratives and challenge stereotypes and prejudices. This required staff to research and discover new materials to incorporate into their schemes of work. Curriculum leaders held department meetings to begin this process in June 2020. Over the subsequent months, departments designed and implemented new units of work and sourced new materials to better reflect the diversity of their subject area and to address racism in the UK.

In response to requests from Year 11 students at the school, staff opened dialogue with students through focus groups with Year 11 and Year 8 students. The purpose of the focus groups was to further understand student views about the curriculum and the school culture. The Year 11 focus group included self-selected students who felt passionately about the topic, while the Year 8 focus group was formed of students selected or recommended by staff. Both focus groups were hosted by the deputy head teacher. Each focus group included a small group of six to eight students from different backgrounds, both white and non-white. The student feedback told us that we could include more explicit teaching about racism in lessons and that more diverse texts and materials were needed in a range of subjects. The feedback from students was insightful and provided us with valuable information about the lived experiences of students in our school from a myriad of backgrounds.

In focus groups, our students delivered clear and insightful feedback to the deputy head teacher that they felt the curriculum did not cover race and racism in sufficient depth. For example, one student said that it 'should not be black children's job to educate white people about racism' and argued that 'if you are old enough to face racism, you are old enough to learn about racism.' This confirmed our belief that the curriculum was a key area for review and improvement.

Later, in December 2021, we arranged further focus groups to gather feedback from our students about the progress we have made and the areas we need to improve in. One was organised and hosted by the Head of PSHE. The group was comprised of student volunteers – six Year 8 students from a range of backgrounds – who were able to speak eloquently about their experiences in school and feedback very positively about their experiences in RE: 'R.E is really good because we talk about different religions and the teacher does it really sensitively so nobody gets offended.'

At Ashlyns School in Berkhamstead, the EDI Lead started by carrying out personal research and attending CPD herself, then conducted a range of pupil, staff and parent voice interviews and, based on the feedback, designed training for all middle leaders to support them in diversifying the curriculum. Students from the focus group have now expressed a desire to work with staff in further diversifying the curriculum:

Ashlyns Secondary School Case Study

The aim of making the curriculum more representative and ensuring that all students could see themselves and their backgrounds presented became a school priority. The SLT lead undertook extensive training and research, and the first action was to gather views from our stakeholders from B.A.M.E backgrounds. This led to a series of meetings with parents, students and staff, which were invaluable in their content and provided both extremely important information and some very galvanising statements. One was particularly powerful – a student from an Asian background who said 'Sometimes I can go to five lessons a day and not see anyone who looks like me on a Powerpoint or on the walls.' It is this statement that has underpinned the work done since and has truly driven us forward.

We then conducted a training session with subject leaders, with a focus on improving representation in the curriculum across all subjects. Subject leaders were asked to do some reading beforehand to inform the session, and all came having read Reni Edo-Lodge's article (later a book) 'Why I'm No Longer Talking to White People About Race.' The aim of the session was to work with subject leaders to agree ways of further diversifying the curriculum, teaching parallel stories and ensuring representation of students from all backgrounds in our teaching. For example, for subjects which frequently use images in presentations as a stimulus, we worked on being very specific in Google searches to ensure representation of all backgrounds.

After the training, staff in subject areas carefully reviewed their classroom and corridor displays, ensuring that they represented people from different ethnic backgrounds, particularly providing positive role models. The impact of this was clear when one of our focus group students commented on the positive portrayal of a Muslim girl in her RS classroom, saying it made her feel like she belonged.

At Summercroft Primary School in Bishops' Stortford, a curriculum audit identified that there was a need for a) topics featuring inspiring people of colour, b) topics looking at the experiences of people of colour and c) more diversity in the remaining topics:

Summercroft Primary School Case Study

Before we embarked upon this journey, our curriculum focused too heavily on a primarily White experience. Although we were following the National Curriculum, opportunities to teach Black history were not exploited.

A formal review of our curriculum highlighted the areas where we lacked diversity. We analysed our existing curriculum and looked for opportunities to incorporate more diverse topics. We knew that we wanted to continue teaching 'umbrella' topics but felt that the format of just six topics per year was too restrictive. Introducing more topics meant that we could still ensure coverage of the National Curriculum whilst giving us more time to include local and diverse learning too.

Teachers tweaked existing topics and designed new topics with diversity at the forefront. For example, Year 1's Dancing Spy looks at the life of Josephine Baker, a Black entertainer, French Resistance agent and civil rights activist. Mary Seacole's contributions are explored in Year 2, while Year 3 learn about the achievements of Frida Kahlo. Year 5 are immersed in the inspirational actions of Malala Yousafzai.

We also included topics which look more at the experiences of people of colour. 'Africa: Past to Present' ensures that we meet the statutory objective of children learning about a non-European society that provides contrasts with British history by teaching Benin. However, we wanted to avoid the 'othering' that could happen when teaching about a historical culture, so decided to continue the topic into today's Africa. Children learn about the myriad countries that make up Africa and the differences between them, as well as their rich culture and resources. 'The Impact of Colonisation: Cecil Rhodes' not only allows local links but provides opportunity for children to question the concept of the Great British Empire and looks at the huge impact on the indigenous people and the repercussions that exist to this day. A topic on immigration and refugees aims to build empathy and look at places of conflict around the world.

We also looked for any opportunity to include diversity within all topics. For example, in 'Heroes,' children learn about Marcus Rashford. As part of their 'UK tour,' Year 2 explore the incredible architecture of Zaha Hadid. People from a diverse range of backgrounds can be found in every topic, from famous mountaineers and adventurers, right through to representation in the fairy tales of 'Happily Ever After.' Our curriculum is now far more reflective of society and inclusive of the achievements and history of everyone.

We can already see a difference in the empathy and acceptance that our children have towards everyone. They are more aware of inequalities in the world around us and want to know what they can do to create better equity in our society. Children from BAME backgrounds feel more valued and have access to a range of books which reflect their experiences. The Year 6 children talked passionately after their topic around Cecil Rhodes. They were outraged about the trickery he performed on King Lobengula and made vehement arguments for why our local road, Rhodes Avenue, should be renamed. They were also inspired to create placards to protest against the racism in our society.

Updating our curriculum has been an eye-opening experience and staff have reflected that it has made them more thoughtful when planning topics, ensuring that they are representative. We have had to be careful to ensure that creating a more diverse curriculum does not become tokenistic, or inadvertently create further 'othering.' We have found that our children are far more able than we had anticipated to reflect thoughtfully about sensitive subjects such as enslavement, even in the younger years. They are also more engaged and keen to make links to their real-life experiences.

Adding diversity to our curriculum has opened up important conversations between children, staff and parents which previously may not have happened.

Embedding the stories of local people, past and present, into the curriculum is a great way to address the impact of colonialism, consider the contributions of people of colour to our society and to explore the multiple elements of migration. Summercroft Primary School exploited the fact that Cecil Rhodes came from the local area to study his contribution to colonialism, with demonstrable impact on their children's views on and understanding of empire. The fact that a local street was named Rhodes Avenue gave the issue direct relevance in a way that the studying of another, remote colonial figure from a textbook would not have.

In *The Good Immigrant*, Reni Eddo Lodge comments on this:

'The black history I learnt at school was about the United States. I learnt in school that on December 1st 1955, Rosa Parks was arrested for refusing to give up her seat at the front of the bus, setting up a chain of events that resulted in a bus boycott in Montgomery, Alabama.' She then reflects that she 'didn't learn that less than a decade later, a similar bus boycott took place in Bristol, roughly 106 miles west from the stuffy south London classroom I was learning these facts in. British black history, positioned across the Atlantic, was as real to me as *The Simpsons* and that was a traged.' (2017:78).

Making it local is a great way to diversify and decolonise the curriculum. It is a requirement of the key stage 3 NC in history to conduct local history studies and such studies are also a crucial component of the geography curriculum. Exploration of the local area by students, as part of the taught curriculum, independent or home learning or as the focus of an EPQ or HPQ provides a myriad 'learnable moments,' as the following case study from an Infant and Nursery school shows powerfully.

Woolenwick Infant and Nursery School Case Study

A whole-school enquiry called 'Diversity Squared – What's Your Story?' explored immigration and a sense of belonging by examining the rich variety of people who come to Stevenage town square.

It was linked to the Stevenage motto – 'The heart of a town lies in its people' – and documented the children's curiosities about and encounters with the people in the town square. The year-long project focused on discussion points including:

Who lives in our town? Where in the world do they come from? Why do they come? What do people do in the town square?

Following the Brexit vote in June 2016, there was considerable negative media coverage concerning immigrants and migration. This was divisive and created heightened tension and fear within our school community. The national vote was 51.9% Leave, 48.1% Remain; the result in Stevenage 59.2% Leave, 40.8% Remain. Comments the children were bringing from home made it evident that we needed to proactively address the issue. We wanted to tackle negative myths and stereotypes whilst being inclusive and empathetic.

We carefully considered how to address the theme of immigration in a meaningful way for both our children and families, especially as our school is diverse. Our children, aged between 3–7 years, considered the theme through philosophical exploration and creative expression. Educators also used sources such as BBC Newsround to encourage safe, energetic discussions within their class.

Diversity Squared – What's Your Story? included:

- town centre visits and interviews with people there, including a Black eco warrior/ street cleaner and a Romanian street musician

- a Paddington Bear enquiry

- a weaving installation

- a family histories study and interviews.

The enquiry culminated in an exhibition which pulled together all the elements of the project.

The children spent extended periods of time in the town square to make observations. As they explored, they discovered new experiences and perspectives. We invited members of the community to contribute to a weaving installation to represent the diversity in our town. Each person was asked to choose a thread to represent themselves from the selection of different textured and coloured wool, ribbons, and lengths of all kinds of fabrics. The threads represented our paths, which are connected and cross in unexpected ways. This opened dialogue, an exchange of ideas and questions, and created new connections – developing new understanding of a community proud to put down its roots in Stevenage.

Linking with the 60th Anniversary of Michael Bond's Paddington Bear, the children were introduced to Paddington and his adventures. The children naturally expressed empathy for Paddington and his predicament when he arrived, alone, in England from Peru. This presented an invaluable opportunity to consider Paddington's feelings and thoughts as well as how he may have been received. The children were also encouraged to think more widely about immigration and the challenges faced by displaced people around the world, in our country, and in our town. They carefully considered the value of one person's life over another.

Sophisticated philosophical discussions developed as the children explored equality, difference and acceptance – core strands of British Values – and learned about how immigration has played a large part in the history of our country. The children learned about why people emigrate, including war and famine. They considered the rights and responsibilities of all.

Interested in the human stories behind the migration of people, the children interviewed family members to uncover their own histories and lived experiences of how they came to be part of the Stevenage community, embedding a sense of belonging. Together, these histories represent the diversity of our school community. They instil values, respect and acceptance; and foster community cohesion by helping children to understand people's different backgrounds, allowing young children to fully participate in a democratic society. These stories were then collated and made into a book. The pupil reflections include:

'Just because people come from different countries, they still have feelings like us.' Ethan

'If you have a different colour skin, it doesn't mean you are different inside.' Aurora

'It is wrong to treat people differently because of how they look.' Reuben

'When someone is being mean to someone because they are different, I will stick up for them. I will tell them to stop being a bully.' Katie

At John Warner Secondary School in Hoddesdon, one of the techniques used for decolonising the curriculum was to introduce 'Meanwhile, Elsewhere' tasks:

John Warner School Case Study

Keen to move away from a narrow, Euro-centric approach, staff in the history department explored ways of amending the existing provision and including new topics that would provide a wider contextual lens on established historical topics, as well as introducing students to histories that have previously been untold. For example, the study of the British Empire (Year 8) was extended to include a case study of The Congo to appreciate the existence of pre-colonial African empires and to assess the impact of European (British, Belgian and Portuguese) involvement.

This widening of the lens has partly been achieved through tasks at Key Stage 3 called 'Meanwhile, Elsewhere' that encourage students to explore global parallel histories to discover what was happening in different societies at the same time as the events prescribed in the syllabus. Examples include:

● Alongside the study of the Battle of Hastings in 1066, students are asked to complete a homework task on the Battle of Manzikert in 1071 in the Byzantine Empire

- Students explore the Mali Empire of Mansa Musa in the 14th century while studying The Hundred Years' War in Europe

- Students investigate the rule of Ivan the Terrible in Russia to enrich their study of Henry VIII and the Break with Rome.

Staff at St Catherine of Siena Catholic Primary School in Watford have sought to create a 'Culture of Encounter,' with the aim being 'to address stereotypes, misconceptions, unconscious bias and preconceptions through educating children (and their families) about differences in ethnicity, religion, race, language and beliefs.'

St Catherine of Siena Catholic Primary School Case Study

A simple but powerful way of celebrating the diverse heritage of the pupils was suggested, namely to mark the Independence Days of heritage countries. Following a short Google Forms survey, sent to all families, it was ascertained that pupils within the school hailed from over 50 different countries. In addition, many families identified as having multiple (in several cases three) heritage backgrounds. This survey is now sent to all new starters, so SLT have detailed information on the composition of the community.

When designing how best to mark Independence Days, it was paramount that the outcomes were multifaceted.

- To educate about colonialism and the effect of the colonists on native communities
- To educate about different cultures around the world
- To celebrate the heritage of our families
- To create a culture of encounter – through first-hand engagement, to dispel the concept of the 'other'
- To instil pride in pupils about where they have come from and the contributions of that country to the world.

In the weekly newsletter, the Head references upcoming National or Independence Days and invites contributions from families. On Independence Days, children and staff wear national colours or national dress and bring in flags, food or personal items associated with their culture. Families can contribute to a Powerpoint which is shared with the whole school and pupils speak about their own experiences of visiting their heritage country and of being of dual/multiple heritage.

'I love the opportunity for children to come into school on cultural feast days relevant to them and celebrate with their class.' Parent Year 2.

'My friends all asked me about Grenada. It makes me feel special to wear different clothes. I am excited to celebrate my day!' Pupil Year 3.

'I liked it when I taught my class about what it's like in Nigeria.' Pupil Year 4.

> **Reflection**
>
> What can you take from these case studies to help you with your own school's action plan to diversify and decolonise the curriculum?

This last case study raises the question of using key anniversaries, theme months and national days as opportunities for a focus on aspects of diversity and anti-racism. And there are now a lot of such occasions in the annual calendar, including Race Equality Week, Martin Luther King Day, Stephen Lawrence Day and the anniversaries of the tragic murders of other people of colour such as George Floyd. Perhaps the most high-profile and contentious is Black History Month.

Black History Month (BHM)

Many educationalists have a strong aversion to the concept of BHM. Nigel expressed to me his view that it 'is patronising. The origins of all history come out of Africa!' My colleague Toks Olusamokun wrote a blog in 2021 about 'Six things that rile me about Black History Month' namely:

'1. It's one solitary month.

2. When done badly, it's reduced to tokenism and stereotypes.

3. There's often an expectation of Black staff to do something for BHM.

4. It can create trauma for Black people.

5. It's not celebratory enough.

6. It rarely includes any discussion about race and racism.'

She continues,

> I resent the idea that the history, contributions and impact of 57 individual nations in the continent of Africa, 13 countries in the Caribbean, let alone the wider diaspora should be confined to one solitary month... The history highlighted during this month is sometimes negative and inaccurate. There is an over-reliance on slavery, African American history and civil rights movements, as well as the ubiquitous entries from Bob Marley (for music), Martin Luther King (for English, politics and history) and a collection of sports and music stars such as Mohammed Ali. Asking the Black teacher(s) is a genuine problem and not just because Black teachers – as detailed in the Runnymeade/NASUWT's report (2016) – are paid less, face structural discrimination and are less likely to be promoted. In brief, they've already got a lot on their plates... Producing something authentic, accurate and detailed requires time, interest and skill. If schools and educational settings are serious

about BHM being done, then they must give staff time to research, increase their knowledge first and work collaboratively... I genuinely worry about the impact that BHM may have on Black children and young people. Imagine being a Black child in a class when a well-intentioned but misguided teacher decides to play a video depicting slavery, hostility towards Windrush migrants or racist booing during football matches? Meanwhile the teacher recounts the statistics: numbers of Black people abused, stolen, beaten, raped, killed and thrown overboard. Your classmates react and you may be left feeling: upset, confused, ashamed, embarrassed, tearful and/or traumatised... Why don't we spend more time explaining why BHM was created? The absence of debate and discussion about racism before and especially during BHM is most odd. The reason we have BHM in schools is because the current curriculum does not adequately reflect the history or contributions of Black people; therefore schools celebrating BHM must surely engage in discussions about race, racism, inequality, unfairness, injustice and the balance of the curriculum.

Reflection

Do you mark BHM and/or other key race related anniversaries at your school? Is this something that you have debated as a staff body, or with your senior leaders, governors or trustees?

If so, do you have a clearly articulated rationale for why you do so and what your aims are?

Reading Olusamokun's critique above, could any of these criticisms legitimately be made of BHM at your school?

If so, what could you do to improve your provision?

Olusamokun concludes that there are significant merits to BHM when done well and in conjunction with a range of other anti-racism actions, but that 'One month won't cut it. A bigger and deeper change is necessary.' BHM, if well planned and driven by a clear rationale, can be a great way of involving members of the community and pupils themselves in designing and leading celebratory, educative and impactful activities, as the following case studies show:

Bishop's Hatfield Secondary School Case Study

In the autumn term of 2020 we established a pupil-led Equality and Diversity Committee. The aim was to create a core group of pupils, approximately 20–25, from Key Stages 4 and 5 to consult with, and who would take the lead on delivering assemblies, activities and focus weeks. We decided to initially offer the role to Key Stage 4 and 5 pupils as we wanted membership of the committee to be a key leadership role within the school community. At all times the group would be supported by the lead teacher and would initially meet twice a half-term to plan and discuss their work. The creation of the new group was publicised during form time, via assemblies and using posters around the school on the pupil noticeboards. Interested pupils were asked to complete an application form, which required applicants to:

- Explain why they would like to be a member of the Bishop's Equality and Diversity Committee

- Give at least one idea/event they think we could undertake to promote equality and diversity this year

Twenty pupils applied to be committee members, all of whom demonstrated through the application form that they were engaged with promoting positive change. Using feedback from focus group interviews, the committee created an initial calendar of events which included Human Rights Day, World Religion and Culture Week and Ramadan assemblies.

Staff have commented positively on the work of the committee:'It has been important for pupils to see their peers lead on topics of diversity, such as Black History Month and religious festivals; students have ownership of these topics, and this enhances their role in the school community.'

At Nicholas Breakspear RC School, each tutor group in Years 7–13 elects two EDI representatives and they organise BHM events. Here is an extract from the school newsletter from October 2021 which highlights the work of the EDI representatives in celebrating the contribution of all people to the community and the wider world:

Nicholas Breakspear School Case Study

Black History Month is the time for everybody to be educated on the impact Black people have had on society and the world. Black History Month is a way of remembering important people and events in the history of the African diaspora. We celebrate Black History Month to commemorate the contributions that black people have done unto the world and to show that their doings have not gone unappreciated.

The Equality, Diversity and Inclusion representatives from each tutor group researched inspirational black people who have made an impact on society today and to express why they are so important. The EDI representatives have produced presentations to show to each of their form groups, addressing Black History Month and the importance of bringing awareness to our whole school community, in order to fulfil the school mission to build a better world.

The EDI representatives have also made posters regarding important black figures (relating to department areas), which have been creatively designed. The EDI representatives have been very hardworking with their research and are looking forward to sharing it with the rest of the NBS community around the school.

The Catholic Social Teachings teach that human dignity must be protected and a healthy community can be accomplished only if human rights are protected and responsibilities are met. Therefore, every person has a crucial right to life and a right to those things essential for human decency. This term Bosco House have been presenting assemblies on this theme to the rest of the school. We are also looking forward to the Black History Month assemblies that the Student Leadership Team will be leading in the coming weeks. For the future of this country, we should help make each of our voices heard and ensure that, no matter what physical differences we may have, we remember that we are all equal and play an important role in society.

By LM, Year 9.

Diversifying the wider curriculum

So far in this chapter we have largely been focused on ways of diversifying and decolonising the taught and timetabled curriculum. But, as themed events and focus months show, there are numerous ways in which schools can address representation and promote an anti-racist message in the wider curriculum. Assemblies are a great opportunity for this, as are enrichment activities and extra-curricular clubs.

At Isaac Newton Academy, we worked hard to ensure that our students had regular opportunities to see and talk to great role models from a range of ethnic backgrounds and excelling in multiple fields. For example, once a month on a Saturday we hosted a seminar for around 20 students (different ones each time), led by university undergraduates from the local community, which was very ethnically diverse. They spoke about higher education and what it is like to study at a particular university on a particular course. We invited a great number of visitors to the school to talk in assemblies, lead workshops or discussions or address the students at key events: the physicist Jim Al Khalili officially opened the school, the BBC journalist Mishal Hussain spoke in assembly about her career and ran a workshop on reporting on the Arab Spring, the authors Rohan Gavin and Polly Ho-Yen each gave an assembly to different Year 7 cohorts and led writing workshops, the England Football Manager Hope Powell ran a workshop for girls who excelled at sport, Charlie Dark from Run Dem Crew addressed the sixth form about the music business and Community Night Running, the journalist Secunder Kermani addressed Key Stage 4 students about a career in the media. Most of these speakers were secured by staff or students writing to them to invite them to the school. For every letter that received a positive response, we probably wrote five that went unanswered, and in some instances we got frustratingly close to securing a visit (for example with the England cricketer Moeen Ali) only for the speaker's schedule to change at the last minute. But the time spent on arranging these visits was always well worth the effort; the speakers never failed to inspire the students, and their time and interest impacted most demonstrably on the racially minoritised students, who identified with them, and hung on their every word.

Action planning

To succeed in diversifying and decolonising the curriculum requires commitment from every adult in the school, strong leadership with a relentless focus on the agenda and robust action planning. The schools which have made demonstrable impact in this area have made curriculum representation a key school improvement priority, clearing space and time to deliver on this declared priority. They are clear about the specific actions they should take at the current time to make most impact. They articulate and publicise clear objectives and set smart performance measures against which to judge their success. They have ensured that regular staff INSET time is protected to train and educate teachers in their different CPD needs. Some have encouraged all staff to set themselves a performance development target related to their role in diversifying and decolonising the curriculum and to build this into phase or departmental plans to share the load and to hold all staff equally accountable. They also return frequently to focus groups with staff, pupils and parents to gain feedback and gauge their success in meeting the milestones towards their objectives.

Reflection

How smart is your action planning to achieve an anti-racist curriculum?

Have you agreed clear objectives? And precise performance indicators?

Do all staff have their own targets in this area? How are they a) supported and b) held to account for their individual contributions?

What could you do to further improve or refine your action planning?

References

Adewunmi. B. *What We Talk About When We Talk About Tokenism* in Shukla. N. ed. (2017). *The Good Immigrant.* (London: Unbound). p 208–212.

Eddo-Lodge. R. *Forming Blackness Through A Screen* in Shukla. N. ed. (2017). *The Good Immigrant.* (London: Unbound). p 77–83.

Macfarlane. R. and Catchpool. M eds. (2022) *Great Representation. Collection of School Case Studies.* (Hertfordshire: Herts For Learning Ltd).

Newmark. B. (2019) *Why Teach?* (Woodbridge: John Catt).

Olusamokun. T. (2021). *Six Things That Rile Me About Black History Month.* Blog. Available at: https://thegrid.org.uk/news/black-history-month-october-2022

Rollett. S. (2021). *Curriculum decolonisation as a disciplinary process.* (Confederation of School Trusts) Available at: https://cstuk.org.uk/assets/CST-Publications/CST_Bridge_Decolonisation

Selecting books and resources

If books are mirrors then where are our reflections?

Gemma Bagnall

We want readers to encounter characters with agency, who are identifiable, relatable, nuanced, varied and central to the narrative.

CLPE (2020:12)

In the last chapter we looked predominantly at diversifying and decolonising the curriculum through review and re-design of schemes of learning and programmes of study and by replacing, revising or enhancing topics and content. We also explored ways of ensuring breadth of representation in the additional educational experiences that learners get beyond taught lessons. To date, although we have considered the impact of diversity in displays and textbooks, we have only touched on the importance of diversifying the teaching and learning resources in schools that staff use to deliver the curriculum and that are accessible to learners, for example via libraries, Learning Resource Centres and resource lists on websites. In this chapter, we will focus mainly on the importance of diversifying book choices and stock and look at some practical ways in which schools might do this. But first, we will give some attention to the need to consider diversity of other classroom resources, particularly in the impressionable Early Years.

'I don't see colour (and young children don't see colour either)'

Those of us who were educated in the 1970s will remember a time when many people considered it rude to point out people's ethnicity and the attitude adopted in many schools was a deliberately 'colour blind' one. There are still the remnants of the 'I don't see colour' attitude amongst staff in many schools. Afua Hirsch, who is considerably younger than I am, recalls being 'taught not to see race. We are told

DOI: 10.4324/9781003275220-12

that race does not matter. We have convinced ourselves that if we can contort ourselves into a form of blindness, then issues of identity will quietly disappear. ... But...being taught not to see race only heightened my sensitively to the extent of my difference' (2018:10).

Hirsh says that 'The problem is, there is still race, and there is still racism. Denying it does not solve the problem, it creates two further problems. First, it assumes that seeing race is something bad' (2018:25); in other words, the very act of recognising and acknowledging ethnic differences is somehow racist. 'The second problem is that as long as racism does exist... not seeing race shuts down analysis of the issue. Just because one individual chooses not to "see race", it doesn't mean that the racialised nature of poverty, discrimination and prejudice in society at large disappears' (2018:26). She concludes that 'The effect of both these tendencies is to deny people who do experience race... a sense that they can have their own identity.'

Hirsch reflects that, whilst their intentions are well meaning, the type of people who say they do not see colour are those people 'who have never experienced the disadvantages of being a visible other' (2018:307). Have you ever heard a person of colour say they don't see race?

Akala also addresses this issue. He finds the 'I don't see colour' argument somewhat laughable: 'This idea that racism will just vanish if we refuse to discuss it is rather fascinating. Imagine for a moment if scientists and engineers... said Right, the best way to solve a problem is not to discuss, confront or challenge it but to leave it alone completely and hope it just works itself out' (2018:24).

The 'colour blind' approach is problematic; clearly people do see, and categorise, according to skin colour. And children, including very young ones, notice different skin tones and ask curious questions. They also pickup messages from the media. If educators don't proactively discuss race with children they will, of course, draw their own conclusions and these may well be problematic. They need to be taught that difference exists but that this should not be the basis for inequality. In *Sway* (2020:289). Agarwal reminds us that 'Children... start developing a sense of race from the age of six months or so.' 'While 30-month-olds show a preference for children of the same race when shown photographs of unfamiliar white and black children, demonstrating in-group bias, the majority of children start choosing white playmates by the time they are 36 months old.' In *Wish I Knew What To Say*, Agarwal says that four to six year olds 'create assumptions related not only to skin colour but also to lifestyles, language and religious belief' (2020:83). 'Once they start putting people into categories and assigning labels and value judgements, slowly and steadily they can start forming biases and prejudices' (2020:87). Tatum tells us that the idea of race constancy is not fixed until a child is around six or seven years old. Up until then, they may well express a desire to be White due to the advantages of White Privilege. (1997:122). In *Brown Baby*, Nikesh Shukla describes his young daughter telling him that she didn't like the colour brown (2021:12) and that it was dirty (2021:14). She abandoned her brown doll and said 'I don't want to be brown' (2021:16). He reflects 'you may be four but you are perpetuating tropes that you are yet to even comprehend' (2021:14).

Tatum advises that it is important for young children to see lots of different skin colours and tones around them in books, displays and resources (1997:125). It is also important for educators to encourage children to challenge what they see (and don't see) represented around them. When I was head of an all-through school, I ran an after-school art club for Reception and Year 1 pupils. We explored colours and the colour chart, mixing primary colours to get the shades we sought. The children paired up and, over a series of sessions, created a portrait of their partner, after carefully studying their facial structure, eye, hair and skin colour, hair texture and so on. This was a perfect opportunity to discuss and celebrate differences in skin tone and ethnicity. As Agarwal says in *Wish We Knew What To Say*, portrait activities are also a great way of explaining the reasons for variation in skin colour: 'It is relatively straightforward to say that people who have more melanin will have darker skin. It is also easy to say that children come in different shapes, sizes and appearances, including different skin colours, and that this is what makes us all unique' (2020:100).

Some educators have the attitude that primary aged children, and especially those in Early Years, are too young to be encouraged to talk about colour difference and issues concerning race, that in some way this robs them of their innocence and introduces concepts that it is not appropriate for them to consider. But it is common for children to be considering issues of colour and difference, race and inequity without sharing their thoughts with adults and, sadly, experiencing racism from a young age. As Sarpong reminds us, 'Children of colour are told much earlier (than white children about the realities of life) and the inequalities they will face at some point, no matter how talented or brilliant they might be' (2020:3). In *Wish We Knew What To Say*, Agarwal says 'Often any anti-racism work that is done in schools is focused on adolescents' but that this is too late: 'by the time children are six years old they already have well-formed attitudes...by the age of nine, many of the racial stereotypes have been laid down very firmly' (2020:15).

Kinouani argues that not talking about race is dangerous: 'Silence fosters self-hate and breeds shame.' She explains that 'In silence the child gets the message that there is something that is dreadful, unspeakable...So not only is racism something we do not talk about, it is something we struggle with alone' (2021:106). Her argument is that what is not talked about and processed is not healed.

Have you come across staff/governors/trustees who

a. Have adopted a colour-blind attitude to race issues or

b. Express reservations about younger children considering race issues?

If yes, how have you addressed this? If no, you might like to prepare a response to both scenarios.

Teaching resources

Using carefully chosen classroom resources is a good way of usualising a wide variety of skin colours and enabling learners to see their ethnicity represented in their learning environment. Zaretta Hammond gives good advice about diverse resources: 'Think carefully about what visuals are displayed on the walls. They send a non-verbal message about what and who is valued in the classroom. Unconsciously, we pick up clues about affirmation and validation from our surroundings.' She urges educators to 'find authentic cultural elements that add real value to the classroom', such as prints of contemporary or traditional art representing a range of cultures, photos of murals and others community art work, textiles and handcrafts (2015:144). She advises, 'Think about the cultural values of your students and translate those values into concrete objects and symbols that you can display or integrate into the classroom.'

Sandra Smidt (2020:66) says, 'When they only see images of people like them-selves there is a danger that they think that these are the only important people'… 'This is why the intervention of adults engaging with young children about race, racial identity and discrimination is so important.'

The tiney guide to becoming an inclusive, anti-racist early educator suggests that practitioners should ask themselves how, and how much, their environment enables children to recognise and celebrate difference and develop empathy and what kinds of thought and conversation the environment enables (2021:17). The guide states that 'Children are able to recognise differences from the time they're a baby. They have that awareness and we mustn't postpone this work until children are old enough to have a deep and meaningful conversation about it!' The guide stresses that 'We can begin celebrating difference and championing an anti-racist outlook from day one… Pause to think about everything… children experience with you and the extent to which you're broadening children's horizons' (2021:23). It stresses the importance of having different languages and scripts on display (2021:24).

Primary teachers should also give careful consideration to the clothing and accessories that they stock their dressing up boxes with, to ensure that racial stereo-types are not given oxygen. In *Wish We Knew What To Say*, Agarwal recalls a time when her daughter was given a blonde princess wig to wear and another when her twins were denied the role of angels in the school nativity because 'angels always have blonde hair' (2020:73).

Activity

Design an audit tool that you and your staff might use to assess the diversity of the teaching resources and displays in your school.

Books

Books of all kinds – picture books, fiction books and non-fiction books – can be a great resource for giving children of colour a sense of belonging and for opening up age-appropriate discussions and activities around race and identity, difference and equality, stereotyping, discrimination and anti-racism. But the book stocks of too many schools lack diversity and perpetuate racist stereotypes and messages of White supremacy.

Bonolo told me that as a young child he would 'read books and imagine the protagonist as black until the skin colour was mentioned.' He quickly learnt to adjust his expectations: 'As an adult I now read books and imagine the protagonist as white, until the skin colour is mentioned.'

Chimamanda Ngozi Adichie grew up in Eastern Nigeria. She started reading at around four years old and writing stories aged seven. She had never travelled outside Nigeria but her early characters were 'White, blue eyed, played in the snow, ate apples and spoke about the weather.' They drank Ginger beer. 'We are impressionable and vulnerable in the face of a story.' She said in her TED talk, 'I didn't know that people like me could exist in literature.' Rubia similarly said to me that she had never come across a character in a book that was anything like her, a British Pakistani girl, until she was a late teenager. Darren Chetty, in his essay in *The Good Immigrant*, tells the tragic story from his class. A Year 2 boy who had recently arrived from Nigeria was reading a story that he had written to his friend (born in Britain and identified as Congolese). On hearing the story, the friend say 'You can't say that. Stories have to be about white people' (2017:96). Chetty, who has spent nearly 20 years teaching teaching four to 11 year olds in English primary schools serving 'multi-racial, multi-cultural, multi-faith communities', reflects that he has come to notice that 'whenever children are asked to write a story in school, children of colour will write a story featuring characters with "traditional" English names who speak English as a first language. This has been the case across the schools I have taught in with barely an exception. Yet I don't recall it ever being discussed by teachers in these schools' (2017:96–7).

Disturbing as they are, these stories should not surprise us, given the data on the paucity of children's books with racially minoritised characters. In 2017 just 4% of children's books published in England and Wales featured minority ethnic characters, in 2018 the figure was 7%, in 2019 10% and in 2020 15%.

Ethnic category	% rep in pop of England/ Wales	% total books published featuring ME main character
Arab	0.4	0.2
Asian	6.8	0.7
Black	3.4	2.2

Ethnic category	% rep in pop of England/ Wales	% total books published featuring ME main character
Chinese	0.7	0.3
Mixed	2.2	0.8
Other	0.6	0.5

(CLPE 2020)

In some recent years there has been no presence at all of a demographic group, such as Gypsy, Roma and Traveller (GRT), in newly published children's books. GRT culture is critically underrepresented in literature. Gemma Bagnall speaks movingly on this matter; she never saw her GRT identity in books she read when young. A You Gov poll conducted in 2017 found that 6 out of 10 parents surveyed would not allow their child to go to the home of a traveller for a play date. Is that any wonder, Gemma asked in an HFL workshop in January 2022, when the GRT community has been represented in literature as child snatchers, by characters like Esmeralda in The Hunchback of Notre Dame. There are still very few children's texts with GRT protagonists and those that do exist tend to be about the struggle narrative; she argued that they don't show GRT skills, work ethic, sense of family and moralities.

Children should, of course, have access to a wide range of stories and characters. In an interview with Sky News in 2014, referenced by Chetty, Malorie Blackman said, 'I think there is a very significant message that goes out when you cannot see yourself at all in the books you are reading. I think it is saying "well, you may be here, but do you really belong?"' (2017:102).

In her introduction to the 2020 CLPE report, Louise Johns – Shepherd says, 'Learning to read is a social process and it is intensely linked with self-image. Put simply, the reading experience can be compromised if you never come across a character or story that reflects your life, culture or background.' She argues, 'We also know so much now about how important reading is to developing empathy and broadening outlook; ensuring an opportunity for all children to come across reading material that reflects the wide world in which they live has never been more important' (2020:3).

The report continues, 'It is crucial that all readers are able to encounter characters of colour as a meaningful part of the mainstream. The benefit is twofold as it serves as affirmation in one instance and broadens world outlook in another.' On the one hand, 'to encounter characters and worlds that resemble your own can allow for powerful connections to be forged between the reader and the world of the book.' And on the other, 'to experience people, cultures and worlds beyond your own can deepen and enrich a reader's understanding of the world and their place in it.' The report concludes that 'A representative and inclusive shelf therefore benefits all readers and should be an entitlement for all of our pupils' (2020:7–8).

Professor Rudine Sims Bishop coined the phrase 'Windows, Mirrors and Sliding Glass Doors' in a seminal paper of 1990. She argued that children need to see themselves reflected in what they read (mirrors) and to be able, through books, to see and learn about other worlds and the experiences of other people (windows). Sliding glass doors refers to the experience that the reader has when they walk into a story and become part of the world created by the author – fully immersed in another experience.

Farrah Serroukh is Research and Development Director for the Centre for Literacy in Primary Education (CLPE). In a talk for an HFL conference in January 2022, she stressed the crucial role of the educator in choosing which books to introduce learners to. She argued that we act as gate keepers and curators of literature and that what we provide access to and endorse really matters. Serroukh stressed that books can uphold problematic dominant narratives or challenge and counteract racism. They offer readers opportunities to influence, shape and make sense of the world.

At this point, it is perhaps worth sounding a word of warning about choosing books that we loved when we were children. Most educators can remember favourite books that they read, or had read to them, as children. Mine would include: *The Mill On The Floss*; *The Lion, The Witch and the Wardrobe*; *Three Men and a Boat*, *The Railways Children*. It is tempting for teachers to share the books that got them hooked on reading with their pupils, but this is seldom a good idea. A lot of literature from bygone days is tainted with bygone racist, sexist and other problematic attitudes and tropes. Much better to work as a staff to put together an up to date, diverse and anti-racist book list; there are plenty of examples online to use as a starting point. Smidt has lots of suggestions of books to read to and with very young children (2020:115–124), as does the tiney guide (2021:32–40).

Libraries and librarians

Not all schools are fortunate enough to have a library or Learning Resource Centre, but for those that do, there is a crucial role here to be played in race awareness and education, representation and tackling race inequity. A great librarian builds up links with publishers and bookshops that specialise in texts by diverse authors and featuring diverse characters. They make it their business to source and recommend anti-racist texts for each curriculum area and to support each scheme of learning. They devise and communicate to staff their system for classifying anti-racist texts: by author, by theme, by characters, by setting. And they see it as their role to educate all pupils: to support learners of colour to see themselves and others like them in what they read, to educate White children about the diverse world, and to introduce all students to key issues of race equity via literature and non-fiction.

The best libraries I visit are effectively co-run by student librarians or library ambassadors. Smart librarians ensure that they use pupils as anti-racism allies: to select, recommend and write reviews of texts and to draw their peers into reading materials.

What do you do in your school to ensure that your book stock supports your anti racism work?

What criteria do you use for choosing class readers? And books for story time/ the book corner/book boxes?

Do your staff look for racially minoritised characters in all genres – science fiction, fantasy, comedy, horror – to usualise the presence of people from a range of ethnic backgrounds?

Do children of colour feature in every day narrative and events? Do your books feature people of colour in a variety of places, jobs and experiences?

Are racially minoritised characters given agency and voice?

Have you trawled through your book stock to ensure that none of the texts include racist tropes?

Are stories featuring characters of colour told through a white lens or written by authors from racially minoritised backgrounds?

Do you choose books that will enable your staff to explore issues such as equity, diversity, colourism, refugee experiences and racism with pupils – books that challenge and encourage learners to think? And if so, have staff received adequate training to be able to explore these issues confidently, sensitively and with impact?

Think about the text/literature diet across the whole school from early years to Year 6, or Year 7 to 13, or across all 14 years if you are in an all-through school. Where is the presence of racially minoritised characters?

Do these characters have main roles or bit parts? Are they well developed or one dimensional? Are they empowered or subjugated?

Do you encourage staff to share their own diverse reading, with notices on classroom and office doors or on email signatures?

To end this chapter, here are some examples of actions taken by schools to review, audit and refresh book stock to support their anti-racism work:

Summercroft Primary School Case Study

Our library was in need of updating, not just because of the lack of diverse authors and characters, but also because a number of books contained out-of-date language.

Our first priority was to tackle the lack of diversity in our books. There were three parts to upgrading our book offering:

- Books for Reading for Pleasure

- Books for the library

- Books linked to topics and our English curriculum

We introduced Reading for Pleasure time. This involves teachers reading a high-quality text to children for 15 minutes, every day. This text isn't linked to the current topic or English unit; it is simply a book to enjoy together.

Teachers could choose the books they wanted to read to their class, with the only parameters being that the books must either be by an author of colour or have a person of colour as the main character. The English lead and our librarian were on hand to help teachers to make their choices.

When purchasing the books for our library, we focused on increasing our selection of diverse non-fiction and fiction. To improve our non-fiction offering, we worked with a bookshop to find a range of high-quality texts. We ensured the texts were from a range of genres and provided children with exposure to Black history and inspirational people of colour, both past and present.

With our fiction books, we wanted to improve the diversity both in our picture books and chapter books. We took advice from our TLA, other educators, groups via social media (such as Elevate.uk2020), diversebooks.org and shortlisted books from diverse book awards to help us find a good selection of texts. As well as focusing on shared books for communal areas, we provided each class with £250 to improve the book offerings in their own classrooms.

We ensured that our bookcases in classrooms and around the school included front-facing books, actively choosing books that reflected diversity. This means that children and adults can see the wide range of diverse books available to them easily and know that everyone is being represented by the literature we choose to celebrate.

Our third step towards upgrading our book offering was to ensure that our books for our topics and English units were diverse. We looked at our existing topics and found opportunities to include more diverse figures and texts. For example, in our Year 1 topic, Heroes, which includes work on space and astronauts, we introduced the text, *Counting on Katherine: How Katherine Johnson Saved Apollo 13*. In our Year 6 topic, Adventurers, we used the text Fantastic Female Explorers and looked at the achievements of Jin Jeong and Misba Khan. We were able to add high-quality, diverse texts to almost all topics and are continuing to look for additional books to support these.

Ashlyns School Case Study

In English, the first novel studied in Year 7 had been a novel called *My Sister Lives on the Mantlepiece*, which is a book based around the aftermath of the July 7/7 bombings in London. It explored some very difficult issues surrounding Islamophobia, and the feelings of a white family towards the Muslim community and Islam after the death of one of their children in a terrorist attack. The department had originally brought in this book to bring diversity to their curriculum, and it had been well received by students. This is an excellent example of a well-intentioned decision which did not work in practice; the book may have explored some very important and challenging issues, but it did so by stereotyping Sunya, the Muslim character who takes the role of educating the narrator by becoming his best friend. Following feedback from Muslim staff and students, the English department made the decision to change the text and replaced it with 'Coram Boy', a text that is linked to the history of our own school, which started life as a found-ling hospital, and explores contemporary issues of class and race in a historical setting.

There was some resistance in the department to this change, illustrating perfectly that change in this area can be challenging against the context of backgrounds of a 'colourblind' mentality.

When asked about the changes to the English curriculum, students talked positively of the introduction of *The Other Side of Truth* and of the removal of *My Sister Lives on the Mantlepiece*. One student commented, 'I really liked *My Sister Lives on the Mantlepiece*, but it's by a white author and I feel like we need to be sure that we are hearing the experiences of black writers telling black stories so the other books you've chosen are better.'

Wheatfields Junior School Case Study

Our starting point was that our English Leads and our very knowledgeable Librarian worked together to undertake an extensive review of texts available to children in our school library, particularly focusing on how people from different ethnic backgrounds were portrayed. Part of this involved a rigorous audit of existing texts and included the removal of a number of very outdated books which contained stereotypical representation and inappropriate language. This audit also highlighted that texts which were being used to include some representation of racial diversity were limited to obvious choices by traditional authors, or characters such as Handa from 'Handa's Surprise'. We wanted to ensure our children were able to see themselves and their families represented in the characters and illustrations used.

Senior Leaders included this work as a key priority in the School Improvement Plan. The Governing Body were very supportive of this initiative and approved that a significant budget be allocated to enable the purchase of a wide range of age appropriate, quality texts over the summer ready to use in the new academic year. The school's work around diversity became a standing item on the Full Governing Body meeting agendas so that governors were kept fully abreast of developments.

Texts chosen were carefully selected to include content which allowed children to explore the experiences of others (for example through picture books and novels focusing on the experiences of refugees), or to learn about world religions or which included Black and Minority Ethnic people as main characters and positive role models. INSET time was dedicated to allowing all staff time to explore the new resources and to consider how these could be used effectively to enhance the children's learning about equity and anti-racism.

Our librarian has pro-actively ensured that displays in the library promote diversity and she continually ensures that books are rotated and are prominent, so that children are drawn to these when visiting the library. She also ensures that she is very aware of themed weeks and upcoming events, for example anti-bullying week or religious festivals such as Diwali or Hannukah. She uses her expertise to direct children and teachers to books which will be of particular interest and relevance to them and their classes when they visit the library.

Our next step was to review how texts containing diverse representation could be woven into our English curriculum, ensuring that the same high quality which we had already established was maintained, focusing on diverse characterisation, settings and authors. As part of every unit of teaching in English, we always include 'link reading' texts; it was important that high quality examples of these were also chosen so that teachers and children had access to a broad range of diverse texts. Lockdown provided us with an unexpected opportunity to allow our children to enjoy virtual visits from two authors from diverse backgrounds who had written texts that the children were using in their learning: Humza Arshad and Baroness Floella Benjamin. The children were very inspired by these.

The impact of our work can be seen immediately on entering our school library. Visitors have commented on how prominent books relating to anti-racism and diversity are. Evidence of impact is also clear through staff feedback: 'Children have felt free to ask more questions for clarity and understanding. They have a better understanding of how it feels to face discrimination.' 'It has naturally prompted discussions that involve elements from a variety of cultural backgrounds that I don't think would have come up as often otherwise.' A reluctant reader was enthused to read after encountering 'radio-active samosas' in Humza Arshad's book and commenting:' I like this book. Samosas are my favourite food and the family are from Pakistan like my family'. Another child shared that she had been inspired to read 'Agent Zaiba' by Annabella Sami, saying 'I chose this book because the girl on the cover looked just like me'.

Summative activity

Having read Chapters 7, 8 and 9, you might wish to work with colleagues to devise an action plan for how you will work to further diversify and decolonise your school curriculum and resources over the next five years, with targets and milestones.

References

Adichie. C. N. (2009) *The Danger of the Single Story* (TED talk). Available at: www.bing.com/search?q=Chimamanda+Ngozi+Adichie+The+Danger+of+the+single+story+TED+talk&cvid=2e1bcb7319514e96a78b73ff657cc694&aqs=edge..69i57j69i11004.4723j0j4&FORM=ANAB01&DAF0=1&PC=U531

Agarwal. P. (2020). *Sway: Unravelling Unconscious Bias.* (London: Bloomsbury).

Agarwal. P. (2020). *Wish We Knew What To Say.* (Great Britain, London: Dialogue Books).

Akala (2019). *Natives: Race & Class in the Ruins of Empire.* (Great Britain, London: Two Roads).

Bishop. R. S. (1990) *Windows, Mirrors and Sliding Glass Doors.*

Chetty. D. 'You Can't Say That! Stories Have To Be About White People' in Shukla. N. ed. (2017). *The Good Immigrant.* (London: Unbound).

CLPE Annual Reflecting Realities Report 2020 https://clpe.org.uk/research/clpe-reflecting-realities-survey-ethnic-representation-within-uk-childrens-literature-0

Hammond. Z. (2015). *Culturally Responsive Teaching and The Brain.* (California, London: Corwin)

Henry-Allain. L. and Lloyd-Rose. M. *Our guide to becoming an inclusive, anti-racist early educator.* (tiney). Available at: www.tiney.co/blog/becoming-an-inclusive-anti-racist-early-educator/

Hirsch. A. (2018). *Brit(ish): On Race, Identity and Belonging.* (London: Vintage).

Kinouani. G. (2021). *Living While Black.* (London: Ebury Press).

Macfarlane. R. and Catchpool. M eds. (2022).*Great Representation.* Collection of School Case Studies. (Hertfordshire: Herts For Learning Ltd).

Sarpong, J. (2020). *The Power Of Privilege: How White People Can Challenge Racism.* (London: HQ).

Shukla. N. (2021). *Brown Baby: A Memoir of Race, Family and Home.* (London: Pan Macmillan).

Smidt. S. (2020). *Creating an Anti-Racist Culture in the Early Years.* (London: Routledge).

Tatum. B. D. (2021) *Why Are All The Black Kids Sitting Together In The Cafeteria?* (Great Britain, Dublin: Penguin).

PART FOUR
Recruiting, retaining and developing a diverse body of staff, governors and trustees

10 Recruitment

I feel most coloured when I am thrown against a sharp white background.

Zora Neale Hurston (1928:2)

Not everything that is faced can be changed, but nothing can be changed until it is faced.

Attributed to James Baldwin

In Part Three we explored the ways in which the school that is committed to becoming an anti-racist institution can diversify and decolonise the curriculum. It is far easier to provide a culturally responsive curriculum and pedagogy and to draw on the richness of diverse cultures if the staff planning and teaching the curriculum bring lived experiences from a wide range of heritages to the design and delivering processes. Part Four of this book is all about the importance of addressing the under-representation of people of colour in our workforce. The presence of racially minoritised staff in schools does not, of course, in and of itself indicate race equity and it is dangerous when people point to representation of staff, governors or trustees from a range of ethnic groups as evidence of a 'job done': as one of my interviewees reflected, 'It's not a numbers game.' However, I do argue in this section of the book that race equity is most effectively embedded when inspiring educators of colour occupy a wide range of positions throughout the school – as teachers, leaders, governors, trustees and operational staff. This part of the book examines the link between racially minoritised learners seeing themselves represented on staff and governing bodies and feeling a true sense of belonging, entitlement and ambition. It considers the reasons why we currently fail to appoint, retain, develop and promote representative proportions of racially minoritised adults in schools and how we might address these barriers. In this chapter we start with recruitment.

DOI: 10.4324/9781003275220-14

The current under-representation problem

We have all heard the depressing testimonies of how, not many decades ago, people of colour attending schools in the UK were actively dissuaded from considering careers as teachers. Malorie Blackman, who went on to become a celebrated author and the Children's Laureate, related in an interview with Sian Cain that she was told very directly by a careers adviser at school that 'Black people don't become teachers' (2021). When schoolgirl Betty Campbell told her headteacher that she would like to become a teacher, the response was that the problems would be 'insurmountable.' Deflated, but fortunately not deterred, Betty went on to become the first Black headteacher in Wales.

Stories such as these explain why most readers, especially if educated in non-metropolitan areas, may struggle to remember any teachers of colour at the schools they attended. But the data relating to diversity in the profession today also make sobering reading.

As we saw in Chapter 2, a third of all school children in the UK are from ethnic minorities: the Department for Education's school data for 2020 shows that in primary schools 33.9% of pupils are from racially minoritised backgrounds and in secondary schools the figure is 32.3%. Yet the teaching workforce in England's schools and colleges does not reflect the diversity of the student population. DfE 2020 data shows that 88.6% of nursery and primary teachers are White British, 82.2% of secondary school teachers, and 86.1% of special school teachers. 46% of English schools have no teachers at all from Black, Asian or ethnic minority backgrounds and 26% of schools have no racially minoritised staff in any role, teaching or support (Tereshchenko, Mills & Bradbury (2021:8)). Staff of colour are concentrated in London and other metropolitan areas. In its 2018 data, the DfE reported that only 3% of headteachers come from ethnic minority backgrounds. In the following three years, little changed: the DfE's 2021 School Teacher Workforce data reported that 85.1% of teachers and 92.7% of head teachers are White British.

Under-representation is an issue amongst governors and trustees also. In a 2020 survey conducted by the National Governance Association, 94% of governors and trustees who responded identified as White. Only 1% of respondents identified as Black, African, Caribbean or Black British, 2% identified as Asian or Asian British and 1% identified as of mixed or multiple ethnic groups. The figure improved slightly to 93% in 2021. As reported by James Carr in *Schools Week*, then Secretary of State for Education, Nadhim Zahawi, called in November 2021 for greater diversity across the sector, saying it was 'vital' that boards reflect the 'diversity and richness' of school communities. Addressing the NGA annual conference, he stated: 'We need to do more to encourage those who may not ever have considered volunteering as a governor or trustee but who still have so much to offer, who could bring a fresh perspective perhaps or a specific skill that a board really needs' and that governing boards 'especially need more young people and more people from multi-ethnic backgrounds to come forward.' Worryingly, in September 2022,

Amy Walker wrote in *Schools Week* that a further drop in the number of racially minoritised governors and trustees had been reported by the NGA: just 6% school governors and trustees who responded to their annual survey were Black, Asian or minority ethnic, compared to 7% in 2021.

The problem of under-representation of people of colour in the teaching profession appears to be exacerbated by an ethnic inequality in acceptance rates onto teacher training courses. As cited by Rhia Gibbs in a 2022 essay in *Diverse Educators: A Manifesto*, UCAS data for 2020 shows that White teacher training applicants had an acceptance rate of 71.8% compared to 48% for Black applicants. Another contributory factor is the legislation that does not recognise the teaching qualifications of teachers from the majority of nations with predominantly Black and Brown populations. Teachers wishing to gain QTS to teach in the UK have a significantly easier route if they are from the EU, EEA (European Economic Area), Gibraltar, Australia, New Zealand, Canada, USA or Switzerland than anywhere else in the world.

This data would suggest that we have a long way to go to improve access routes into careers in education, at entry level and even more to the higher tiers, and to present the profession as inclusive and attractive to people of colour. But how commonly known are these inequalities? How keenly are they felt by those responsible for recruiting, promoting and developing teachers, operational staff, governors and trustees? And what can be done to achieve greater ethnic diversity in our education system?

Uncovering the scale of the problem and declaring a determination to address it

It isn't always easy to calculate exact figures around the ethnic composition of staff groups. It will clearly be simpler in a small village primary school than across a large trust, county or region. For very understandable reasons, employees may prefer not to declare their ethnicity and many people of colour find the ethnic categories used by employers problematic. In her book *Why Are All The Black Kids Sitting Together In The Cafeteria?*, Beverly Daniel Tatum says 'The language we use to categorise each other racially is imperfect. These categories are still evolving… The original creation of racial categories was in the service of oppression. Some may argue that to continue to use them is to continue that oppression.' She continues, 'Yet it is difficult to talk about what is essentially a flawed and problematic social construct *(race)* without using language that is itself problematic' (2021:97). Furthermore, the fact that the data collected may be imperfect is not an acceptable reason for failing to carry out this analysis: we will never impact the problem if we cannot track our progress.

When school leaders and governors do analyse their workforce by ethnicity, they invariably find under-representation of people of colour, relative to the percentages of children of colour in the UK education system. And that feels very uncomfortable. It can lead to defensive explanations ('We don't tend to get many applications from people of colour') or 'justifications' ('This is a very White area') and such responses can result, worryingly, in subsequent inertia ('We'd love to appoint some BAME staff but they clearly aren't out there so there's not much we can do').

However, some leaders feel sufficiently moved by the under-representation they have uncovered that they determine to signal in the wording of future recruitment material their openness and desire to receive applications from people of colour. You will have read statements in job packs along the lines of 'We are an equal opportunities employer,' 'We are keen to have a diverse workforce' or 'We are an inclusive school and welcome applications from suitably qualified applicants regardless of race, gender, disability etc.' Such statements, I would argue, do little to 'own' the problem or attract applicants from minority ethnic communities. In fact, they may be seen as tokenistic and put people of colour off. The 'regardless of...' wording is actually, I would suggest, rather offensive!

When I have challenged leaders in the past around what are sometimes called 'vanilla' statements of inclusivity, I have been presented with two types of nervousness:

Some colleagues have verbalised a concern about admitting that there is an issue of lack of ethnic diversity at their school. This is articulated as a worry that candidates of colour may be put off applying to the school if they sense that it has a predominantly White workforce. We will return to this issue later in the chapter, but my response (informed by conversations with many people of colour) is always to say that to acknowledge the problem and a desire to redress it sends a very strong message of genuine anti-racist commitment to a potential applicant. Where analysis of the ethnic breakdown of staff shows a lack of diversity, I would encourage leaders to discuss the findings openly with staff, governors/trustees, students and parents. This shows a healthy level of accountability and ownership and could well lead to very profitable discussion as to possible strategies and actions that could be taken to redress the balance.

The other understandable source of nervousness derives, ironically, from the Equalities Act itself. Miller (2021:10) writes that 'The Equality Act 2010 stipulates that it is illegal to discriminate against anyone with nine protected characteristics in any area of public life, including in recruitment and progression. However, the Act also stipulates that it is illegal to take any of the protected characteristics into account when making decisions about recruitment or progression.' This leads Miller to conclude that the law acts 'both as a lock and a key' or as 'both the motor and handbrake of progress as far as equality practice is concerned.' Notwithstanding this challenge, it is perfectly possible to state a commitment to diversity in recruitment messaging. How much more powerful than the somewhat platitudinous phrases above would a statement along the following lines be:

We strive to achieve a diverse workforce, fully representative of our pluralistic society and the ethnic make-up of the student population in the UK. People of colour are currently under-represented on our staff team/governing board. We are keen to attract applications from a diverse pool of candidates and determined to be a fully inclusive employer, and a great workplace for people of Black, Asian and ethnic minority heritage as well as White heritage.

Remember, it is not illegal to encourage applications from a particular demographic. In *Maybe I Don't Belong Here*, David Harewood comments that, when he went to LA as an actor, he was struck at his first audition by the message printed in bold at the top of the signing in sheet which read 'Please send more actors of colour. These roles are open to all ethnicities' (2021: 174).

What does a genuine commitment to achieving an ethnically diverse staff body look like? We all know that we are far more likely to strive to achieve a goal if it is publicly declared and regularly revisited. Schools which open their recruitment policy with a bold commitment to attract and appoint a greater number of people of colour are demonstrating that they mean business. Leadership teams, governing bodies and trust boards that have open and rigorous debate about what success would look like in terms of the number or proportion of people of colour in various roles within the institution are more likely to keep a central focus on this agenda. Discussions that involve considering the pros and cons of setting numerical targets and what might make appropriate targets that show commitment to tracking progress and gauging success.

Have you analysed your staff/governing/trust body make-up by ethnicity?

And shared the outcomes with staff, students and governors/trustees in order to generate debate?

Do you have a statement in your recruitment literature designed to encourage applicants from racially minoritised backgrounds?

If so, is it strong enough to catch the attention of applicants you would like to attract? How do you know? Have you asked people of colour for their views?

Have you considered setting targets for establishing a more diverse workforce? Who has been involved in such discussions? What might success look like in your school's/trust's context?

Some schools and trusts have set themselves a goal of, for example, ensuring that the ethnic diversity of the staff reflects that of the student body within five years and have then agreed annual milestone objectives for each interim year. Others have applied the Rooney Rule (named after former National Football League diversity chair Dan Rooney) when recruiting to certain posts: this is the practice of ensuring that at least one racially minoritised candidate is shortlisted for the post, provided they meet the minimum requirements. Jon Coles, CEO of United Learning, explained, in an interview with Tom Belger, that his Trust had decided to adopt the Rooney Rule in recognition of the fact that 'something was going wrong. We had great people, appointed on merit, but they didn't look like our students.'

It is important to acknowledge that this is a controversial issue. Not only is it illegal to recruit a weaker candidate over one who meets the person specification more demonstrably and objectively, simply to fulfil a race quota or target, but such practice is also insulting to people of colour. No one wants to feel that they have been offered a job because they are from a minority ethnic group or to be offered a post for which they are not as qualified or capable as other candidates. The footballer Thierry Henry, quoted by Michael Holding in *Why We Kneel, How We Rise* (2021:235) says 'I'm a winner. I'm a competitor. So don't give me a free ride. Don't give Black people jobs because it's a good thing to do. I want a fair call.' Holding reflects that 'If you start filling positions...because you need to tick a box based on ethnicity...instead of employing the best person for the job, you don't solve a problem, you create one.' He adds, 'That person may not be capable of doing the job...How is that good for inspiring someone or being a role model? It will also embolden the racists who can stoke resentment, arguing, 'Told you they shouldn't be there' or shouting, 'Look, they're taking our jobs and they can't do them' (2021:239). Sufian Sadiq, Director of the Teaching School for The Chiltern Learning Trust, speaking at the Great Representation seminar in December 2021, said 'I don't want positive discrimination. I don't want to be the solution to your problem.'

However, setting objectives around ensuring that job descriptions and person specifications don't disadvantage people of colour and implementing actions and strategies that are likely to result in the generation of a greater volume of applications from people of colour is neither risky nor contentious. We will return to this a little later in the chapter.

Getting people on board: ensuring clarity about why lack of staff diversity is such a problem

In my experience, many schools set about attempting to address the lack of diversity amongst the adults they employ without having taken the time at the outset to reflect on why a predominantly or solely White workforce is an issue. It is perhaps assumed that everyone will see this state of affairs as problematic and feel equally compelled to take action. Also, it can be assumed that everyone has a common understanding of the reasons why lack of staff diversity is a problem, when in fact there are a multitude of different reasons, some more or less applicable in different contexts.

As a headteacher, I was committed to ensuring that my students saw themselves reflected in the staff and governors of the school, but I do not recall creating the time and space to discuss what motivated me to seek diversity or to compare my drivers with those of my peers or the governors. I wish I had, for together I know we would have produced a compelling set of reasons which would have made an arresting case if laid out in our recruitment policy. In recent years, since working in a very geographically diverse county with some schools serving largely White populations, I have been challenged on several occasions as to why it is so important to strive for ethnic diversity in the staff body if the representation is broadly in line with, or indeed greater than, that in the student body. Such challenges can come when least expected and from various quarters (parents, governors, trustees) and it is much better to have rehearsed the response in anticipation of the need to present a strong argument when the circumstance arises than to be caught off guard and ill-prepared.

I'd strongly advise undertaking an activity with students, staff and governors/ trustees if you haven't already to brainstorm all the reason why staff diversity, at every level in the organisation, is so important and enriching for everyone in the educational community. When I did this, in a remote training session in breakout rooms, with my team of consultants and advisers a couple of years ago, we came up with the following list:

1. It is important for children of colour to see themselves reflected in the staff who teach and guide them.

2. White staff have limited understanding and experience of the diverse heritages and lived experiences of their racially minoritised pupils.

3. The student population may be predominantly White at the moment, but the demography of the UK is changing and there will be an increasing proportion of children of colour in all UK schools over the coming years.

4. Children are gaining experience at school for life in the wider world and that is a multi-racial world.

5. It is no more healthy to have an all-White staff body in a school with little racial diversity than it is to have an all-male staff in a boys' school or an or all-female staff in a girls' school.

6. A school led by all White leaders is less well-placed to eliminate racial inequity.

7. Unless we have strong minority ethnic role models in the education profession, it will always be hard to persuade students of colour to become teachers.

Let's unpack each of these reasons a bit more.

It is important for children of colour to see themselves reflected in the staff who teach and guide them

White people need to remind themselves regularly of how infrequently ethnic representation is experienced in society, and in school, by most people of colour. Jeffrey Boakye comments that 'Growing up Black and British was like a cultural "Where's Wally?", searching for racial representations of myself in a very white (specifically British, even more specifically, English) landscape' (2019:10–11).

The importance of racially minoritised children being able to see themselves reflected in the staff around them, and who teach and lead them, was illustrated perfectly by a tweet that I read a while ago from a primary teacher who shared that the previous week she had been talking to a Year 4 pupil who was overjoyed when the teacher told her that she was Ghanaian like the girl. The pupil even asked the teacher to speak Twi to prove it. The tweet said that when she saw the same girl again, she started telling her friends, 'she's just like me!'

To be a sole child of colour or one of very few minority ethnic children at school can be extremely isolating. When I conduct race equity reviews in schools, I always talk to children of colour about their experiences of school. They speak movingly of how much it means to them to see Black and Brown people represented in class-room displays, to come across a Black or Brown protagonist or hero in a book and, most importantly, to have adults around them who look like them, share cultural and linguistic references and with whom they can connect with ease. Invariably they can list every adult of colour in the school community, however infrequently they are likely to interact with them: 'There is a Black English teacher but I have never been taught by her and one of the lab technicians is Indian and I heard that the careers adviser comes from Somalia.' I was similarly struck by how vividly the teachers and leaders I interviewed could recall precisely how many staff of colour there were in the schools they attended as pupils and taught in at various stages of their career, even citing the names and roles of people they had not seen for 40 years.

We know how powerful and impactful good relationships are between staff and pupils. And it makes sense that children are more likely to form strong bonds with adults with whom they feel a connection and have something in common. A study in the United States, referenced by Irena Barker in *TES*, found that Black students of both sexes were more likely to graduate if they had at least one Black teacher in grades 3–5 (Years 4–6 in the UK), the effect being greatest for boys from low-income backgrounds. Paul Miller, speaking at a Great Representation conference in September 2021, reflected that 'the co-existence of the Black child and the Black teacher is significant: I see you. I hear you. I belong.' Children of colour get a sense of security, safety and entitlement from being surrounded by adults of colour; the sense of belonging that White children have every minute of every day. And we know that we perform best when we feel safe and entitled, when we are not having to decode every message because it is culturally or linguistically alien to us. It is logical that such conditions lead to greater attainment.

It is also logical that children of colour will respond better innately to being pushed, challenged and stretched by adults with whom they can make a natural connection. One teacher I spoke to during a race review of a predominantly White secondary school shared an interesting observation when telling me about a Black student who was displaying challenging behaviour and whose punctuality was an issue. She described how the girl would frequently fly off the handle when challenged for arriving late to class. On one particular day, the teacher had invited a guest speaker to the lesson, a local African poet. The girl arrived 10 minutes after the session had started and the poet was in full flow. The guest chastised the girl quite publicly in front of the class. The teacher held her breath, fully aware that, had she handled the situation in this way, it would have most likely resulted in a verbal outburst from the girl. To her amazement, the student apologised and sat down quietly. She then listened attentively, hanging on the poet's every word. The rapport between the two, the teacher reflected, was tangible and powerful to observe.

White staff have limited understanding and experience of the diverse heritages and lived experiences of their racially minoritised pupils

Many White staff who teach and work in schools invest considerable time and effort educating themselves about the culture and heritage of the racially minoritised groups represented in and beyond their school communities and striving to increase their racial literacy. When I was a teacher in the East End of London at a school in which 97% of the students were Bangladeshi, I made it my business to brush up on my knowledge of South-East Asian history, to learn about the features of Sylhet (the region from which the pupils' families originated) and to teach myself some Bengali phrases. I spent time getting to know the local area, forging relations with the East London mosque, shopping at the Brick Lane markets and, in my role as senior teacher overseeing community liaison, meeting with parents and visiting a number of homes. I was honoured to receive invites to key family events and gained cultural and religious insights from attending weddings of siblings of children I taught. Yet, I would be the first to admit that my understanding of Bengali culture was elementary at best. No amount of time spent with members of the community could compensate for my lack of the lived experience of the Bengali families. It was crucially important that the school employed staff from the Bengali community to help the staff body ensure that the needs of the families were fully met and that they received an equitable education.

All schools will declare that they are committed to achieving equality, diversity and inclusion; many will have an EDI lead teacher. But if they do not have people of colour on their staff and governing bodies, how can they really know that their policies, systems and procedures are achieving EDI? It is much more difficult to hear and respond to the voice and perspectives of those most affected by race equity issues if you are a White only or predominantly White group of staff, or to look at practices through the lens of race equity if you have never experienced racism yourself. Can you imagine a group of male only staff being asked to evaluate the success of a school in tackling the Everyone's Invited agenda?

If the school population is ethnically diverse and the staff and governing body isn't, it is much harder for them to truly represent and have the confidence of the pupils and the community. We all lack awareness of cultures that are different to our own. White staff will inevitably lack cultural awareness in relation to their racially minoritised students and that is problematic. I recall a time when, as a headteacher in East London of a school with a sizeable Pakistani population, I received a complaint from a group of parents that some of the staff who had led a residential trip to Barcelona had got drunk one evening when out having a meal with the students. It was a very sensitive matter to investigate and resolve. The (White) staff who had organised the trip were committed and highly responsible professionals who had given up their precious holiday to lead an educational trip for their pupils. They freely admitted that some of them had had a small glass of wine with their meal one evening but they were wounded that this had been seen and interpreted by some of the pupils as the staff being drunk. They struggled to empathise with the perception of teenage girls, brought up in a Mirpuri Muslim tradition, who felt concerned and anxious about the behaviour of some of the adults. Had there been a more ethnically diverse group of staff on the trip, the issue would probably not have arisen.

Racially minoritised leaders are able to draw on their own experiences to challenge racial stereotypes and drive changes in their schools, helping to address issues of discrimination and create more inclusive environments. My interviewees spoke of how they confront issues of racism through their teaching; Rubia explained that she frequently addresses topical race issues with her classes and incorporates references to equality and diversity in her Maths lessons.

Antonina Tereshchenko and Martin Mills say in an article for *Impact Magazine* in 2021: 'Teachers from minority ethnic groups are in a position to provide culturally sensitive teaching and to understand, communicate or identify with students from non-dominant cultural and linguistic backgrounds in ways in which non-minority educators are unable to do.' She explains that 'minority ethnic teachers use their cultural knowledge and own experience as "other" to develop deeper understandings of minority students and their needs. Exposure to teachers from a similar background thus has the potential to help disadvantaged students from minority groups, in greater danger of school exclusion and drop-out than their white peers, to attain greater educational success.'

The student population may be predominantly White at the moment, but the demography of the UK is changing and there will be an increasing proportion of children of colour in all UK schools over the coming years. Children are gaining experience at school for life in the wider world and that is a multi-racial world.

These two arguments are inter-related, so I shall respond to them together.

It is even more important that there is staff and governor/trustee diversity where the number of children of colour is small as the degree of isolation felt by them is likely to be greater. Furthermore, if the local community is predominantly White, it is likely to be harder for the staff to draw from a pool of inspiring role models from ethnically diverse backgrounds to come to the school as visitors, speakers, assembly deliverers and prize-givers. There is a real danger that the children will progress through school seeing no one but White adults, which is hugely problematic given that, as educators, we are preparing our children to thrive in a country and society that is racially diverse. It is tempting for White staff to console themselves with arguments that perhaps they are more sensitive to the lack of ethnic diversity than their pupils, especially the younger ones. But this does not wash. Ibram X Kendi in *How to be an Anti-Racist*, describes going to look around a potential school with his parents when aged seven. They were taken on a tour by a Black teacher but the young Ibram noticed that in all the class photos on the walls the teachers were White. He asked the direct and perceptive question 'Are you the only Black teacher in the school?' (2019:36). It is precisely in Early Years and Key Stage 1 that we most need to ensure that children are surrounded by ethnically diverse educators as it is in the formative years that our views on race and equality are fashioned.

White children living in White areas need to have their experiences challenged, their horizons widened and their cultural capital enriched. As they progress from one school to the next and then to higher education, training or the world of work in society at large, it is important that they are equipped with the skills to respect, understand, gel with and relate to new and diverse people. The demographic make-up of the UK is rapidly changing: Hashi Mohamed says that 'between 2004 and 2017, the foreign-born population of the UK grew from 5.3 million to nearly 9.4 million' (2020:59). If White children lack opportunities to encounter and see people of colour in a range of roles, there is a danger that biases, stereotypes and even an unconscious 'fear of the unknown' could develop. In *Sway*, Pragya Agarwal writes powerfully of how 'in group' and 'out group' bias works: 'the more positive contact we have with people from different ethnic groups, the less likely we are to form the notion of threat associated with unfamiliar faces' (2020:93). This leads us on nicely to the next point.

It is no more healthy to have an all-White staff body in a school with little racial diversity than it is to have an all-male staff in a boys' school or an or all-female staff in a girls' school. A school led by all White leaders is susceptible to group think and less well placed to eliminate racial inequity.

These two arguments are also linked.

Matthew Syed's book *Rebel Ideas* is a powerful manifesto to the power of diverse thinking. In it he cites numerous examples of the 'collective blindness' that groups which lack diversity in their make-up are susceptible to. Blindness, for example, to procedures and practices that might unintentionally cause or perpetuate systemic race inequity. In *The Power of Privilege* June Sarpong, citing a McKinsey study of 2015, explains why this might be the case: 'diverse teams have been proven to be smarter and more effective than homogenous ones; they have a tendency to focus more on facts; are more objective; process data more carefully; and are more innovative' (2020:21–22). If decision makers are too similar to each other in background, experiences and heritage, they are inevitably considering issues through a narrow lens and unlikely to make the best decisions. Smart leaders seek racial diversity in their staff, governor and trustee teams in order to be as effective as possible.

Sally Tattersfield, writing in *Impact Magazine*, stresses that racially minoritised students need to see that people like them can succeed as inspiring educational professionals and leaders. She argues that 'it matters for the staff who will benefit from the diversity and it matters for society and the future' (2021:38). If those people with power in our school – staff, senior leaders, governors and trustees – are all White, what sort of message is that sending our students about how things should be, our beliefs about equality and our commitment to inclusion and diversity? In a school with predominantly White students, it is even more important that students see people of colour achieving success in positions of power, to challenge their assumptions and open their eyes. If staff of colour do not see people like them in leadership, this is a barrier.

Unless we have strong ethnic minority role models in the education profession, it will always be hard to persuade students of colour to become teachers

When Paul Miller shared the mantra at one of my race equity conferences of 'I see you, I hear you, I belong' he added to it: 'I can be that.'

I had the pleasure of hearing the scientist and doctor Kevin Fong speak at a headteachers' conference in October 2021. He explained that he wanted to be a scientist as a result of watching Starship Enterprise as a child and seeing someone like him, a person of East Asian heritage, piloting the Enterprise – one of the actors/characters looked like him. He said that his friend, the journalist and broadcaster Samira Ahmed, had told him that the show had had a similar impression on her. He reflected that in 1970s popular media Black, Asian and minority ethnic people were nowhere to be seen except in science fiction!

Students of colour benefit from seeing staff of colour in leadership positions, as role models for them. The reverse is also sadly the case. I remember well some poignant comments made by two 14-year-old students I interviewed when conducting a school race review recently. They were part of a larger group who were taking part in a student voice activity. When the session ended and everyone left the room, these two girls hung back, clearly wanting to talk further. One of them reflected that at her primary school there were no Black or Asian teachers. She said that it wasn't until she came to the secondary school that she had ever considered that people of colour might be teachers. I asked the girls (one African and one Asian) whether teaching was a career that interested them. They said that, although they now knew that it was possible to become a teacher as a person of colour, the fact that it was 'so unusual' made them think that it would not be a profession in which they would feel comfortable. Maybe things have not changed much since the days when Malorie Blackman and Betty Campbell were schoolgirls. As David Harewood, quoted by Afua Hirsch in *Brit(ish)* says, 'A lack of diversity breeds a lack of diversity' (2018:230). We desperately need to increase numbers of staff of colour in schools to augment the number of graduates of colour entering the profession, in order to accelerate the pace at which we work to eliminate racism in education.

As Hashi Mohamed stresses in *People Like Us*, 'Never underestimate the power of seeing someone who looks like you – someone with whom you share a similar background, someone whose struggles you may relate to – occupying a place where you hope to be one day' (2020:4).

Having established why it is so important that our schools have ethnically diverse staff and governor/trustee bodies, how can school leaders achieve success in appointing staff from a broad range of heritages?

This is a task in two parts: firstly attracting applications from people of colour and secondly ensuring that these candidates are able to demonstrate their potential in the appointment process.

Attracting racially minoritised applicants for teaching posts

Schools spend thousands of pounds on advertisements for staff. Sadly, they are often read by a very small and unrepresentative pool of potential applicants. By tracking applications received over time for different types of posts and sorting them by ethnicity and by the place in which the candidate heard about the job, it is possible to gauge those publications and social media channels more likely to be read/visited by people from minority ethnic communities. For example, you could find that using *The Voice* or *Black Men Teach* to advertise for teachers from the Black community is more effective than using the *TES*. Many schools now make use of Twitter to promote vacancies, in the knowledge that the followers of their staff represent a more diverse population than the readership of some national recruitment sites. When recruiting recently for director posts at HFL Education, we promoted our roles on the following Diversity Networks, amongst others:

- Diversity Channel – Diversity Jobsite Official UK BME Recruitment Job Board

- Asian Media Channel – Asian Jobsite is dedicated to e-recruitment within the Asian community

- BAME Channel – Ethnic Jobsite Official Site for Diversity Network.

Some posts are more suited to advertisement on local forums, in local papers and on local notice boards. As a head, I was always keen to ensure that a healthy proportion of my staff came from and lived in the local area, as I knew that their insight into and investment in the community that the school served would enrich the school. I was fortunate in that the area was extremely ethnically diverse so an advert in a local community centre would be likely to result in applications from people of colour. In a mono-ethnic area this requires a bit more thought.

Christine Callender, in a talk to the Great Representation programme in January 2022, advised that schools wanting to attract a more diverse pool of applicants to teaching posts should seek to make links with training providers and universities, to attract the attention of people of colour amongst cohorts of trainees.

Attracting racially minoritised governors and trustees

I was recently asked by a senior leader of a school in a very White part of Hertfordshire how she might go about reaching members of minority ethnic communities with an advert for a governor. My advice was to

1. target the town three miles down the road which had a much more ethnically diverse demographic

2. publicise the vacancy on the school website and in the headteacher's newsletter, with a clear message about the school's desire to increase the ethnic diversity of the governing body (and the reasons for this)

3. approach key parents of colour to ask for their support and to seek their suggestions as to where else to advertise the role

4. ask key contacts from the community (at the local mosque, gurdwara, temple, synagogue, companies and organisations owned and run by Black, Asian and minority ethnic business people, CEOs and leaders) for support in promoting the vacancy

5. contact ex-students of colour to explore possible interest in becoming a governor.

Where do you advertise your a. teaching posts, b. operational/support staff posts and c. governor/trust vacancies and why?

Could you increase the diversity of your applicant pool by diversifying the places in which you advertise?

Who could support you with ideas for effective places to advertise?

In 2021, a group of governors from Camden schools, with logistical support from Camden Learning, conducted some research into the experiences of racially minoritised governors, leading to the production of a set of recommendations for increasing the diversity of governing boards. These included:

Improve promotional materials for governors, including where and how vacancies are advertised

Governing bodies should consider how they promote governor vacancies, ensuring that these are appealing and accessible to all our communities. This should include simpler language, a clear explanation of the support and training available, and a reasonable assessment of the commitment required.

These updated materials should be tested with people from Black, Asian and other ethnic groups to ensure their effectiveness as part of the outreach recommendation.

Other specific recommendations to schools are:

● Ensure that parents are approached early – as the children enter the school system – to normalise spending time as a school Governor. Year 7 and Nursery is crucial for this.

● Use the student and the school council members to speak to their parents and promote the idea of being a school governor, with a particular focus on the benefits of a diverse governing body.

● Make better use of video in promoting the role of School Governor, using community languages.

● Consider the blend of in-person and online meetings and whether the latter is more likely to attract diverse governors.

Better explain and promote the roles of governors and governing bodies across our ethnic communities, demystifying the role with outreach work and promotional events

Work together with governors from Black, Asian and other ethnic communities to develop a strategy for community outreach, which will aim to promote the role of governor amongst Camden's diverse communities. This may involve visits to community associations, places of worship and supplementary schools, and will serve to promote the role, sense check the promotional activity, deepen understanding of school governance and inform further development in this area.

Conduct a review of the application process and how it works for Black, Asian and other ethnic communities

Schools should review their applications processes to ensure that these are not disadvantaging or discouraging individuals from any community (2021:14–15).

One of my interviewees advises school leaders to 'call BAME parents and tell them "Your school needs YOU to be a school governor" and to talk to BAME parents at parents' evenings or events to encourage them to become governors and to explain the post in person.'

Lydia Bower, in a Diverse Ed blog of 5 May 2021, states that 'The changes we saw in 2020, specifically the move to virtual governance, has opened up the possibility of having remote governors join boards.' She stresses that 'This new way of meeting has led to an increase in the number of schools now considering remote governance and inviting those who don't live locally to join the board. It's an opportunity for boards to get the perspective and experience they need and opens up hard-to-reach vacancies to a wider pool of volunteers.'

At Isaac Newton Academy one of the founding cohort of students, Adarsh Ramchurn, who is of Mauritian descent, sits on the local governing board. His recent experience of having been a student at the school and his links to the immediate community are invaluable to the board.

Smart leaders ensure that they keep in touch with their alumni and encourage them to consider returning to the school to support with careers days, mock interviews, to work as volunteers at summer schools, sports coaches or intervention tutors, to apply to join the governing body or the staff team as teaching assistants or teachers. In ethnically diverse communities this is a great way to ensure good representation amongst the adults in the school community.

Adarsh's story

Initially, the idea of being a governor for the school sprouted whilst I was studying in the sixth form. I wanted to give back to the school that had provided a lot for me in my personal development journey. I had a conversation with the Principal, Ms Spencer, one day when I passed her in the corridor. I just posed the question; one day would it be possible to be a governor of the school? I spoke about how other governors at the school coming to visit the students had a positive impact and inspired me to potentially one day become a school governor. Her response was great; she said that it would, of course, be possible.

Fast forward to the completion of my A-Levels, and I had started my degree apprenticeship in Business Management with Social Change. In December 2019, INA students were invited to come back into the school to collect their A-Level certificates. There was also a gathering where we could reconnect with our teachers to let them know how university was going. I was in conversation with Ms Spencer again, and she posed the question:'Would I like to be a governor of the school?' I was pleasantly surprised, but knew I definitely wanted to contribute to the school in a positive manner. A few months later, I was able to join the governing body.

As a former student on the governing body, I've found the experience rewarding and captivating. Seeing the decision making, influence and challenge that the governing body brings to the school was unique and seeing it from the perspective of a governor as a former student was eye-opening. I think that having been a student helps when it comes to being a governor. I've always had an opinion of what the school is really great at, what makes it special, but also where it can improve to really enhance student learning and experience. This has helped me contribute and offer my thoughts, experiences and know-how, as well as act as a voice for students, which I think is really important for a board to offer and understand.

I also hope I bring my experience of growing up in Ilford and the area to the board. I think there is a huge underrepresentation of young people from diverse backgrounds on boards across businesses and organisation, but particularly in schools. I hope that by being on the board I can act as a role model to students.

The following case study shows the methods employed by one school to recruit more governors of colour.

Bishop's Hatfield Girls' School Case Study

Our governing body does not reflect our pupil population in terms of race: around 40% of the pupil cohort is BAME yet we had just one governor from a BAME background. We recognised that this lack of diversity amongst our governing body had the potential to narrow our decision-making. As headteacher, I presented to governor committees and to the full governing body the reasons why I felt it was important to try to diversify our membership The FGB agreed that we needed to take a more pro-active stance and that we should work to co-opt onto the FGB a governor to champion equality and diversity. The Chair and I then wrote to the whole school community, encouraging them to express an interest in joining the governing body. The letter said:

'The governors of the school (also known as the Trustees) are keen to promote and encourage diversity at Bishop's. We are aware that our current group of governors do not fully reflect the diverse make-up of our pupil population and would like to change this. We recognize that bringing different skills, backgrounds and experiences to our membership is likely to improve decision-making and also give our pupils strong role models that they can relate to.

We are therefore seeking to bring onto our Governing Body new co-opted governors who feel that they can represent and champion diversity at Bishop's. In particular, we would like to increase representation from the BAME community. Co-option means that there is no requirement for an election and anyone joining the Governing Body would become a Community Governor for a four year term.

If you are interested in finding out more about this opportunity to help shape and uphold the strategic vision of our school please get in touch with either of us via the school email. Alternatively, you may feel that you know somebody else who would be well suited to the role who is not necessarily a parent/carer at Bishop's and we would be interested in hearing from them too. This could be a family member, work colleague or friend.

We look forward to hearing from you and would be happy to answer any questions you may have.'

Historically, there have been very few nominations when parent governor vacancies arise and no need to hold an election since the field is so small. The response to our letter for a diversity champion was fantastic. We had 12 expressions of interest. These were followed up with a Zoom meeting with myself and the Chair where we talked through our aims and aspirations and answered questions. We asked those still interested to write to us, briefly outlining what they felt they could bring to the body. The majority of the 12 did this and we have taken the decision to co-opt two new governors, both from BAME backgrounds.

The Camden governors' research in 2021 into the experiences of governors from minority ethnic groups in Camden schools shows that having a close connection with a school, as a former pupil, increased the likelihood of a person of colour applying to become a governor. The familiarity with the setting and determination to improve ethnic representation on the board overrode any anxiety about not fitting in: 'I knew the (first) school (where the interviewee was a governor). I knew the teachers because I went there myself. So, I felt comfortable. I felt at home. And so, I was confident and comfortable. At the primary school and the second time being a parent governor, I didn't feel part of the board because I was the only BAME person, everybody else was white' (2021:9).

Attracting people of colour to apply to work in majority White schools

Once a person of colour has heard about a vacancy at your school what do you do to persuade them to apply to work with you, especially if they would be joining a predominantly White workforce?

There are many factors that attract staff to work in particular schools: proximity to family, the Ofsted rating, the academic track record of the pupils and the reputation for positive behaviour for learning being common considerations. Added to this, for many people of colour the ethnic diversity of the school population is, understandably, a key priority. Yasmin told me that, having done her teaching practice in a tiny village school in Northamptonshire where the children had never seen anyone like her 'I knew I didn't want to work in a school like that. I applied for a job back in Southall (where I had grown up). The head was Asian, lots of the staff were Asian, 95% of my class was Asian.'

Many Black, Asian and minority ethnic teachers gravitate to London, drawn in part by the diversity of the population. Around 35% of teachers in outer London and 40% in inner London are from racially minoritised groups. Staff of colour express a preference for more diverse schools. For Rubia 'working in London was a significant factor which I felt would open opportunities to work in diverse settings. Having mostly attended predominantly White schools/colleges as a student I was excited to be in BAME settings.' For Ayeesha the pull of London was both the opportunity to work in an ethnically diverse environment and also to serve disadvantaged communities: 'I was asked to apply for an NQT job in Dorset after my PGCE, which I flatly turned down. My reason was mostly because I was not White (and a little because it wasn't London which was where I was looking). I didn't feel I had anything to offer schools in Dorset because I felt I didn't share anything with the community. I disliked my first placement so much I wanted to leave the course; the entire community was White and I was the only PoC. Thankfully, I was only there for 10 weeks! I will not work in a school which is mainly White and middle-class. I want to empower communities who are the "underdog" rather than groups who already have a culture of aspiration and cultural capital. I firmly believe in education as a leveller.'

Given the above, I frequently remind school leaders that most potential applicants will peruse their website to get a feel for the school and advise them to take a close and objective look at the messages conveyed through this window to the school. The following are all features of websites that I have seen when conducting race audits that would be likely to put off a person of colour from applying to a school:

- No images of Black or Brown pupils, despite the school's having an ethnically diverse population.

- No photos of Black or Brown staff or governors/trustees, despite there being some.

- Culturally exclusive references in policies e.g. rulings about no braids or hair extensions in the uniform policy or no reference to headscarves or turbans/top knots for Muslim or Sikh pupils (even when, in reality, provision is made for these requirements and accessories).

- Euro and Christian centric references in details of PTA activities, such as Christmas Fairs and BBQs.

In contrast, I have seen websites for schools which serve quite mono-cultural areas with the following features:

- Prominent statements from the student council, staff body and governors/trustees about the school's commitment to an anti-racist culture and the BLM agenda.

- Details of the current EO and EDI objectives that the school is striving to attain and progress made towards their goals.

- Soundbites (with photos) from a range of students, including children of colour, about the school's induction practices, leadership opportunities and inclusive ethos.

- Testimonials given by staff of colour.

- Staff team photos with Black and Brown staff prominently featured.

- Images of staff of colour engaged in staff development activities.

One school website I know has videos of pupils declaring the mantra 'I see you, I hear you, I belong' in all the languages represented in the school's community and a song featuring the same phrase, composed by staff and performed by the pupils. What a statement that makes!

A potential applicant for a post at such a school might well decide that this was an environment in which (s)he could feel safe, valued and honoured and could contribute to a compelling vision. Bonolo told me, 'Now I ensure that diversity is a determining factor when choosing a school. Staff diversity which reflects the make-up of the local community is very important to me. Inclusive policies and statements are also a determining factor when applying for roles.'

When did you last look at your school's website through the eyes of a potential job applicant of colour?

What opportunities are you missing to promote the diversity of your staff, governing and student bodies and to share your EDI practices?

NB: Addressing the above will increase the sense of belonging felt by your racially minoritised children. It will also make your school more attractive to prospective parents of colour considering applying for a place for their child and looking at your website.

Enabling promising applicants of colour to be successful in the recruitment process

Most schools take pride in having robust and formalised selection processes, with detailed job descriptions and person specifications and experienced appointment panels. They design rigorous interview activities (the specifics of which are not shared in advance to guarantee that no external assistance can be offered to the candidate) to ensure that no unfair advantage is given to the first or last interviewee, the internal or the external candidate, the known or unknown applicant. As a head with two decades of interviewing experience, I felt pretty confident that I had eliminated from my schools' recruitment practices any possible opportunities for one candidate to have an unfair advantage over another. I now look back and see all too clearly the pitfalls of our practice.

As we considered in Chapter 6, we all have biases, some conscious and some unconscious. This applies every bit as much when we are engaged in selecting staff as in any other activity. Pragya Agarwal, in *Sway*, argues that the higher your status in the hierarchy, the more biased you are likely to be: 'those who have social privilege …are more likely to use shortcuts that use stereotype-consistent information' (2020:111). And very often appointment panels are all White (a reflection of the under-representation of people of colour in the more senior positions in schools). There is a real danger that, without addressing this head on and discussing it openly, such a panel will find itself unconsciously looking for people like them. Agarwal says 'We are biased towards anything that is more familiar to us, as the repeated exposure is a sort of conditioning signalling about the lack of negative consequences and protecting against the fear of novelty' (2020:185). In *Just Work*, Kim Scott argues that 'the "cultural fit" screen in interviews – ostensibly designed to make sure the person will work well with others on the team – is too often a giant back door for bias, an unconscious code for "looking for someone who looks like us"' (2021:180).

In addition, I am ashamed to admit that I paid insufficient attention as a school leader to the impact that an all-White selection panel might have on candidates of colour. Paul Miller reflects that he has, at times, felt as if he was appearing before a parole board hearing when sitting in front of an all-White panel. I had a Black Assistant Headteacher on the SLT in one of my headships and appointed an Asian Vice Principal and Asian SENCO at INA, as well as many racially minoritised middle leaders, so very often interview panels were ethnically diverse. However, if I were leading a school today, I would make it a requirement of my recruitment policy that all appointment panels must include at least one person of colour.

In addition to ensuring representation of people of colour on panels or confronting the implications of lack of ethnic diversity on the panel with anti-bias training if this is unavoidable, employers like KPMG, HSBC and Deloitte, as well as many schools, have taken steps to minimise unconscious bias in selection processes. One way of doing this is to anonymise CVs and letters of application by redacting the names, ethnicities and other key details of applicants. Anyone who might consider such action unnecessary or excessive should be minded that name bias in recruitment is still, sadly, very much in evidence in the UK. *The Daily Record* ran the story on 2 August 2021 of Scottish health secretary Humza Yousaf being denied a place for his child at the pre-school that he and his wife chose but, on applying again with a Scottish sounding name, being offered a place. In an article for the World Economic Forum in 2017, cited by Hashi Mohamed, Stephanie Thomson refers to several research studies from around the world that all indicate that people with Chinese, Indian, Pakistani and North Africa names are between 28% and 60% less likely to be called for interview than applicants with English sounding names (2020:19).

Tom's experience of name bias

I was recently reacquainted with a member of my tutor group and history class in the early 1990s. Much to my pride, he is now a primary headteacher in Hertfordshire. On a visit to his school to discuss race and unconscious bias, he shared, and subsequently wrote up, the following experience:

My full name is Thomas Mohamed Hassan. My middle name was my paternal grandfather's name; his family had emigrated to British Guyana from India. My paternal grandmother's family had also ended up in Guyana, having emigrated from Madeira. My grandfather moved his family to London in the early 1960s. They quickly integrated into British society. My father married my mother, who is of British and Irish decent.

I would describe my appearance as white, although often people assume I am Turkish or Greek, and culturally my upbringing was what you would expect of a typical White British working-class family. Despite what people assume from my name, I have never entered a mosque and was christened as a Methodist.

Growing up, my name did not initially cause me any undue anxiety. In fact, I would say that I was very proud of it. This was until I entered my mid-teens, when I started to become very aware that I was being judged because of it. I would actively avoid telling people my surname when I met them because, inevitably, it would lead to questions about where I was from, or at the very least a quizzical look. In 1980s/90s North London, at least where I grew up, the term Paki was fairly ubiquitous and widely used to describe anyone of Indian/Pakistani/Bangladeshi heritage. On reflection, I was trying my best to fit in, and didn't want to be thought of as a 'Paki.' As I grew older and Islamophobia began to gain a foothold in society, this added a new nuance to my experience of name bias.

When I finished my A-Levels I opted to have a year out of education before going to university. I needed a job and handed my CV in to a local kitchenware shop who were advertising for help in their window. A week or so passed and the advert was still up so I popped in to ask if they would be shortlisting soon. It was a very busy day and the assistant at the till went to check with the manager. He came out, had a look at me, invited me to his office for chat, and I was offered a trial. I ended up working at the shop for the duration of my gap year and went back during university holidays to earn some extra cash.

I got on well with the owner and would often go for a drink with him after work. On one such occasion, about half way through the year, we were discussing how good the team was and how efficient the whole operation had become and he dropped in to the conversation that if I hadn't come back in to check on the shortlisting process I wouldn't be there as he had taken one look at my name on the application and thrown it in the bin, saying something along the lines of 'not thinking a foreigner would fit in.'

At the time I laughed it off, and even convinced myself this was perfectly normal and something that I just had to deal with. It was never mentioned again.

At HFL Education, the school improvement company for which I work, we started anonymising application forms early in 2021 by redacting the name, age, gender, ethnicity, address, place of work and place of study (e.g. university) of candidates. The HFL Recruitment Team which supports governing and trust boards with the appointment of headteachers across Hertfordshire did the same and encouraged leaders to anonymise applications for all appointments. We also now prominently state that this is our practice on our website and have had feedback from minority ethnic hires that this was one of the details that attracted them to apply for a position with the company. Over the intervening months we have monitored the impact on our internal recruitment. There are early indications that this practice has led to an increase in the number of racially minoritised candidates being called to interview. This, coupled with greater organisational awareness of unconscious bias and ongoing race equity training, has contributed to an increase in hires of people of colour. In July 2018, 36 of 432 (8%) HFL employees surveyed were recorded as identifying as non-white. In March 2022: 67 of 449 (15%) HFL employees identified themselves as non-white.

In a recent evaluation of the process, the HFL Executive team decided to retain anonymisation of names, age, gender and address but to stop redacting the place of employment and places of training or education. The place of study had originally been removed in recognition that students from minority groups are underrepresented at so-called top universities but should not, along with racially minoritised candidates who have studied and qualified abroad, be disadvantaged by this when interviewers considered their CVs. The counter argument posed was that racially minoritised students who have worked their way to study at 'top' universities against the odds should not have this achievement overlooked. We were also finding it hard to determine whether the nature of the courses studied by some applicants would have equipped them for the roles advertised. The rationale for anonymising details of the current employer or school at which the applicant worked was that teachers from minority groups might have found it harder to secure posts at highly regarded institutions and should not be further penalised as a result of any bias they had suffered from earlier in their career. However, for the posts to which we appoint at HFL we tend to look favourably on candidates who have taught in tough environments such as less popular schools and those requiring improvement as this can equip them with a highly desirable skill set for advisory work. Thus, we were finding that the level of redaction we were imposing might actually be disadvantaging candidates from more diverse backgrounds or who had pursued less orthodox careers.

We have also had in-depth discussions at HFL about possible bias in our job descriptions and person specifications. We have taken a hard look at those qualifications, experiences and qualities which are really essential as opposed to just desirable (because they are teachable) in the knowledge that, in a racially unequal society, White Privilege (see Chapter 5) inevitably results in it being harder for racially minoritised candidates to be in a position to tick all of the essential requirements.

A further change we have introduced when interviewing for posts at HFL is to include a question (and follow up discussion) about unconscious bias. We now state the following in our job details packs: 'We encourage you to view our Black Lives Matter statement which gives clarity on our anti-racist stance. Please note that if you are invited to interview, we will expect you to be prepared to discuss unconscious bias with us; we find these conversations more than any others give us all a good idea of what working together will be like.' The type of questions that might be asked at interview are:

- What do you understand by unconscious bias?

- Tell us about a time when you challenged a colleague when they were showing unconscious bias.

- What unconscious biases do you have and how are you working to address them?

These questions and the subsequent discussions ensure that panellists are reminded of their biases and enable recruiters to assure themselves that they are hiring employees, of whatever ethnicity, who are racially literate. This practice also, of course, sends a message to potential applicants about how seriously the organisation takes its responsibility to become anti-racist.

Addressing the biases of interviewers

Once applicants of colour make it to the interview stage of a recruitment process, they can then face voice discrimination. In a recent survey, cited by Hashi Mohamed, 28% of British employees thought they had been discriminated against because of their accent and 80% of employers admitted accent discrimination (2020:221–2). Mohammed urges us to 'be more imaginative, more acutely self-aware when we are making those instantaneous judgements about others, and look beyond the voice to what the person in front of you at interview... is actually saying' (2020:233).

In *People Like Us,* Mohammed argues the case for recruiters being prepared to take on an unpolished gem, saying 'Too often, employers are allowed to get away with presenting recruitment as a process of making a choice between finished products' (2020:262). He encourages recruiters to tell candidates that it is fine to ask for a question to be rephrased or repeated. He urges interviewers to rephrase a question if they can see that the candidate has missed the point. What is essential? He makes a case for looking beyond the immediate strengths to see future potential. His challenges beg the question as to whether formal interviews in which candidates are asked to give immediate responses to questions fired at them out of the blue is the smartest and most equitable way to select staff.

If I were a headteacher now, I would radically revise my recruitment methods, introducing a greater number of activities for which candidates could pre-prepare in an attempt to level the playing field between the more and less privileged.

Do you track your minority ethnic representation at every step of the recruitment process (expressions of interest, invitation to interview, progression from longlist to shortlist, successful appointment)?

If so, what does this show? And what action might be required?

Have you introduced the practice of anonymising applications? If so, what information do you redact and why? What has the impact of this practice been? Are you satisfied that it is having the desired effect?

Have you considered whether voice bias could be at play in your school? If so, what can you do to counter this?

Have you looked at job descriptions and person specifications through the lens of race equity? If so, what has this thrown up and have you made any adjustments as a consequence?

How do you avoid the 'parole board experience' for applicants of colour? If it is not possible to have a racially minoritised member of staff or governor on the appointment panel, could you invite a racially minoritised parent onto the panel or at the very least ensure that candidates are shown round the school by a pupil of colour or engage with staff of colour in an activity as part of the recruitment process?

To finish this chapter, here is a case study from a Hertfordshire primary school where leaders started to address the under-representation of people of colour on their staff and governing bodies in 2015. Interestingly, they considered anonymising application forms but instead went for a different approach. In a small school with relatively few staff involved in recruitment and high levels of confidence that all of the selection panel members are committed to increasing the ethnic diversity of the adults in the school community, this has proved to be an effective strategy.

This case study is an uplifting example of how the appointment of one minority ethnic staff colleague or governor can generate a momentum, making the next hire easier and leading in time to a level of ethnic diversity that no longer requires such a degree of strategic intervention to maintain healthy representation. However, a note of caution should be raised to guard against the phenomenon whereby the appointment of one person of colour disincentivises the organisation from seeking to appoint others due to a sense of 'job done.' Worryingly, Nafisa Bakkar, writing in the collection *It's Not About The Burka*, references a study showing that when companies hired racially minoritised staff, these colleagues were less likely in turn to advocate the appointment of other racially minoritised staff, fearing that if they favoured applicants from their own group they might be penalised themselves for seeming to be impartial (2020:56).

Windermere Primary School Case Study

With a predominantly White staff team and an exclusively White British governing board, leaders recognised that the staff and governors were not representative of the pupils they served – at this time only 42% of pupils were White British. The predominant ethnic minority group was Bangladeshi, representing 18% of pupils. The school had two Bangladeshi employees: one midday supervisory assistant (MSA) and one newly-appointed teaching assistant (TA). Leaders embarked on an ambitious strategy to recruit staff and governors from BAME communities.

Leaders had noted that pupils from an Asian background joining the Reception class made slower progress initially compared with their White British counterparts. At the end of Reception only 14% of Asian pupils achieved a good level of development (GLD) compared with 81% of their peers. Pupils and parents commented that they sometimes felt staff did not understand their culture or accommodate their cultural needs. This provided an additional incentive to diversify the staff body.

Whilst the recruitment process offers the opportunity to anonymise applications, leaders chose instead to be proactive in including applications from BAME candidates in the shortlisting process. This gave them the opportunity to interview a broad range of high-quality candidates. This meant on occasion overlooking grammatical and spelling errors made in letters of application from BAME candidates, accepting that they might not have the home support to identify these errors in their forms.

Furthermore, leaders acknowledged when shortlisting that certain key skills could be developed through experience and training and so were not essential prerequisites if the key personal qualities were evident.

One of our Bangladeshi parents was first approached by senior leaders to see if she would be interested in applying for the MSA vacancy, her youngest child having just started school. She was successful in her application and her firm but fair interactions with pupils at lunchtimes meant that, when one of the class teaching assistants was absent, she was quickly offered an opportunity to gain some in-class TA experience.

She enjoyed this and expressed an interest in any future vacancies. When a vacancy arose, colleagues helped her to complete the application to the required standard. Although senior leaders acknowledged that she lacked the TA experience of some other applicants and would require some support and additional training for the role, they used their knowledge of her commitment to the school and the skills that she brought with her to 'sanction' her appointment. In this role, she is not only a successful adult role model for BAME pupils, but she has also encouraged other BAME members of the community to put themselves forward when opportunities arise. Creating additional opportunities to support BAME employees in accessing better paid and more interesting or challenging jobs has resulted in two more taking on the role of teaching assistant in the school.

Two vacancies arose as parent governors' terms of office came to an end. Enlisting the help of the Chair of Governors, specific parents were approached and asked to consider standing in the parent governor election. Ultimately three candidates were nominated: one Bangladeshi, one Chinese and one Russian. The Bangladeshi and Chinese parents were duly elected to the governing body, providing a more representative school leadership. Some adjustments have been made to ensure that proceedings are inclusive, for example avoiding meeting during Ramadan. It is also recognised that a Muslim governor may need to join a meeting later or remotely to allow for daily prayers.

The school has benefited from a better understanding of BAME concerns and interests. BAME teachers are able to empathise with some of our pupils, particularly when discussing racial abuse and Black Lives Matter. BAME staff are also able to influence policies and the curriculum. Their presence helps other staff to ensure that diversity is part of the school's ethos; for example, guided reading groups that are named after children's authors including BAME authors, not just White ones. Children and parents have benefited from having a greater representation within the school's leadership. Governors have encouraged the senior leadership team to review the school's curriculum in order to increase diversity.

Having a governor from our local Asian community has not only provided support and advice for the school's leadership team, but it has also broadened the school's links with the wider community. In the summer of 2021, the school offered its facilities to the St Albans Youth Project. This is a registered BAME charity that promotes activities that foster understanding and inclusion between people of diverse backgrounds to build a stronger community.

When the school's first BAME teaching assistant was employed in 2015, it was expected that communication with parents would improve and children's early language skills would benefit, but in fact the whole school has benefited from a greater awareness of cultural differences, a review of the school's teaching and learning provision and improved links with the local community.

References

Agarwal. P. (2020). *Sway: Unravelling Unconscious Bias*. (London: Bloomsbury).

Bakkar. N. *On the Representation of Muslims: Terms and Conditions Apply* in Khan, M ed. (2020) *It's Not About The Burka* (London: Picador). p 45–63.

Barker. I. (2021). *Racial Bias and Attainment*. (TES). Available at: www.theguardian.com/education/2021/sep/23/black-girls-in-england-twice-as-likely-to-be-excluded-from-schools-as-white-girls

Boakye. J. (2019). *Black, Listed*. (Great Britain, London: Dialogue Books).

Bower. L. (2021) *Getting Diverse And Skilled Governors On Board*. (Diverse Educators). Available at: www.diverseeducators.co.uk/getting-skilled-and-diverse-governors-on-boards/

Belger. T. (2022) *Biggest academy trust turns to NFL for inspiration in diversity drive*. (Schools Week). Available at: https://schoolsweek.co.uk/diversity-racism-academy-trusts-united-learning-oasis/

Cain, S. (2021). *Malorie Blackman: 'Hope Is The Spark.'* (The Guardian). Available at: www.theguardian.com/books/2021/sep/11/malorie-blackman-hope-is-the-spark

Carr. J. (2021) Zahawi calls on schools to increase diversity of governors. (Schools Week) Available at: https://schoolsweek.co.uk/zahawi-calls-on-schools-to-increase-diversity-of-governors/

Department For Education (2020). National Statistics: School Workforce In England: November 2019. Available at: www.gv.uk/government/statistics/school-workforce-in-england-november-2019

Department For Education (2022). School Workforce in England Reporting Year 2021. Available at: https://explore-education-statistics.service.gov.uk/find-statistics/school-workforce-in-england

Gibbs. R. *The Recruitment And Retention Of Black Teachers In The UK* in Wilson. H and Kara. B ed (2022) *Diverse Educators: A Manifesto* (London: University of Buckingham Press). p 306–310.

Harewood. D. (2021). *Maybe I Don't Belong Here: A Memoir of Race, Identity, Breakdown and Recovery*. (London: Bluebird).

Hirsch. A. (2018). *Brit(ish): On Race, Identity and Belonging*. (London: Vintage).

Holding. M. (2021). *Why We Kneel, How We Rise*. (London: Simon & Schuster).

Hurston. Z. N. (1928). *How it Feels To Be Coloured Me*. (The World Tomorrow). Available at: www.bing.com/search?q=Zora+Neale+Hurston+1928&cvid=29e719fb7b374e8d83514e7444eff1d1&aqs=edge..69i57j0l2.6327j0j4&FORM=ANAB01&DAF0=1&PC=U531

Kendi. I. X. (2019). *How To Be An Anti-Racist*. (London: The Bodley Head).

Macfarlane. R. and Catchpool. M. eds. (2022) *Great Representation. Collection of School Case Studies*. (Hertfordshire: Herts For Learning Ltd).

Miller, P. (2021). *'System Conditions,' System Failure, Structural Racism and Anti-Racism in the United Kingdom: Evidence from Education and Beyond*. MDPI Available at: www.mdpi.com/2075-4698/11/2/42

Mohamed. H. (2020) *People Like Us* (London: Profile).

National Governance Association (NGA) (2021) *Increasing participation in school and trust governance*. Available at: www.nga.org.uk/Knowledge-Centre/research/Increasing-participation-in-school-and-trust-gover.aspx

Sarpong, J. (2020). *The Power Of Privilege: How White People Can Challenge Racism.* (London: HQ).

Scott. K. (2021). *Just Work: Get it Done, Fast and Fair* (London: Macmillan).

Syed. M. (2019) *Rebel Ideas: The Power of Diverse Thinking* (London: John Murray).

Tattersfield. S. (2021) *Representation matters: How do we increase diversity in our school staff body?* (CCT Impact Magazine). Available at: https://my.chartered.college/impact_arti cle/representation-matters-how-do-we-increase-diversity-in-our-school-staff-body/

Tatum. B. D. (2021) *Why Are All The Black Kids Sitting Together In The Cafeteria?* (Great Britain, Dublin: Penguin).

Tereshchenko. A. and Mills. M. (2021) *The Retention and Progression of Teachers from Minority Ethnic Groups.* (CCT Impact Magazine). Available at: https://my.chartered.coll ege/impact_article/the-retention-and-progression-of-teachers-from-minority-ethnic-groups/

Tereshchenko, A, Mills, M, Bradbury, A. (2020) Making progress? Employment and reten-tion of BAME teachers in England. (UCL Institute of Education: London, UK). Available at: https://discovery.ucl.ac.uk/id/eprint/10117331/

Umeadi. N., Ferdinand. K. and Boyland. M. (2021) *The experiences of Governors of Black, Asian, and other ethnicities on Camden School Governing Bodies: Qualitative Research Report for Camden Governing Bodies and Boards, Camden Learning and Camden Council* (London: Camden Learning).

Walker. A. (2022) *School governing boards becoming less diverse, research suggests.* (Schools Week) Available at: https://schoolsweek.co.uk/school-governing-boards-becom ing-less-diverse-research-suggests/?utm_source=rss&utm_medium=rss&utm_campaign= school-governing-boards-becoming-less-diverse-research-suggests&mc_cid=3847561 2e6&mc_eid=24623934f7

Retention of staff of colour

If you are neutral in situations of injustice, you have chosen the side of the oppressor.

Attributed to Desmond Tutu

Prejudice is a burden that confuses the past, threatens the future, and renders the present inaccessible.

Attributed to Maya Angelou

Having recruited staff and governors/trustees of colour, it is obviously vital that they are well inducted, feel well-integrated into the school, are supported and invested in. This chapter starts by taking a look at the concerning rate with which teachers of colour leave the profession. In order to better understand the retention issues for racially minoritised staff and governors/trustees, it examines, through personal testimony, the experiences of adults of colour in schools. It then offers suggestions for actions that school leaders might take to better include, protect and demonstrate commitment to adults of colour.

We have, for many years, had a significant issue in the UK with teacher retention. In 2020, 34,100 or 7.8% of all qualified teachers left the profession, as cited in the School Workforce in England report of June 2021. And we face a particular issue with those new to teaching choosing to leave: 22% of teachers who joined the profession as NQTs in 2015 were not working in the state sector two years later (DfE 2018a). Some of the key factors cited by teachers for leaving the profession, as discussed in the DfE report 'Factors affecting teacher retention: qualitative investigation.' are stress and ill health; school leadership, policy and approaches; enforcement of inflexible teaching protocols; government policy; professional development and pay. But 'workload remains the most important factor influencing teachers' decisions to leave the profession' (2018b:6).

Given their scarcity, it is particularly concerning that teachers from minority groups leave at a higher rate than White British teachers. The percentage of racially minoritised teachers still in service in the 2017 school workforce census, one year after becoming NQTs was 83% (compared to 86% for White counterparts). Five years after becoming NQTs, just 69% of the White teachers were still in the profession but the figures for racially minoritised teachers were even lower at 65% (2018a:65–6). Interestingly, 'BAME NQTs have a higher retention rate than white NQTs in Inner and Outer London, but a lower retention rate across the rest of the country' (2018a:65) – likely to be linked to their even greater under-representation outside the capital.

In *Making Progress?*, Tereshchenko, Mills and Bradbury reported that their 'qualitative research found that some of the factors influencing minority ethnic teacher retention are the same factors influencing teachers of majority background in England. Unsurprisingly teachers were happiest in those schools where they felt valued, respected, had autonomy, connection with, and support from, colleagues and senior leaders, and clear paths for career progression' (2020:14). Yet they also found that 'racism and associated inequalities are at the forefront of BAME teachers' minds in conversations about retention, not workload' (2020:4). 'Our participants highlighted how both overt and covert racism takes a toll on BAME teachers' well-being, progression and job satisfaction. BAME teachers had the same high levels of workload as all teachers, plus an additional 'hidden workload' of coping with racism' (2020:4).

Antonina Tereshchenko and Martin Mills, in an article for *Impact Magazine* (2021), explore racism and inequalities as significant reasons for teachers of colour leaving the profession. They say that many of the racially minoritised teachers interviewed by them 'were dissatisfied and planned to leave because of the perceived low expectations or negative attitudes about minority students, lack of support from school leaders for culturally relevant and inclusive teaching, colour-blind approaches to dealing with students and staff, and limited dialogue about race and equity in the school.' They, and the interviewees in the *Making Progress?* study, also cite barriers to getting awards and promotions as a key retention issue, which we will examine in more detail in the next chapter.

If school leaders are serious about creating and maintaining staff and governing teams which benefit from rich ethnic diversity, it is essential that they ensure that each and every incident of racism towards pupils and staff is dealt with directly, swiftly and effectively. At the same time, they must prioritise work to develop the racial literacy of their staff and governing bodies (as discussed in Chapters 5 and 6), to ensure that their workplace is a safe, nurturing, respectful and stimulating space for staff and governors/trustees of colour.

What are the experiences of staff of colour in our schools?

Clearly, the experience of every member of staff, whatever their ethnicity, will be different. However, the uncomfortable truth is that very many staff of colour experience racial discrimination and ethnic stereotyping in the workplace. In the interviews I conducted with racially minoritised teachers and leaders, I listened to numerous harrowing accounts of direct and indirect racism that they had experienced in their careers, from so called 'micro aggressions' to near career ending traumas. I have grouped the following examples into several categories. They do not make for comfortable reading. I am aware that for staff of colour these accounts may surface distressing memories of similar experiences you have faced in your careers. For White readers, I am sure the stories will lead to considerable soul searching and self-reflection. You may wish to read the remains of the chapter in several sittings.

'Hard to prove' racism

We considered 'microaggressions' in Chapter 4 and Chapter 5. As isolated incidents they may not seem too significant, but the fact that they can occur frequently and at any time means that their effect builds up to cause considerable detrimental impact. Tatum says 'Social science research has demonstrated that the cumulative effect of microaggressions "assail the self-esteem of recipients, produce anger and frustration, deplete psychic energy, lower feelings of subjective well-being and worthiness…deny minority populations equal access and opportunity in education…"' (2021:53)

Here are some of the microaggressions cited in my interviews with racially minoritised teachers and leaders:

- One colleague reflected 'I wonder, "Are they faffing about because it's me?" when someone keeps me waiting.'

- Rubia shared a recent experience: 'I was working at a workbench in the departmental office, above which there are shelves that we keep resources on. A white teacher suddenly climbed up onto the workbench, their feet in front of my face, my desk without any communication at all, disturbing my work and invading my space. I felt shocked and left the room. I didn't follow it up because this kind of microaggression is very difficult to prove.'

- Yasmin told me 'I was once delivering some INSET at a local school. I had my resources in a black bag. A member of staff asked me in an aggressive tone whether I was going to take my rubbish home with me.'

Have you discussed the concept of 'microaggressions' with staff at your school?

Have you supported staff to understand behaviours that could be termed as microaggressions? And to reflect on whether they have ever been responsible for them?

Do staff of colour feel safe and supported to share racial microaggressions that have happened to them? Do they feel confident that microaggressions are dealt with appropriately? How do you know?

Incidents like those cited above cause anxiety, insecurity, worry, anger, indignation, frustration and pain. It is essential that they are not allowed to go unchecked.

Ignorance of racially illiterate staff colleagues

It stands to reason that incidents of unintended racism, ignorant attitudes and lack of race awareness will exist in schools as in all workplaces; after all, working communities are made up of people of varied ages, backgrounds, levels of education and life experience. Schools which prioritise developing the racial literacy of their staff and keeping attuned to the behaviours of staff are able to pick up and deal with such incidents quickly and effectively. But, left unattended, they will not dissipate of their own accord. Below are some examples cited by my interviewees of the racial illiteracy of colleagues with whom they have worked in schools:

- An elderly school secretary who would talk of 'that little coloured boy,' regardless of how many times the Asian headteacher told her she couldn't use language like that.

- A senior leader agreeing with the headteacher that it was important to ensure that pupils experienced more ethnic diversity through assemblies, saying 'We could do more assemblies about Blacks.'

- A member of staff saying to a headteacher from a minority group 'I don't see your colour. I just see you as you.'

Lucky recounted: 'A call came into the office for "Lakhbir" – that's my real name but everyone knew me as Lucky. The member of staff who took the call said "What sort of name is that?" "How should I know that's you?" I was so shocked that I didn't respond. Everyone around me looked embarrassed.'

Bonolo told me: 'One teacher in a previous school often referred to me as "coloured". Even though I corrected her numerous times, she failed to change her language as she thought it was less offensive and believed that the term "Black" was too harsh. She continued to call me "coloured" even after I told her not to. I felt that I could not complain because these conversations happened in the staff room but no one else defended me. It was also difficult because I was the only Black member of the teaching staff at the school.'

What is striking about the last two examples is that Lucky and Bonolo's colleagues did not give their support or assume the role of race allies. Due to shock and/or a sense of the futility of addressing the racist behaviour alone, the offensive behaviour of the perpetrators went unchecked and the subjects of the racism experienced a reduced sense of belonging to the institution.

How would you deal with each of the five examples of racial illiteracy cited above if you were the leader of the school in which they happened?

Staff racially stereotyping and demonstrating race prejudice towards people of colour

Here are four contrasting examples given by my interviewees:

- A White Ofsted inspector saying to a student 'You're Black, you must like music.'

- A contractor seeing the Asian headteacher and White office manager in conversation and addressing the office manager as the headteacher.

- A teaching resource about British Values which featured a stylised cartoon image of an Asian Muslim girl throughout.

- Staff in a predominantly White school assuming when a theft had taken place that the culprit must have been a Nigerian boy and wanting to search his bag.

Activity

Discuss the four examples above with your colleagues.

Which would cause you the most concern and why?

How would you wish for each to be addressed and by whom?

What impact do you think each scenario would have on staff of colour at the school?

If one of these incidents happened in your school, what would you do to ensure that staff of colour retained their confidence in the school's commitment to being an anti-racist institution?

Failure of leaders to address or deal effectively with incidents of racism

Activities like the one above are really important to ensure that the racial literacy of the senior staff in schools is well developed. Heads, deputies and assistant heads have multiple roles and pressured jobs, and we know that only a very small minority are people of colour. Sadly, but perhaps inevitably, not all senior staff are sufficiently trained and skilled at dealing effectively with racist incidents in school and many lack confidence. What is not understandable or acceptable in any way is that in some instances senior staff do not prioritise dealing with racist incidents and leave issues unresolved. And it should be noted that it is not only White senior leaders, of course, who can find it challenging to address incidents of racism in their schools effectively. This causes untold harm and leads to staff of colour feeling unsupported, under-valued and disillusioned. The following testimony from my interviewees illustrates these points.

An incident between two pupils happened on a day when I was not in school. One of the children had made a racist comment to the other. When I came into school the next day, I checked that the incident had been dealt with by the senior leader who had picked it up. Her response was that she had not yet called the perpetrator's father as he was known to be a difficult parent. I felt very angry. I told her to deal with it and had a discussion with her about why she hadn't dealt with it immediately.

I remember in my first term at the school witnessing an awful physical altercation where a pupil was hit with a metal pole in the head. I was quite shaken by the event. When the headteacher, who is Black, came to speak to me she said, 'I'm just grateful it wasn't a White middle-class pupil.' The headteacher also decided that we would not celebrate Black History Month at the school as she didn't want White students feeling 'bad about themselves.' I felt that her own fears around dealing with White middle-class parents were being projected onto staff and having a detrimental effect on the inclusively of the school.

A student called out 'Curry, Curry' at me. I was very shocked – this was the first and only experience of racism in the classroom I have ever experienced. But what followed was very distressing. I was questioned about what the student had said and 'what I did to encourage the student to say this.' Then, when the White senior leader responsible for behaviour met with the parents and explained why calling out 'Curry, Curry' was racist, the parents asked 'If the teacher had said fish and chips to our child, would that be racist?' The leader said 'yes, of course!' When the leader explained to me what had been said at this meeting, it was relayed in my office which I share with two other members of staff. Both colleagues were shocked by his comment and felt that saying 'fish and chips' is not racist. I didn't feel I could discuss this with the Principal; both he and the senor leader are White. A few days later, the Principal said he would catch up with me about the incident but he never did. Instead, he gave me the same look as colleagues when they were investigating the incident, as if to say that it was my fault and that I had made the student say 'Curry, Curry.'

I was an assistant headteacher. It was a hot summer day and I was doing some strategic planning with the headteacher and the maths lead. The headteacher left the room. I commented on the fact that the day was so hot and the maths lead said 'I'd have thought you'd be able to tolerate temperatures like this given where you're from.' I replied saying 'What, Wolverhampton?' (I am of Indian heritage but I was born and brought up in the West Midlands). The comment upset me and afterwards I told another teacher who said it was wrong and advised that I should tell the headteacher, which I did. The head said I should leave the matter with her. She met with the leader. We were then both invited to attend a mediation meeting with the head. At the meeting the maths lead said, 'What did I say that was so wrong? It's just an assumption that I made. I can't help it.' She got angry and defensive. The head sent the maths leader out and sent me back to class. The next thing I knew, the maths leader's husband had come up to the school and threatened to take further action and seek legal support. The maths lead then got the unions involved. I was not kept informed about what was happening. I was then told that I was not allowed to talk to the maths leader and I should ensure that I was not alone with her without a chaperone. The matter was never formally resolved. I never received an apology.

Activity

Take one or more of the examples above and examine them with colleagues (senior leaders, governors/trustees/staff).

What errors were made in the handling of the situation? To what would you attribute these failures? What training needs did the leader demonstrate and how could these needs be addressed?

How do you think the member of staff subjected to the racism was left feeling? What do you imagine the short and long term effects of the incident would have been? What support should they have been given?

What are your collective learning points from analysing this example?

Being punished for calling out racism

In all walks of life, when Black people stand up against racism and call out a problem, they are frequently made to feel that they have become the problem and, in too many instances, they get excluded and punished. We saw this in the previous section where one of my interviewees was made to feel that she must have caused a pupil to make the 'Curry, Curry' comment to her and my other colleague was told that she must never meet alone with the maths leader, as though the perpetrator of racism needed protecting.

When Colin Kaepernick took the knee throughout the 2016 NFL season to highlight racial inequality and police brutality in the USA, he paid the price: no team would sign him for the next season. The same happened to Adam Goodes (the Aboriginal Australian Rules player); he identified a 13-year-old girl who had shouted out 'Goodes, you're an ape!' to security at a match and was vilified for his actions, portrayed as a bully and a villain. Again, his career was ended. Michael Holding concludes, 'If you stay silent, nothing changes. If you pushback, you are a troublemaker' (2020:70).

What follows is a truly shocking story, told by one of my interviewees. In this case, a dedicated middle leader, committed to supporting Black students in the schools in which he worked, effectively lost his job and nearly his career. This incident took place over 30 years ago, but the colleague is still teaching in London and, inevitably, carries the effects of the experience with him to this day. And, as William Faulkner said, 'The past isn't dead and buried. In fact it isn't even past.'

Interviewee's testimony

'I was teaching at a Secondary Boys' School in London, which had a significant number of Black pupils. There were six Black teachers in total at the school. There was no ethnic representation in the curriculum so I wrote and taught a module on African history. I then designed and ran a course on demeaning stereotypes. The school had a Foundation Department, which educated students working below the CSE and O level. 60% of the African Caribbean children were in that department, despite the fact that many were performing at a more advanced level than was taught in that provision. Added to that, there were no Black boys in the sixth form at all and there had never been. I was active in the arena of supplementary education; I was part of the Black Teachers' Alliance and taught in a supplementary school.

I went to see the headteacher to pitch a proposal I had written for community outreach to extend support for Black families and help raise outcomes for their children. He gave me permission to take the proposal to a staff meeting. It was met with hostility from many staff who declared it racist and asked "What about the White children?" But the head could see that there was a problem and that there was structural racism in the school. He was near to retirement but gave me a role to develop community outreach with the Black community, an office and a phone.

Then the head retired and a new head arrived at the school. The new head questioned why I had an office. I had to go back to the staff and re-present my case for the work I was doing. I highlighted the inequalities in the school, such as no Black children in the sixth form, as part of my case. The head took offence and took out a grievance against me. I was suspended. I could have been barred from teaching. I had to attend a hearing at the town hall and defend a gross misconduct charge in front of the chief education officer. I represented myself and presented over 150 documents which showed the systemic racism at the school (minutes of staff meetings, memos, details of the head making appointments without interviews). After the hearing I was written to and told that there was some merit to what I had said. I was offered a post at another school but it was made clear to me that returning to my school was not an option. To this day I have never received written confirmation of the outcome of the hearing.'

In research conducted for the NUT/NEU and the Runnymede Trust, *Visible and Invisible Barriers: the impact of racism on teachers of colour*, Dr Zubaida Haque and Sian Elliott report that 'Black teachers in particular spoke about being labelled "troublemakers" or being viewed as "aggressive" if they challenged any decisions' (2017:6). Christine Callender, in an article entitled 'Black male leaders, White education spaces,' describes phenomenon whereby many Black teachers, particularly males, mute their voices and 'employ silence as a coping mechanism – a strategy used to avoid confrontation or misunderstanding' (2020:3).

Is it any surprise that many staff of colour choose to suffer discrimination and inequality in silence or to move out of our schools, rather than call racism out and seek to right wrongs?

Staff demonstrating negativity to anti racism initiatives

As many organisations and institutions in society, including schools, strive to address racism and become anti-racist, one of the sinister consequences and challenges can be White staff displaying fragility and fear of expressing their conscious or unconscious racist views. The following examples were cited by my interviewees:

- White teachers in the staffroom expressing annoyance that they were not invited to attend meetings of the BAME forum in the school.

- White staff commenting that 'everyone is equal, nobody should get special treatment' in response to the school's work in support of the Black Lives Matter movement.

- A staffroom conversation, in front of a Muslim teacher, about Muslim staff taking leave for religious observance for Eid and whether they should therefore come in to work on Christmas Day instead.

- Staff commenting that they felt the practice of the England football team taking the knee was over the top and unnecessary.

It is little surprise that many employees from racially minoritised groups feel a disconnect from some of their work colleagues. Sally Tattersfield, in her *Impact* article of spring 2021, cites CIPD research that half of Black, Asian and minority ethnic employees say that they feel the need to censor what they say about their personal lives while at work, compared to 37% of white British employees. (2021). Sadly, schools are not always places of psychological safety for staff of colour. The following examples are particularly shocking. They illustrate the fact that staff of colour, including headteachers, can sadly experience the most violent racism and are not always supported when such incidents occur.

Direct racist aggression from parents and community members

Yasmin recalls an incident at the school entrance one day when pupils were being collected by their parents. There was an unsafe degree of vehicular congestion and Yasmin asked a particular parent to move his car. The parent wound down the window of his car and, in a loud, exaggerated and slow voice, shouted 'Can you understand English?' for all the other parents to hear. No one supported Yasmin. No action was taken against the parent.

How typical are such stories? What lessons can we learn from this harrowing testimony?

How do your staff of colour know that, if they were to experience any racism from members of the community or parents, they would have the unconditional support of the senior leaders/governors/trustees? Where is this stated?

Does every member of staff from a minority group know to whom they should report it if they are subjected to racism?

Is training provided to your governors and trustees on how to challenge racism directed towards school leaders by parents or community members and on how to support staff and leaders subjected to racism?

Is counselling available to staff who require it?

Feeling either invisible or hyper-visible

Racially minoritised staff can feel invisible and like an outsider in schools where the majority of staff do not share or understand their heritage, culture and lifestyle. In their article *Professional development for career progression: through the lens of ethnic diversity and gender*, Youlande Harrowell and Aretha Banton state that 'It is not only about having a seat at the table – it is about feeling as though we belong at the table.' They stress that 'While there is absolutely an onus on the individual to forge their own alliances and find their own space, the question persists: how does one 'fit in' to a community in which you feel marginalised and isolated, and which does not often represent, consider or acknowledge the contributions of diverse groups?' (2021).

But as well as feeling invisible, staff of colour can also feel hyper-visible when the staffroom goes quiet and conversation stops as they walk in, when they find themselves under surveillance or when they are seen as the spokesperson for all staff of colour.

Bonolo told me that 'people approach me for advice on issues of injustice which I am not always qualified to speak on. I then feel obligated to find out the processes and requirements so that my colleagues are supported. I feel that this only happens because of my ethnicity.' Lucky reflected, 'There have been occasions when colleagues would assume that I have all the answers. They often say "ask Lucky" about information on cultural festivals, even those that are nothing to do with my culture or religion. I would prefer genuine questions that seek to find out what I do to celebrate certain festivals or about my culture and background as opposed to assuming what may be portrayed as the norm.'

As well as feeling pressure to be a resident expert on all things race-related, or to take on additional work related to race equity, racially minoritised staff often report feeling pressure to serve in racialised roles. For example, Black men are often encouraged to take on pastoral roles working with disaffected Black boys, rather than seeking academic or curriculum-related responsibilities. Callender says, 'The "othering" and isolation experienced by black male teachers in schools runs along-side arguments which assert an assumption that they are ideal disciplinarians of black boys. This logic assumes that black teachers possess knowledge, cultural skills and attributes to improve the outcomes of black boys...that any black male teacher, regardless of background, could be a successful teacher of black boys' (2020:3). Sufian Sadiq reflected, amusingly, at a Great Representation seminar, 'The Black physics teacher is just as rubbish at dealing with the naughty boys as the White physics teacher!' The Haque and Elliott Barriers report found that 'BME teachers from all ethnic groups complained about being given stereotypical responsibilities (e.g. behaviour responsibilities or Black History Month) instead of challenging intellectual TLR roles' (2017:6). One of my colleagues told me, 'I was determined to fight that expectation and become a Teaching and Learning Leader rather than a Pastoral Manager.'

In *Living While Black*, Guilaine Kinouani writes powerfully about the emotional energy expended by many workers of colour in the process of assimilation: 'it's the expectation that Black people leave their Blackness at the door to get in, that they whiten themselves to be accepted by their peers or to not face barriers in relation to promotion.' She gives examples: 'It includes (but also goes much beyond) how our hair is worn...not discussing our lived experience (particularly that of racism) and adopting modes of communication that may be alien to us to get ahead' (2021:122). This is what was termed code-switching by John J. Gumperz.

In conclusion, racially minoritised staff experience a hidden, additional work-load on top of the workload that all teachers face: they have to work harder to get noticed and they are turned to by others and feel pressure to represent people of colour (children and adults). And this is in addition to having to deal with the emotional load of covert racism and, too often, direct racial aggression and discrimination. Haque and Elliott's Barriers report (2017) stated that 31% of minority ethnic teachers had experienced racism in the last year. A review conducted by Paul Miller for a university in the North of England into equality and diversity within the university's recruitment and selection, promotion and disciplinary processes found that more grievances are raised against racially minoritised staff and the sanctions are harsher. It also concluded that grievances are more likely to be sorted informally with White staff. Tereshchenko, Mills and Bradbury reported that their 'participants highlighted how both overt and covert racism takes a toll on BAME teachers' wellbeing, progression and job satisfaction. BAME teachers had the same high levels of workload as all teachers, plus an additional 'hidden workload' of coping with racism' (2021:4).

Harrowell and Banton are right to stress that 'Representation is hugely important and plays a powerful role in staff retention...schools with more minority ethnic leaders have a higher overall minority ethnic teacher retention rate' (2021). But by taking steps to address all the causes of additional workload and emotional stress, all school leaders, even those in schools with few racially minoritised staff, can reduce the attrition rate of staff of colour.

Here is a top ten of tips designed to help to ensure that minority ethnic staff enjoy a sense of belonging in their school – that they feel valued, included, respected and equal to their colleagues.

Top Ten Tips

1. Allocate each new racially minoritised staff member a buddy who has been trained to be racially literate to assist with their induction to the school and their integration into the staff team.

2. Seek feedback from staff of colour (via questionnaire or informal meeting) as to their experiences of race and act on it.

3. Ensure that all staff activities are socially inclusive of all religious and cultural practices (e.g. not centred around the consumption of alcohol or meat, not requiring participation on Friday evenings or other times of religious observance).

4. Don't allow staff to see racially minoritised staff only through the lens of their ethnicity or to allow conversation to be too focused on their identity – pick individuals up if you see this happening.

5. Prioritise the development of a culture in which it is understood that it is everyone's role to look out for and tackle microaggressions or covert racism.

6. Ensure that all staff members have a target around the development of their racial literacy, encourage them to share their personal objectives and seek support from their peers in achieving them. Create a culture where it is OK to make mistakes but not to remain racially illiterate.

7. Communicate to all staff that you have a collective responsibility to ensure that staff of colour do not experience the additional workload that racially minoritised staff in so many schools do.

8. Ensure that all staff of colour know the person they should got to if they experience any racism of any kind from anyone in the school community.

9. Ensure that you have access to a high quality, independent and free counselling service for anyone who has experienced racism in the workplace; publicise details of it and encourage staff to colleagues to make use of it.

10. Share examples of colleagues calling out and standing up to racism. Thank those who bring incidents to your attention and so reinforce that your school is a safe community and committed to anti-racism.

Additional barriers faced by governors and trustees from racially minoritised groups

All of the barriers (and suggestions for tackling them) considered in this chapter apply to governors and trustees as much as they do to school staff. But there are additional obstacles that can be off-putting to those serving on trust or governing boards. The interviews conducted for the Camden Learning study of 2021 showed that the bureaucracy and formality associated with many board meetings can lead to new governors and trustees feeling as if they are entering an alien and unwelcoming world, especially if they speak English as an additional language, have not been to school in the UK and/or are the only person of colour on the board. The following are extracts from the Camden Learning interviews:

'There's so many acronyms and a lot of lingo, the language ... is really complicated. You're sort of struggling to get to grips with it.'

'I'm a lawyer by profession and so I don't mind being sent loads of papers...But ... I think the whole structure is very bureaucratic...the chairman's structures and commands and ... the vice chair's comment and all the rest of it. I do think it's very intimidating for new governors, if you're not experienced in that kind of field.'

'If someone ... speak(s) English as a second language, and they feel it's not their world anyway, they will find it tricky. I mean, the acronyms are an issue. I have to basically Google throughout while I'm reading.' (2021:11)

These accounts chime with the reflections of relatively well-educated former parent governor quoted by Karamat Iqbal in his essay in *The Birmingham Book* (2022:57). This man told Iqbal: 'I frequently felt unable to participate in meetings. I could understand what was going on, but it was hard to contribute to the discussion...It was hard to find the right words to express myself.'

In response to their research findings, Camden Council and Camden Learning are recommending:

Being more inclusive for new and nearly new Governors

Governing bodies should ensure that they are as welcoming to new governors as possible. Governing bodies should encourage observation meetings – where potential candidates can attend as observers. London Borough of Camden via Camden Learning should commission training for governors, including headteachers, on how to be inclusive in meetings and make this available to all governors via video.

Provide support for Black, Asian and other ethnic governors and make this explicit in the communications and promotional materials

Communications should make clear that training and support is available to all governors, showcasing examples of governors from Black, Asian, or other ethnic groups, noting that those who take up the role largely thrive in their roles and make a huge contribution to our schools. However, Camden Council and Camden Learning should also seek to identify whether additional sessions and/or programmes would aid recruitment, retention, or progression for governors from underrepresented groups.

2021:14–16

How does your trust/governing board welcome new governors?

How do you demystify the role and identify the support and induction needs of governors/trustees?

Are all your new governors/trustees given a buddy? And are the expectations of the buddy made explicit?

Do you interview governors/trustees after they have been in role for a while to get feedback about their experiences? Are there particular barriers that your governors/trustees of colour have faced? What have you put in place to address them?

References

Callender. C. (2020). *Black Male Teachers, White Education Spaces: Troubling School Practices of Othering and Surveillance.* (Institute of Education). Available at: https://discovery.ucl.ac.uk/id/eprint/10091514/

Department For Education (2018a). Analysis of teacher supply, retention and mobility. London: DfE. Retrieved from: https://assets.publishing.service.gov.uk/government/uploads/system/uploads/attachment_data/file/748164/Teachers_Analysis_Compendium_4_.pdf

Department For Education (2018b). Factors Affecting Teacher Retention: A Qualitative Investigation. Available at: www.gov.uk/government/publications/factors-affecting-teacher-retention-qualitative-investigation

Department For Education (2021). School Workforce In England Reporting Year 2020. Available at: https://explore-education-statistics.service.gov.uk/find-statistics/school-workforce-in-england/2020

Haque. Z. and Elliott. S. (2017). *Visible and Invisible Barriers: the impact of racism on BME teachers.* (The Runnymede Trust). Available at: https://neu.org.uk/barriers-report-impact-racism-black-teachers

Harrowell. Y. and Banton. A. (2021). *Professional development for career progression: through the lens of ethnic diversity and gender.* (CCT Impact Magazine). Available at: https://my.chartered.college/impact_article/professional-development-for-career-progression-through-the-lens-of-ethnic-diversity-and-gender/

Holding. M. (2021). *Why We Kneel, How We Rise.* (London: Simon & Schuster).

Iqbal. K. *Unrepresentative and ill-equipped education bureaucracy* in Diamond. C. ed (2021). *The Birmingham Book.* (Carmarthen: Crown House). p 53–72.

Kinouani. G. (2021). *Living While Black.* (London: Ebury Press).

Tattersfield. S. (2021). *Representation matters: How do we increase diversity in our school staff body?* (CCT Impact Magazine). Available at: https://my.chartered.college/impact_article/representation-matters-how-do-we-increase-diversity-in-our-school-staff-body/

Tatum. B. D. (2021). *Why Are All The Black Kids Sitting Together In The Cafeteria?* (Great Britain, Dublin: Penguin).

Tereshchenko. A. and Mills. M. (2021). *The Retention and Progression of Teachers from Minority Ethnic Groups.* (CCT Impact Magazine). Available at: https://my.chartered.college/impact_article/the-retention-and-progression-of-teachers-from-minority-ethnic-groups/

Tereshchenko. A., Mills. M., Bradbury. A. (2020). *Making progress? Employment and retention of BAME teachers in England.* (UCL Institute of Education: London, UK). Available at: https://discovery.ucl.ac.uk/id/eprint/10117331/

Umeadi. N., Ferdinand. K. and Boyland. M. (2021). *The experiences of Governors of Black, Asian, and other ethnicities on Camden School Governing Bodies: Qualitative Research Report for Camden Governing Bodies and Boards, Camden Learning and Camden Council* (London: Camden Learning).

Development and promotion of staff of colour

'Life in the shadow of the snowy white peaks'

Shilpa Ross

'One is always in the system. The only question is whether one is part of the system in a way that challenges or strengthens the status quo.'

Harry Brod (1989:29)

Across our society, the vast majority of institutions and organisations are led by White people. This is one of the clearest signs of systemic racism in the UK. The term 'snowy White peaks' describes the phenomenon of workforces becoming increasingly monoethnic the more one moves up the hierarchy. The quote above is from the title of a report into race inequalities in the NHS workforce, produced in 2019. Sadly, the description applies equally well to our education establishments.

This chapter starts with an examination of the data on under-representation of people of colour in senior leadership positions in schools. It shares the personal testimony of my interviewees who have encountered a glass ceiling in terms of career development. It then considers ways in which anti-racist school leaders can strive to ensure that there are no barriers faced by staff of colour in gaining promotion and progressing to headship or CEO level. The chapter ends with the reflections of one of the country's very first female Muslim headteachers, now a MAT CEO.

So what does the data on the ethnic diversity of senior leaders in schools show?

Schools Week's annual diversity audit in 2021 found just two of the 117 trusts with 15 or more schools had non-white leaders. An NFER report of 2022 found that 96% of headteachers were White and that 86% of state schools had an all-White SLT.

DOI: 10.4324/9781003275220-16

When Paul Miller spoke at a Great Representation conference in September 2022, he reminded leaders that there are 411 secondary schools in London and that this is more than the entire number of headteachers of minority ethnic heritage in the whole country. When my colleague Dr Michael Catchpool spoke to me about his appointment to a primary headship, he explained that, at the time, 'there were only 19 others like him in the country out of a possible 21,281.' He was referring to being a male, black headteacher in a primary school. Given that statistic, he joked that perhaps he ought to have had it printed on a T-Shirt: 'One in a thousand.'

The link between the retention of staff of colour in schools and the ethnic diversity of the SLT

Apart from the plethora of reasons considered in Chapter 10 for ensuring that we have more ethnically diverse senior staff, governors, trustees and trust leaders, there appears to be a greater likelihood of retaining staff of colour in schools with leaders. Tereshchenko, Mills and Bradbury found from their research that 'All of the teachers interviewed disapproved of the universal whiteness of senior leadership teams (SLT) in otherwise diverse schools. This issue plays a role in teachers' decisions to move schools because of a perceived negative impact on the organisational culture. The racial literacy of all school leaders and their commitment to equity and social justice are important for creating a supportive organisational culture' (2021:4).

Their interviews also revealed that stalled opportunities for career progression is a key retention factor for experienced racially minoritised teachers and that there is a greater degree of trust in an ethnically diverse leadership team to demonstrate racial literacy and ensure equity in career progression than an exclusively White one. Experienced teachers of colour interested in senior promotions felt unfairly passed over for such opportunities, leaving many considering positions outside the state school sector. Most interviewees reflected that this 'glass ceiling' was not obvious to them in the early stages of their career (2021:4). 'As the tenure of our participants progressed, they developed a particularly keen eye for discerning the place of White privilege in school power hierarchies. Teachers who had been in the profession for over ten years highlighted their concerns about barriers to securing rewards and promotions, which they said were not obvious to them at the beginning of their career' (2021:17).

Experiences of the 'glass ceiling': you're 'not ready yet'

Between January and March 2021, 16,565 staff across 380 schools supplied data for an Edurio report into equality, diversity and inclusion in schools and MATs. In response to the question 'How confident are you that decisions impacting promotions are made without bias in your workplace?' only 49% of minority ethnic respondents said they were very or quite confident, compared to 60% of their White British/Irish counterparts, and 23% said they were not very or not at all confident (2021:33). The question 'How confident are you that all staff are treated equally in your workplace?' also elicited concerning findings. Here only 29% of ethnic minority respondents declared that they were very confident, compared to 37% of White British/Irish respondents (2021:20). The report found that '7 in 10 staff feel all staff are treated equally. However White staff, men and staff without a disability feel more positive than their peers.'

Tereshchenko, Mills and Bradbury reflect in their report that 'Notably, we observed that the majority of participants who had been in the school system for a number of years were successful in obtaining middle leadership roles. For some it took less than five years to secure mid-level appointments such as heads of year and pastoral units, subject leaders, curriculum coordinators, and heads of department in secondary schools.' They noticed that, once reaching middle leadership 'they often felt stuck in those posts. Those teachers who were interested in further career progression into senior leadership roles emphasised that their racialised status prevented them from entering what they perceived as all white, and predominantly male, senior leadership circles' (2020:18). Alice Bradbury expanded on these findings in a talk to the Great Representation programme in December 2021. She described the feeling that 'you can be promoted, but only so far' and that 'you have been invited to the table but only to be seen, not heard.'

Sufian Sadiq, speaking at the same seminar, said 'As a leader in education I feel like a trespasser (not an imposter). It's difficult to feel that every day. White men can fail upwards. They screw up and they're forgiven. BAME candidates have to be the absolute finished product.'

This was corroborated by testimony from my interviewees. When Yasmin started applying for headships, she recalls going to one particular interview and getting the sense that her 'face didn't fit.' She was asked about her views on religious education – 'What should RE be about?' – and was left wondering whether that question was asked of all the candidates.

Here is the testimony of another of my interviewees, a middle leader in a secondary school in East London:

'Always the bridesmaid, never the bride' is the expression that I would use to describe the glass ceiling that many BAME leaders face in educational settings. There's a sense that BAME teachers manage to climb to middle management but somehow fall short when endeavouring to become senior leaders. No matter how much we've 'proved ourselves' in our current roles or the amount of discretionary effort we put in at work, we are made to feel that we lack the 'polish' that our White counterparts possess and that we're 'not ready yet.' We'll be recognised for our work ethic, maybe even publicly praised, but not be trusted with a high-profile, senior position.

At my school there is one Assistant Head who is a person of colour. I noticed last year that she shared several responsibilities with other SLT members. Apart from the line-management of two departments, she did not have any remit that she was solely in charge of, unlike her White counterparts. I first noticed this when a head of department was promoted to be an Assistant Headteacher. The recently appointed Assistant Headteacher was given big ticket remits such as staffing and whole school data. However the minority ethnic Assistant Headteacher, who had been part of the senior leadership team for over five years, was still not allocated any whole-school responsibilities.

Issues around equity became more glaringly evident to me when I applied for a SLT secondment. I was not successful. The Deputy Head informed my line manager that it was very close between myself and the two successful candidates. When I received my feedback, I was told that there was only a point or two between three of the four candidates and that I had slimly missed out on being appointed. I was given conflicting information by members of the interview panel as to the criteria used for selection and the weighting of the various tasks carried out by candidates. A week later, it was announced that one of the school's Assistant Heads had decided to step down and that, in the interim, another staff member would be taking up his duties. This member of staff was one of the applicants for the secondment. No new advert went out and no interviews were held.

Possibly aware that I was told during my feedback that I was the close second, during a meeting my headteacher made a point of informing me that the other candidate was shoe-horned into the post in an acting capacity due to his expertise in data. This confirmed what I already knew about unconscious/conscious bias. I had read about it and heard about other people's experiences, but this was the first time I had experienced it so overtly for myself. I didn't try to challenge the decision and call it out as I knew that very little would be achieved. Instead, I decided to create a micro-climate for my department, actively promoting race equity, and to seek a senior leadership elsewhere in the near future so that I can champion race equity on a larger platform.'

So what can be done to ensure that staff of colour cannot be faced with feedback that they are 'not ready yet' and are enabled to progress to headships and trust leadership roles? In the remainder of this chapter, I will explore the following strategies:

- Building confidence and resilience and encouraging applications

- Ensuring staff of colour get access to high quality CPD and careers guidance

- Providing mentoring for teachers of colour

- Ensuring that appointees have undergone impactful unconscious bias training

- Ensuring open and fair recruitment practices

- Using White Sanction to positive effect.

Building confidence and resilience and encouraging applications

For understandable reasons, many Black, Asian and minority ethnic teachers lack the confidence to put themselves forward for consideration for senior leadership posts in schools. They are aware that they are applying to enter an almost exclusively White space, they are likely to face a White appointment panel exhibiting unconscious biases and prone to seeking to appoint in the image of the other senior leaders. They may well have faced rejection at interview on previous occasions and experienced a multitude of microaggressions or examples of covert racism in their career to date. This has affected their self-esteem. Christine Callender, when addressing the Great Representation cohort in January 2022, explained that often minority ethnic staff won't put themselves forward for posts unless they are completely confident that they meet every single aspect of the person specification and can demonstrate that they can deliver on the entirety of the job description. They sense that the benchmark is higher for them and that they are less likely to be afforded flexibility and room for growth than White candidates. And they have less confidence than their White colleagues. Here there is also an issue of intersectionality, in that female leaders of colour appear to have less self-belief than their male colleagues. A third of the sample of racially minoritised teachers surveyed by Haque and Elliott for their Barriers report had never applied for promotion, and over 80% of this group were female (2017:5).

Let's return to the incident described in the last chapter of the racism experienced by one of my interviewees when the maths leader at her school made an ignorant racist comment on a hot day 20 years ago. The failure of the headteacher to deal with this incident appropriately, indeed the fact that she directed my colleague not to have contact with the perpetrator, as though she was somehow responsible for the incident, had a profound effect. It led to her making the decision not to apply for headships: 'I thought, what if a similar thing happens when I am head? I made excuses not to go for jobs. I didn't want to put myself in a position where I could have been rejected.' When her colleagues, seeing her potential and her readiness for headship, encouraged her to apply for various posts, she deflected their appeals. She didn't even tell her husband the real reasons. She reflected in her conversation with me, 'Throughout the last twenty years, I have doubted myself to move into headship (a feeling I didn't have before the incident) because of the risk of not being accepted.'

This tragic illustration serves to remind us of why it is so essential that we pick up every single incident of racism that takes place in our schools and also of how alert leaders need to be to the potential for the self-esteem of leaders of colour to be dented. Leaders of colour who have the potential to be great senior leaders need extra encouragement, additional confidence-boosting and repeated entreaties to apply for senior positions.

And yet Haque and Elliott cite a study by Harris et al. (2003) 'which found that BME teachers were less likely to be encouraged to apply for promotion than their white colleagues' (2017:14). Josephine Okokon, head of St Martins-in-the-Field High School for Girls, London and quoted in a 2022 *Guardian* article written by Amelia Hill, said

> I was often the only female teacher of colour and I soon began to see the white teachers getting more encouragement, more support and more mentoring than me. I was left to fend for myself. Whenever I tried to put myself forward for promotion, I was told that I needed more experience but I'd look at the white teachers who had moved up and think, they've got the same, if not slightly less experience than me. I always had to go over and above to show that I could do the job well.

Ensuring staff of colour get access to high quality CPD and careers guidance

Haque and Elliott's Barriers report found that 'less than half of BME teachers in primary and secondary schools agree with the statement "my line manager supports me in my career development and progression" (42% and 40% respectively)' (2017:24). Moreover, the authors refer to a study by Clare et al. (2016) which found 'BME teachers were more likely to have requests for CPD rejected than their white colleagues' (2017:14). In her article for *Impact Magazine* (2021), Tattersfield cites research in which only half of employees across most ethnic groups felt able to talk to their manager about career aspirations.

Increasingly, there are great training courses and programmes being set up specifically for racially minoritised teachers to address these inequities. Nadine Bernard, head of school at Van Gogh Primary in South London, became a leader at the age of 31, but faced many challenges on route to headship as a young black woman. She founded Aspiring Heads with her husband Ethan, with an aim to equip Black teachers with the 'resilience, skills, and mindset to secure leadership roles.' The organisation runs a six-month online leadership programme, delivered by Bernard and other school leaders. And it puts participants in touch with a support network. Sufian Sadiq, Director of the Teaching School at the Chiltern Learning Trust, runs a BAME into Leadership programme. This programme puts a big emphasis on personal development and growing resilience. It supports recruits with application writing, developing the essential skills and knowledge for leadership, understanding data, school governance, school improvement and finances. It provides mock interviews, shadowing opportunities and networking events.

Sadiq's BAME into Leadership programme also provides guidance on how to create a great first impression at senior leadership interviews. Christine Callender addressed this issue in her presentation to the Great Representation leaders. She talked of how important it is to ensure that candidates appreciate the need to be 'suited and booted' and to comply with all the Euro-centric cultural expectations of candidate behaviours in senior leadership interview activities. She said, 'I see this as a performative act, one which BME candidates need to know about and perform in order to be seen to "fit in" and considered suitable for the role.'

This is understandably problematic to people of colour. Ross Ashcroft, now a primary headteacher, quoted in Hill's *Guardian* article of January 2022, said 'Appearance is... a hard one for teachers of colour.' She related a story from very early in her career when she was asked by her manager whether she thought having canerows in her hair 'was "appropriate or professional". These were professionally done, in straight lines and not patterned. I asked another member of staff who was also a teacher, with bright pink hair, a nose piercing and several visible tattoos, if management had ever asked her about professionalism. She said that they hadn't, ever.' Why should an Asian candidate not wear a shalwar kameez to interview? Why should a Black candidate think twice about declaring their favourite poet to be Audre Lorde? Or to state that they like relaxing to hip hop music? Remember the reference in Chapter 6 to Brent Staples, the *New York Times* columnist who noticed White people crossing to the other side of the street in fear when he was walking at night? His story explains the title of Claude M. Steele's book, *Whistling Vivaldi*: 'Couples locked arms or reached for each other's hand when they saw me... Out of nervousness I began to whistle... I whistled popular tunes from The Beatles and Vivaldi's Four Seasons. The tension drained from people's bodies when they heard me. A few even smiled as they passed me in the dark' (2010:6).

It is depressing to think that, in order to connect with some White interviewers, candidates of colour might be wise to stress their understanding of and engagement with European linguistic, cultural or lifestyle tropes. But it may well serve to increase a sense that they will 'fit in.' Likewise, some teachers of colour I have spoken to find the concept of leadership programmes designed for and specifically marketed at racially minoritised leaders problematic. It could be seen to imply that the candidates themselves have particular deficiencies or additional needs. Why, they say, is the time and resource not invested in unpicking and eliminating the biases and prejudices of the appointees? My personal view is that if courses such as those led by Sadiq and Bernard increase the number of racially minoritised senior leaders in the UK's schools then that is a good thing. Hopefully we will arrive at a point in the not-too-distant future where programmes like this are no longer required because we have reached a state where the representation of our school and trust leader is at least equal to that of children of colour in the UK's education system.

Here are some questions for school and trust leaders to consider in order to gauge what next they might do to ensure equity in training and CPD for staff of colour:

1. Does every person of colour in your staff body have a high-quality line leader/manager?

2. Have those line leaders/managers been trained in the role and is their work quality assured?

3. And are they aware of the research showing the particular importance to staff of colour of being encouraged to engage in CPD and supported in seeking career development opportunities?

4. Do you keep detailed records of the training and CPD that each member of staff has engaged in each year? And analyse this (and the monies spent on each colleague's training) by ethnicity? If so, what does the data show and what do you plan to do as a result of your findings?

5. Do you have a clear and well-publicised CPD programme and progression route at your school? Does each member of staff have a CPD planning discussion each year, written up into a plan of intent? If so, how do you monitor adherence to it?

6. How do you additionally demystifying progression routes into leadership for any staff who would benefit from additional support (e.g. recent arrivals from overseas?)

7. Do you monitor the length of time that each member of staff has served in their current role? And analyse this data by ethnicity?

8. Do you analyse internal applications and promotions by ethnicity? If so, what does the data show you and what actions are you taking as a result of your findings?

9. Do you produce pay gap data annually based on ethnic groups (as well as gender and other protected characteristics)? With whom does such data get shared? What does it show and what actions have you agreed to take?

10. Do you seek regular feedback from your staff of colour about the quality of their line leadership/management and whether they feel both supported and challenged to undertake training and progress their careers (if desired)?

Providing mentoring for teachers of colour

One of the most powerful ways that people of colour can be supported to progress their careers is through high quality mentoring. A well-chosen mentor can act as someone to look out for, induct, open opportunities for and, if required, support teachers and governors of colour to develop social and cultural capital. In summary, they can ensure that promising racially minoritised staff don't miss out on the benefits of being 'someone like us.' Hashi Mohamed talks in *People Like Us* about a good mentor giving four things:

1. Access to people, things and information that you couldn't find for yourself

2. A safe space where there are no stupid questions and you can ask and discuss anything

3. Honesty about your strength, weaknesses and challenges and

4. A belief in you to have a future that you might not believe for yourself yet. (2020:196–7)

He sees the role of the mentor as centring around equity, being 'about getting them to the same starting line as everyone else' (2020:197–8).

Callender and Miller found that mentoring was crucial in facilitating the progression of aspirant teachers from minority ethnic backgrounds into headteacher roles. Mentoring and support from leaders with similar backgrounds who were able to relate to the experiences of their mentees was even more powerful, they argued (2018).

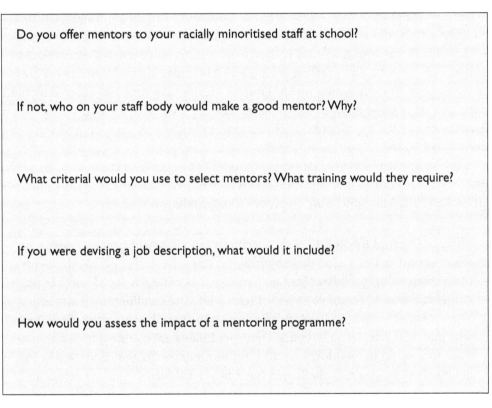

Do you offer mentors to your racially minoritised staff at school?

If not, who on your staff body would make a good mentor? Why?

What criterial would you use to select mentors? What training would they require?

If you were devising a job description, what would it include?

How would you assess the impact of a mentoring programme?

Another initiative used by some schools is reverse mentoring, whereby racially minoritised junior colleagues mentor White senior colleagues. In a *Schools Week* article of 7 January 2022, Tom Belger quotes CEO of United Learning, Jon Coles, who has 40 junior ethnic minority staff mentoring senior leaders. The aim is to facilitate 'dialogue between people from different backgrounds' and support career progression. Allana Gay, co-founder of BAMEed, warns in the same article, however, that 'reverse mentoring also places the onus on junior staff to educate, and power dynamics can limit openness.'

Ensuring that appointees have undergone impactful unconscious bias training

Let's return to the Edurio research question put to 16,565 staff in schools in early 2021: 'How confident are you that all staff are treated equally in your workplace?' What is fascinating here is the disparity between the perceptions of senior leaders and staff not in leadership roles (regardless of their ethnicity): 88% of senior leaders said that they are very or quite confident, compared to just 70% of staff not in leadership roles (2021: 22).

Given the evidence of Agarwal, cited in Chapter 10, that the more senior the role of the interviewers, the more likely that their decisions are impacted by bias, it is essential that those recruiting to senior posts in schools have undergone bias awareness training. As we know, leaders are likely to recruit in their own image and likely to be unconsciously seeking to replace their previous post holder (who will probably have been White) if they were strong. Interviewers can make snap judgements, selecting on a feeling or a hunch. It is important that they are supported to confront their own biases and prejudices and to take time before making their decisions. It is good practice for panel members to write down and declare their impressions of the candidates. This can lead to healthy discussion and flush out unfounded biases.

It is also advisable to avoid a panel comprising people who know each other too well, share viewpoints and think in ways which are too similar. Christine Callender advises putting in a 'wild card' to provoke and challenge. She says,

> This is to disrupt the 'local logics.' Generally, appointment panel members are selected on the basis of their knowledge of the school, the job requirements, their relationship with the Head and so on. This creates a set of 'local logics' which mirrors and reinforce a view of who is an ideal candidate and who is not. The wild card is there is challenge and disrupt the local logics so that candidates who may not necessarily be considered appointable are included in the discussion. In a sense the wildcard 'speaks for' and represents the candidate in the deliberation process and challenges the role of local logics in decision making.

When I was Principal of Isaac Newton Academy, I would always invite the Chair of Governors to sit on the panel for key strategic appointments. This was not just because he was Chair; it had more to do with the fact that his experiences, viewpoints and insights were so different from mine and my team members.' Gerard was an ex-hedge fund manager, an American and had been to a progressive independent school in the US as a child. He had a fierce intellect and the ability to throw disruptive and novel suggestions into a discussion. His challenges were immensely useful. He ensured that my colleagues and I regularly articulated and reviewed our presumptions and practices from a fresh perspective. In effect, he interrupted the cloning effect by asking insightful and important questions and injecting a sense of outsider perspective.

Tereshchenko, Mills and Bradbury suggest that 'school leaders in diverse schools should be required to demonstrate the experience, training and skills that allow them to develop equitable learning environments that support diverse learners and BAME teachers.' They stress that 'A better preparation of school leaders and a conscious effort by them to improve the racial literacy and diversity within the SLT is paramount for a favourable racial climate for BAME teacher retention' (2020: 5).

Ensuring open and fair recruitment practices

I will keep this section brief. In my opinion, it is never acceptable for school leaders or governors to appoint to a position in the school or trust (unless to a fixed term 'acting up' role where deputising for your leader is a part of your job description) without advertising the vacancy, producing a job description and inviting expressions of interest, if not applications, from anyone who feels they can carry out the role and would like to be considered. Ensuring that all recruitment opportunities are advertised (for teaching and support staff posts and for governors and trustees) and therefore open to interested parties is crucial. Too often, recruitment in schools is a closed process. Youlande Harrowell and Aretha Banton in their article *Professional Development for Career Progression: Through the Lens of Ethnic Diversity and Gender* (2021) argue that 'By engaging in closed recruitment practices (e.g. creating "acting/associate roles" for specific individuals), senior leaders miss out on crucial conversations with Black and Asian women who want to progress.' Where these conversations do take place they 'enable employers to gauge the interests, skills and hidden experiences and aspirations of Black and Asian women and provide a space for candidates to practise their application and interview technique and set out their career progression aspirations clearly.' Thus 'creating a legitimate space for these conversations is vital for supporting career development and progression for everyone.'

Using White Sanction to positive effect

We explored the concept of White Sanction in the introduction to this book. It is a term coined by Professor Paul Miller who writes:

> In order for BME teachers and academics to progress in their careers, it appears that they need to go through a process of 'white sanction'... 'white sanction' occurs where the skills and capabilities of a BME individual are, first, acknowledged and, second, endorsed/ promoted by a White individual, who is positioned as a broker and/or mediator acting on behalf of or in the interests of the BME individual. 'White sanction' can be 'indirect' (e.g. a

verbal reference and/or nomination for an activity) or 'direct' (e.g. a written reference, joint publication, joint appearance at a conference or joint grant application).

2016

When addressing the Great Representation programme in September in 2021, Miller acknowledged the ways in which he had been supported by white sanction, for example to get his professorships.

White heads, governors and trustees have the positional power to support people of colour into leadership roles. They need to see this as a solemn and crucial responsibility and action plan accordingly.

Key Question

If you are a White leader, how have you used your power of White Sanction in the past 12 months to support, promote and develop leaders of colour: directly? indirectly?
The above would be a good discussion to have with your leadership team, governing body or trust board.

Which members of your staff team can you support with White Sanction next? How will you go about doing this?

Summative Activity

Having read Chapters 10, 11 and 12, devise an action plan for how you will work to recruit, retain and develop your racially minoritised staff over the next five years, with targets and milestones.

I close this chapter with testimony from Bushra Nasir CBE, CEO of the Drapers MAT and one of the under 3% people of colour to occupy the role of CEO in the UK.

When I became headteacher of Plashet School For Girls in East London in 1993, I was one of the very first Pakistani Muslim heads in the UK. I felt a lot of responsibility. Being at the table enables you to influence and I was determined to be a strong role model to female leaders and leaders of colour. It was an honour and a privilege to be a headteacher but I remember feeling that doing a good enough job wasn't enough – I needed to be an outstanding leader.

I had been the deputy headteacher at Plashet for just two and a half years when the headship vacancy arose. I didn't feel ready to be a head; I had anticipated being a deputy for ten years before considering applying for a headship. But I loved the school and, when I looked at the girls and considered my decision, I realised that if I was going to be a head it was of Plashet School, so I need to apply. I had no direct role model; I had never come across any Asian headteachers. I was, however, inspired by an Asian senior adviser in Newham who ran a Women Into Leadership course that I had attended.

The appointment panel was predominantly White and male and I remember one of the appointees telling me that the school had never appointed an internal deputy to the headship! However, I was used to working in predominantly White, male environments, as a science teacher, and facing monocultural panels. In retrospect, I think that the fact that I, and the quality of my work, was known to the appointees, was an advantage to me, as was the fact that the student demographic was female and mostly Asian – I reflected the school community. At the end of my interview, I remember saying that I only wanted to be appointed if the panel thought that I had the skills to do the job better than the other candidates. Yes, I would bring additionality to the role, but that was not why I wanted to be chosen.

Minority ethnic leaders require lots of confidence and lots of support. I did not have a mentor when I applied for my headship but I did have lots of support and encouragement from my family, some key governors and parents and the staff. Over the years I have coached and mentored lots of aspirant leaders and new heads, formally and unofficially because I know how vital this role is. This was how I came to be involved with the Drapers MAT. I was asked by the headteacher of Drapers Academy whether I would do some School Improvement work for him and the school. I recall going to Drapers Hall, the home of one of the oldest liveries companies in the City of London, to meet with the Chair and Vice Chair to discuss the role. This was a much less diverse world than Newham; I expect that a woman in a shalwar kameez was a rare sight there! I felt somewhat out of place and if I had been a less experienced and confident leader (by then I had a CBE and had been a headteacher of the year) I might have been unnerved. I moved from being a school improvement partner (SIP) to a headteacher mentor to then being appointed as CEO. So, I was promoted from within, as I had been at Plashet. Who knows whether my application for CEO would have been successful if I had been an unknown outsider.

When I trained as a SIP, I deliberately asked to be deployed in Essex rather than in Newham, Redbridge or Tower Hamlets, as I wanted to work outside of my community and to have an impact in a predominantly White area. I wanted to change perceptions and to use my influence to help others to become leaders. I smiled when one of the heads I worked with told me that one of the members of her office staff had asked her 'Who is that Indian lady in the sari who comes into our school?', to which she had replied 'She's not Indian – she's Pakistani, it's not a sari – it's a shalwar kameez, and she's my boss!'

I now coach on a number of Women into Leadership and BAME into Leadership courses and programmes. I advise on CVs, give mock interviews and provide leadership shadowing opportunities. In the future, hopefully such programmes will not be needed but at the moment I see the great impact they have. When I attend online trust leader forums, I look around me and see hardly any people of colour. I was very worried about race relations around the time of Brexit; it reminded me of the 1970s and 1980s with the BNP and skinheads. But, overall, I feel very positive about the future in terms of race equity in education. We are slowly seeing more presence of people of colour in influential jobs and that is a great thing.

References

Belger. T. (2022) *Biggest academy trust turns to NFL for inspiration in diversity drive.* (Schools Week). Available at: https://schoolsweek.co.uk/diversity-racism-academy-trusts-united-learning-oasis/

Brod. H. (1989). *Work Clothes and Leisure Suits: The Class Basis and Bias of the Men's Movement* in Men's Lives, ed. Kimmel. M. S and Messner. M. (New York: Macmillan).

Haque. Z. and Elliott. S. (2017) *Visible and Invisible Barriers: the impact of racism on BME teachers.* (The Runnymede Trust). Available at: https://neu.org.uk/barriers-report-impact-racism-black-teachers

Harrowell. Y. and Banton. A. (2021). *Professional development for career progression: through the lens of ethnic diversity and gender.* (CCT Impact Magazine). Available at: https://my.chartered.college/impact_article/professional-development-for-career-progression-through-the-lens-of-ethnic-diversity-and-gender/

Hill. A. (2022). *'There is absolutely systemic racism': BAME headteachers share their views.* (The Guardian). Available at: www.theguardian.com/world/2022/jan/25/there-is-absolutely-systemic-racism-bame-headteachers-share-their-views?CMP=Share_iOSApp_Other&fbclid=IwAR1M2FvSrO0kk3XlrQP3M9dsahB7V9pER9i-ZCyZwVM99kzV8QT9IOIy0Ts

Miller. P. (2016). *'White sanction,' institutional, group and individual interaction in the promotion and progression of black and minority ethnic academics and teachers in England.* (Power and Education v8 p205–221). Available at: https://eric.ed.gov/?id=EJ1266803#:~:text=%27White%20Sanction%27%2C%20Institutional%2C%20Group%20and%20Individual%20Interaction%20in,England%20has%20been%20the%20subject%20of%20much%20debate.

Miller. P. and Callender. C. (2018). *Black Leaders Matter: Agency, Progression and the Sustainability of BME School Leadership in England* (University of Huddersfield). Available at: https://pure.hud.ac.uk/en/publications/black-leaders-matter-agency-progression-and-the-sustainability-of

Mohamed. H. (2020) *People Like Us* (London: Profile).

Ozolins. K., Jackson. I., Caunite-Bluma. D. and Jenavs. E. (2021) *Equality, Diversity and Inclusion Among School Staff: Staff Experience In Schools and Multi-Academy Trusts.*

(Edurio). Available at: https://home.edurio.com/blog/equality-diversity-and-inclusion-ser ies-race-and-ethnicity#:~:text=In%20the%20spring%20of%202021%2C%20Edurio%20 ran%20England%E2%80%99s,schools%2C%2033%20trust%20central%20teams%20 and%2050%20trusts

Ross, S. (2019). *Life In The Shadow Of The Snowy White Peaks: Race Inequalities In The NHS Workforce.* Available at: www.kingsfund.org.uk/blog/2019/06/race-inequalities-NHS-workforce

Schools Week (2021). *Annual Divesity Audit* Available at: https://schoolsweek.co.uk/acad emy-ceo-diversity-audit-more-women-bosses-but-work-to-do/

Steele, C. M. (2011). *Whistling Vivaldi.* (New York: Norton).

Tattersfield. S. (2021). *Representation matters: How do we increase diversity in our school staff body?* (CCT Impact Magazine). Available at: https://my.chartered.college/impact_arti cle/representation-matters-how-do-we-increase-diversity-in-our-school-staff-body/

Tereshchenko. A., Mills. M., Bradbury. A. (2020). *Making progress? Employment and reten- tion of BAME teachers in England.* (UCL Institute of Education: London, UK). Available at: https://discovery.ucl.ac.uk/id/eprint/10117331/

Worth. J., McLean. D. and Sharp. C. (2022). *Racial Equality In The Teacher Workforce* (NFER, Ambition Institute and Teach First). Available at: www.nfer.ac.uk/racial-equality-in-the-teacher-workforce/

13 Conclusion

And so we lift our gazes not to what stands between us, but to what stands
before us.

Amanda Gorman

I refuse to accept the view that mankind is so tragically bound to the starless
midnight of racism and war that the bright daybreak of peace and brother-
hood can never become a reality... I believe that unarmed truth and unconditional love will have the final word.

Martin Luther King Jr

In an essay called *Shade*, in *The Good Immigrant*, Salena Godden tells a story of a
giant who is separating people as though sorting glass at a bottle bank: 'brown skin
glass there, yellow skin glass here, white skin glass over there.' She says, 'I wish
the giant would pick the glass people up and hold us all up to the light. Then he'd
see that together and united as a people we are a beautiful picture, a multicoloured
mosaic, a glorious stained glass window' (2017:183).

Audre Lorde said that racism stems from 'an inability to recognise the notion of
difference as a dynamic human force, one which is enriching rather than threatening
to the defined self, when there are shared goals' (2017:12). You wouldn't have
chosen to be part of a school, educational setting or trust if you didn't see difference as a dynamic human force and the diversity of your community as enriching.
And I suspect that you would not have read this far in the book if you were not
committed to tackling racism in your institution.

You will be fully aware by now of what a complex, challenging and relentless
task this is. But you will also appreciate that standing by and not taking action is not
an option. As Amanda Gorman said in her wonderful poem at Joe Biden's inauguration, 'We've learnt that quiet isn't always peace.' Racism threatens the lives and
futures of your staff and your students. Tatum reminds us that 'As a society, we pay
a price for our silence. Unchallenged personal, cultural and institutional racism
results in the loss of human potential, lowered productivity and a rising tide of fear

 DOI: 10.4324/9781003275220-17

and violence in our society. Individually, racism stifles our own growth and development. It clouds our vision and distorts our perceptions. It alienates us not only from others but also from ourselves and our own experiences' (2021:337). We have a duty to everyone in our school communities to tackle racism – to improve young people's educational experiences and to equip adults to thrive in and to enrich a racially diverse society.

Creating an anti-racist school is about educational excellence for all. It is synonymous with whole school improvement. Energies invested in this priority will see the quality of education improve for all learners and the attainment levels rise for all groups. As Oprah Winfrey said, 'excellence is the best deterrent to racism.' Sarpong agrees: 'diversity, and the dismantling of systemic racism, is better for everyone, even those who will need to share a little more than they have previously' (2020:90).

Where should you start? Of course, the answer will be different for every reader. It will depend on your role, your position on the road towards racial literacy and your school's context.

For all of us, committing to being upstanders rather than bystanders is essential. This is arguably most important for those in education communities that are predominantly White, where people of colour are especially likely to need allies to confront bias, discrimination and under-representation. In *The Power of Privilege*, Sarpong suggests seven roles that allies can take: 'The Sponsor, The Champion, The Amplifier, The Advocate, The Scholar, The Upstander, The Confidant.' (2020:103–104). Muna Abdi, quoted by Aisha Thomas, talks of going further than allyship: 'The conversation can no longer be about standing beside those impacted by oppressive systems but (by) working with them to effect change. It's time to move beyond allyship and into a space of solidarity' (2020:151).

For each of us, there will be systems and processes that we can influence and change and others that we cannot impact so easily. Having said that, never underestimate your power to make a difference; as the saying goes, anyone who has ever slept in a room with a mosquito knows the impact that a small being can have! Paul Miller advised the leaders on the Great Representation programme in September 2021 that they needed to decide where they were going to put their energies and efforts, in what order and with whom. It is important to know your institution well (and from the perspectives of everyone in it) so that you can pinpoint and then target what it is in your institution that prevents there being race equity. And, as Miller says, it helps you to manage your energies and capacity if you know what your anchor point is and those of others in your setting. Once you know what will get your colleagues going, and how to trigger their anchor points, you have a force with which to tackle racism. And it is important that we work together and network smartly as this is too big a task to tackle alone. As Kara reassures us, 'The support for creating diverse schools is out there. You only have to scratch the surface of social media to find organisations and teachers who will give you ideas and advice' (2021:74).

Lorde reminds us that 'Certainly there are very real differences between us... But it is not those differences between us that are separating us. It is rather our refusal to recognise those differences, and to examine the distortions that result from our misnaming them and their effects upon human behaviour and expectation' (2017:95). 'Too often, we pour the energy needed for recognising and exploring difference into pretending these differences are insurmountable barriers, or that they do not exist at all...Either way, we do not develop tools for using human difference as a springboard for creative change within our lives' (2017:96). I hope that this book will have given you some ideas for how you might use difference as a springboard for change within your school community.

Ultimately, as Mahatma Gandhi taught us, 'Our ability to reach unity in diversity will be the beauty and the test of our civilisation.'

References

Godden. S. *Shade*, in Shukla. N. ed. (2017). *The Good Immigrant.* (London: Unbound)

Gorman. A. (2021). *The Hill We Climb.* Poem delivered at President Biden's inauguration.

Kara. B. (2021). *Diversity In Schools.* (London: Corwin).

King. M. L. Jr. (1964). Nobel Peace Prize Acceptance Speech.

Lorde. A. (2017). *Your Silence Will Not Protect You.* (UK: Silver Press).

Sarpong. J. (2020). *The Power Of Privilege: How White People Can Challenge Racism.* (London: HQ).

Tatum. B. D. (2021). *Why Are All The Black Kids Sitting Together In The Cafeteria?* (Great Britain, Dublin: Penguin).

Thomas. A. (2021). *Representation Matters.* (London: Bloomsbury).

Index

Ingram Content Group UK Ltd.
Milton Keynes UK
UKHW031939120623
423341UK00009B/60